AF324311

The Concert Composer's Business Handbook

Steven L. Rosenhaus

ROWMAN & LITTLEFIELD
Lanham • Boulder • New York • London

Rowman & Littlefield
Bloomsbury Publishing Inc, 1385 Broadway, New York, NY 10018, USA
Bloomsbury Publishing Plc, 50 Bedford Square, London, WC1B 3DP, UK
Bloomsbury Publishing Ireland, 29 Earlsfort Terrace, Dublin 2, D02 AY28, Ireland
www.rowman.com

British Library Cataloguing in Publication Information Available

Library of Congress Cataloging-in-Publication Data

Names: Rosenhaus, Steven L., 1952- author.
Title: The concert composer's business handbook / Steven Rosenhaus.
Description: Lanham : Rowman & Littlefield, 2025. | Series: Music pro guides | Includes bibliographical references and index.
Summary: "This book is written for composers of original music-mostly or completely within the world of concert or classical music-as a one-stop resource of relevant information on earning income from music that they write. Drawing on a breadth of experience, Stephen L. Rosenhaus addresses a variety of music business and industry topics"—Provided by publisher.
Identifiers: LCCN 2024055833 (print) | LCCN 2024055834 (ebook) | ISBN 9781538188835 (cloth) | ISBN 9781538188842 (paperback) | ISBN 9781538188859 (epub)
Subjects: LCSH: Music trade. | Copyright—Music. | Music publishing. | Music trade—Vocational guidance.
Classification: LCC ML3790 .R66 2025 (print) | LCC ML3790 (ebook) | DDC 338.4/778—dc23/eng/20241127
LC record available at https://lccn.loc.gov/2024055833
LC ebook record available at https://lccn.loc.gov/2024055834

For product safety related questions contact productsafety@bloomsbury.com.

∞™ The paper used in this publication meets the minimum requirements of American National Standard for Information Sciences—Permanence of Paper for Printed Library Materials, ANSI/NISO Z39.48-1992.

Contents

List of Figures

Introduction

I didn't have anything like this book when I studied composition. There still weren't any books like it decades later when I began teaching composition and my students need the sort of information provided here. When I would ask how they expect to make a living as a composer of concert music, many students simply didn't know. Some assumed they'd be doing something completely different; one thought "outside the box" and eventually became a pest exterminator, one of those careers that pays well and can't be outsourced or replaced by A.I. Some students thought of going into teaching music (though not necessarily composition) to fund their own creative efforts. Over the last decade many have turned to focusing on writing music for film, video games, and other media; some of my students are doing just that and doing well, I'm happy to say. But not one, in all my years of teaching, ever thought to consider trying to earn income as a concert music composer. They had no idea, until I would mention it, that it was even remotely possible.

Let's face the facts: *more often than not, you can't make a living as a concert music composer*. It can't be said any plainer. All too often music pays less than any non-artistic endeavors, and composers of concert music (aka "classical" music) experience this to an even greater degree. This is the current reality and unlikely to change any time soon. Most universities, colleges, and conservatories have not until very recently prepared composition students properly for the non-academic world. The few that do cobble together information from a wide variety of resources. There has been no single, reliable resource for composers, students, or teachers to depend upon.

The Concert Composer's Business Handbook is written for writers of original music mostly or completely within the world of classical or concert music, so they can earn income from their music. It does not consider other means of earning income beyond mentioning many of them and providing some resources.

Many books deal with the music business, but most are either theoretical in approach, deal only with legal issues, or focus on making money with pop music or scoring for media. Few tackle concert music. There are many online resources available, but all seem to suffer from similar insufficiencies. There are overlaps among all of these various resources and some apply to concert music composers' situations, but there hasn't been a single practical source for the variety of information emerging composers—or even those further along in their careers—need to help support themselves. While *The Concert Composer's Business Handbook* is primarily meant for composers at the beginning of their careers, I hope more established composers will find this book useful as well.

I say this disclaimer repeatedly throughout this book: **Topics touch on legal and financial matters, but I am neither an attorney, let alone one specializing in copyright and other intellectual property law, nor a CPA or any kind of accountant, tax lawyer, or anyone else trained and allowed by law to give advice on taxes.** Anything I write throughout *The Handbook* is based on my own experience as a longtime composer and arranger, and on the research I've done in writing this book. To put it more formally:

The information provided in this book is not, and is not intended to be, legal, financial, or tax advice. All of the information, content, and materials found here are for informational purposes only. No legal or financial action should be taken without first consulting with an attorney, CPA, or certified financial advisor.

There is a truism that things change at astounding rates. Specific information offered here will change over time—certainly anything dealing with technology (the proliferation of artificial intelligence, aka A.I.), numbers (percentages, etc.), copyright law, or specific resources (websites, government agencies, etc.). In fact, just as I was putting the finishing touches on this manuscript, those of us who use music notation programs were rocked by the news that the makers of the Finale program were discontinuing its support effective immediately. The repercussions will certainly have shaken themselves out by the time you read this, but it should give you an idea of just how unpredictably and quickly things can change. Still, the basic concepts needed and provided here will not. This includes the overriding concept behind this book: Composers deserve to be paid for their creative work. It is my hope that you, the reader, will find *The Concert Composer's Business Handbook* a useful tool in securing that payment for your music.

Steven L. Rosenhaus, Ph.D.
New York City, 2024

Acknowledgments

To Ruth, first and foremost, my life mate and secret weapon.

I could not have written *The Concert Composer's Business Handbook* without help. My thanks to my editor, Michael Tan, for considering my proposal in the first place and guiding me as I wrote, rewrote, and re-rewrote to get the book into proper shape. My thanks, too, to my composer colleagues and friends, as well as my other friends and colleagues in music publishing who have known about this project and whose enthusiasm for it has been infectious, inspiring, and supportive. Thanks, too, to Roger Vasquez and Allen Cohen for "beta testing" several chapters before I unleashed the manuscript on Michael. Last but not least, my thanks to all of my current and former composition students for making this book a necessity. To them I only ask in return that, whatever they set out to do, they ask themselves, "What would happen if . . . ?"

Chapter 1

COPYRIGHT

Only one thing is impossible for God: To find any sense in any copyright law on the planet.

—Samuel Clemens, aka Mark Twain

WHAT IS COPYRIGHT, AND WHY SHOULD I USE IT?

Let's begin with what should be the most important thing to know about dealing with the music you've written: *Protect your work*. When you create any work of art, there are things you want: the quality of the work to be high, of course; the recognition as the work's creator; and, most importantly, control over the use and dissemination of the work. It is your creative work. It is, to put it into legal terms, *intellectual property* (or "IP"). (When hiring an attorney, make sure that person specializes in IP.)

Copyright is a type of intellectual property. It gives its owner the exclusive right to copy, distribute, adapt, print, publish, perform, or record the owner's original work, or to authorize others to do the same. Anyone who creates an original work and puts it into "fixed form" is automatically considered the copyright owner according to U.S. copyright laws.[1] Works covered by copyright include literary works (such as this book), visual art works, and, most importantly for the reader, musical works. Copyrights are meant to establish the timeline of the work's creation and to protect its creator and/or an authorized other party, like a publisher, from infringement or plagiarism.

Infringement is the use of a copyright-protected work without permission. Publishing a work without the express permission of the work's copyright owner is considered an infringement. *Plagiarism*, which may or may not occur simultaneously as infringement, is the false claim of a work's creation and/or ownership. Putting your name as the composer of a work written by someone else is plagiarism.

Under U.S. copyright law, an original work is one created by a human author or authors and must have a "minimal degree of creativity." Works created by artificial intelligence (A.I.) means are not currently considered eligible for copyright. Anyone who creates a work of art, be it music, drama, visual art, or literature, can copyright that work.

Music created and fixed on or after January 1, 1978, will have its copyright in force for the life of the author plus seventy (70) years. If you have collaborated with someone, say on an opera for which you've written the music and someone else the libretto, the term lasts for seventy years after the last surviving author's death.

A *work for hire* is something you've created but have turned over all of your rights for, including but not limited to the copyright, to a third party. Works for hire have a copyright term of 95 years from the work's publication or 120 years from its creation, whichever is shorter. There are other situations in which the 95-year/120-year terms apply, but they occur rarely for concert music composers.[2]

Although a work is considered copyrighted once it is put into fixed form, that alone doesn't always go far in a court of law. If someone is infringing on or plagiarizing your work, or someone has accused you of doing the same, you will need the full protection of the copyright laws. The best way to have that protection is to *register* the copyright with the Library of Congress Copyright Office. Registration is voluntary, not mandatory, but a registered copyright is legal proof of ownership of a work, and provides other benefits as well.

* Registration of a copyright establishes your claim to the copyright of the work.

* Registration (or its refusal) is required before an infringement suit can be filed.

* If registration is made prior to infringement, or within three months after a work's publication, a copyright owner is eligible for statutory damages, attorneys' fees, and other costs.

* Registering your work permits you to establish a record with U.S. Customs and Border Protection for protection against the importation of infringing copies.

* Lastly, copyright registration is considered *prima facie* evidence (a Latin phrase used in law meaning "true on first impression") in plagiarism and infringement cases.

For years there has been a misconception about what is usually called "the poor person's copyright." This involves sending yourself a physical copy of your work by registered mail and never opening the envelope. There has never been a provision in any copyright law providing such possible protection. It doesn't prove you created the work, only that you mailed it to yourself on a particular date. Even if you use it to prove the work was not created after the postmarked date, no court has ever accepted it, or will accept it for purposes of determining damages for infringement or plagiarism. In short, do not use "the poor person's copyright" as a substitute for copyright registration.

There are also benefits of copyright registration if your music is made available outside the United States. Registered copyrights are protected not only in the United States but also in countries with which the United States has copyright agreements. Participating countries honor each other's citizens' copyrights. Not all countries have such agreements however, and the list of countries that do changes frequently. The Copyright Office keeps that list up to date.[3]

HOW DO I COPYRIGHT MY MUSIC?

The first and most important step in securing copyright protection of your music is to put it into "fixed form." It needs to be "perceptible either directly or with the aid of a machine or device."[4] Sheet music printed by any regular means (offset printing, "Ozalid" or "white printing," or laser printing, are examples) is a fixed form that is directly perceptible. The Copyright Office also requires that a submission of a published work must be the "best edition" of that work, but the term isn't defined beyond saying that it must be determined to be "most suitable for its purposes." This only applies to printed sheet music, not to unpublished works. PDF files and, in an increasing number of cases, sound files that cannot be changed (mp3 and wav formats *et al.*) are perceptible with the use of computers, phones, tablets, and so on, and cannot be easily altered. Music notation and sound creation files, which can be changed at will, are not considered to be in fixed form. Since almost all music creation involves a digital component these days, physical copies of the work (printed scores or physical records) aren't even necessary. These days most copyright registrations are done online through the Copyright Office website by uploading your work in a "fixed form" format, filling out the appropriate information, and paying a registration fee. Here is a current selection of acceptable file formats relevant to music scores, as of 2024. Please note that PDF files are the most commonly used, as most music notation files can "print to PDF" either directly or with the use of an additional program. There are several of these programs available. PDFs have the advantage of containing multiple pages. The only other format listed that can contain multiple pages is Microsoft Publisher's .pub, but for anyone to read it, they must use that particular program or convert the file to PDF:

    .gif or .giff (Graphics Interchange Format) (single pages only)
    .jpg, .jpeg, or .jfif (Joint Photographic Experts Group) (single pages only)
    .pdf (Portable Document Format) (multiple pages allowed)
    .pic, or .pict (Picture File) (single pages only)
    .png (Portable Network Graphic) (single pages only)
    .pub (Microsoft Publisher) (multiple pages allowed)

Sound files are considered acceptable by the Copyright Office in these formats:
    .aif or .aiff (Audio Interchange File Format)
    .au (Audio File)
    .mp3 (MP3 Audio File or Layer 3 Audio Compression)
    .wav (Windows Wave Sound File)
    .wma (Windows Media Audio File)
    .mp4, .m4a, or m4p (MPEG-4 Part 14 Apple)

Some music notation file formats are considered useful for preservation and other archival purposes (MusicXML, Music Encoding Initiative [MEI]), but none is considered suitable for registering a musical work's copyright. Do *not* upload a Finale, Sibelius, Dorico, or other music notation file in its native format. Create a PDF or similar "fixed-form" file and submit that. And for those who wish to register works using physical (paper) scores, remember to send *copies only*, no original scores (especially handwritten ones!).

Until 1989 all works submitted in fixed form were required to have a *copyright notice*. This is literally an announcement, a notice to tell the public that a copyright owner is claiming ownership of the work.[5] A copyright notice consists of three things:

    * The symbol "©," the word "Copyright," or the abbreviation "copr."

    * The year of publication or, for unpublished works, the year in which the work was completed.

    * The name of the copyright owner.

Copyright notices are no longer required and are considered optional for works published on or after March 1, 1989, unpublished works, and foreign works. In fact, unpublished works have never required a copyright notice, but the legal benefits of using one makes it worthwhile. First, it makes potential users aware that a copyright is claimed in the work. Secondly, a copyright notice provides additional (but not sole) evidence of the work's genesis. A copyright notice makes it easier for those seeking to obtain permission to use the work to contact the copyright owner. Also, a notice including the year of publication or creation may be utilized in determining the term of copyright protection for works of pseudonymous, anonymous, or "work for hire" works. It is recommended that a copyright notice is used in all cases of creating a "fixed form" version of your music. When used, copyright notices need to be provided as a single continuous statement, for example: "© 2024

[Your Name Here]." Notices should be placed on copies or phonorecords in a way that is "permanently legible to an ordinary user of the work and could not be concealed from view upon reasonable examination." Copyright notices on sheet music usually appear at the bottom of the first page of music, centered along the bottom margin. If the work has multiple movements, only the first page of the entire score needs to have the notice. When used for works requiring more than one musician, notices should appear on the first page of the score and each of the parts. Figure 1-1 is an example of a copyright notice and its placement.

COPYRIGHT REGISTRATION FORMS

When copyright registration was only done with physical materials—paper forms, printed scores, etc.—a composer would fill out printed Form PA, submit it along with a physical copy of the score to be registered (not the original!), and include a check or money order. It would then take anywhere from six weeks to just over a year to have that work acknowledged as registered. On the upside, the date the materials were received at the Copyright Office was considered the date of registration, no matter how long it took to process. (That much is still true.) Musical works can still have their copyright registered this way, but it costs more and takes at least as long a time; the most efficient way to register a copyright is to do it online. Here is the process:

Step One

On the Copyright Office website, www.copyright.gov, click on "Registration" to see the menu of options. Click on "Register Your Work: Registration Portal." Figure 1-2 shows what you expect to see. As of this writing there is an "Important Note Regarding Registering a Group of Unpublished Works" at the top of the page. Read it. It gives the welcome option to register up to ten unpublished works separately, but grouped on the same application. A "group" is not a "collection," and the distinction is important: "group" here refers to two or more individual works to be copyrighted at the same time (like a symphony, a string trio, and a wind quintet), while a "collection" is several works being treated as a single composition (such as several songs to be performed as a cycle). Make sure you choose the appropriate method of registration. Trying to register two or more works as a collection when they should be registered individually could result in the Copyright Office only registering one of those works, and you would have to resubmit those left out in a new application.

Let's assume for the moment you're only registering one composition. On the new page choose "Log in to the Electronic Copyright Office (eCO)

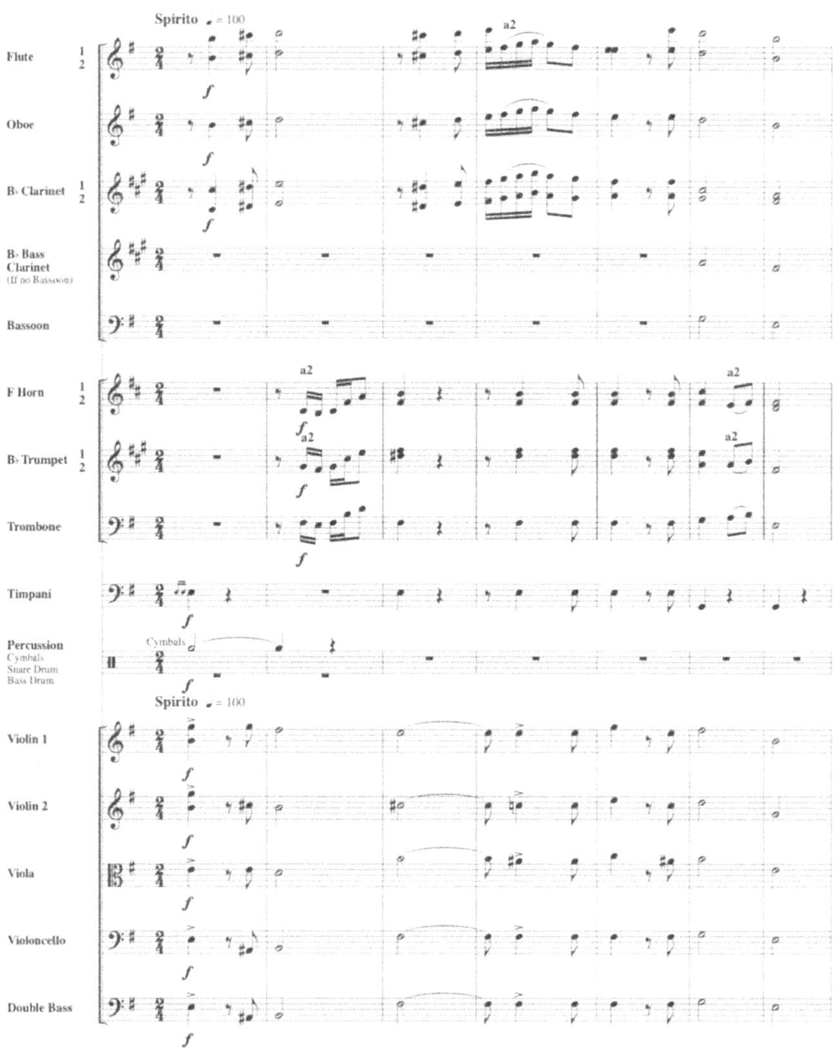

Figure 1-1   First page of score, *Valiant* **for orchestra, © 2022 Steven L. Rosenhaus, demonstrating typical wording and placement of copyright notice,** author created

Register Your Work: Registration Portal

IMPORTANT NOTE REGARDING REGISTERING A GROUP OF UNPUBLISHED WORKS

You may register up to 10 unpublished works on the same application, but **YOU MUST SELECT** the new application for a **"Group of Unpublished Works."**

Click here if you need help finding the application for a "Group of Unpublished Works," and click here to watch a video that provides step-by-step instructions for completing this application. Click here for answers to frequently asked questions related to this application.

The "Standard Application" **MAY NOT BE USED** to register a **"collection"** of unpublished works. If you submit 2 or more works on the "Standard Application" the Copyright Office may register only 1 of your works and remove the remaining works from the claim. To register those works you will need to resubmit them using an appropriate application form.

Welcome to the Registration Portal. This is your starting point for all things related to the registration of copyrights.

To get started registering your work, log in to the Electronic Copyright Office (eCO) Registration System at the link below or you may learn more about the different types of works typically registered with the U.S. Copyright Office.

Figure 1-2 **"Register Your Work: Registrations Portal" page from https://www.copyright.gov/registration/,** partial screenshot of https://www.copyright.gov/registration/

Registration System." If you would prefer to get more information before registering your work, first scroll down to "Types of Work" followed by "Performing Arts." If you then click on "Learn more" you will go to a page with links to tutorial videos including one for registering "standard applications."

Step Two

You may see a dialog box warning that the system you are using is the property of the Library of Congress and may be monitored; click on "Close." Additional dialog boxes may pop up; just click as necessary until you get to the page with the words "Welcome! Welcome to the Electronic Copyright Office" (eCO). On the left side of the page, you will see a "User Login." Log in or, if you are not already a registered eCO user, follow the instructions to enroll. You must be a registered user in order to file a copyright registration.

Step Three

Fill out the required information. The information you provide will be the same whether you're filling out the form online or using the paper Form PA. Figure 1-3 is a screenshot of what you see when you start the registration process on the Copyright Office website. Note the menu/checklist on the left side; this is to help you keep track as you go. Also, you don't have to complete the registration all at once. You can save whatever you've done so far and come back another time to complete the process. Lastly, you'll automatically be assigned a case number (blocked out here). Save the number somewhere for future reference.

From this point on we'll use the paper form as a visual reference because all of the information requested is shown in one place. The first two pages of Form PA consists of detailed instructions, while pages 3 and 4 make up the form itself. Page 3, shown in Figure 1-4, is where you enter: the title(s) of your work, your name and the nature of your creative contribution to the work, the same information for any additional creators of the work, the year in which the work was created, the date and nation of the work's first publication (if any), and the name(s) and address(es) of the copyright claimant(s). As you fill the form out, note the following:

   * Titles themselves cannot be copyrighted; only the content (the work itself) is afforded those rights.

   * When asked "Was this contribution to the work a 'work for hire'?" be sure to answer correctly. Answer "No" for most circumstances and "Yes" *only* if you have agreed to give up all of your rights to the work to a third party.

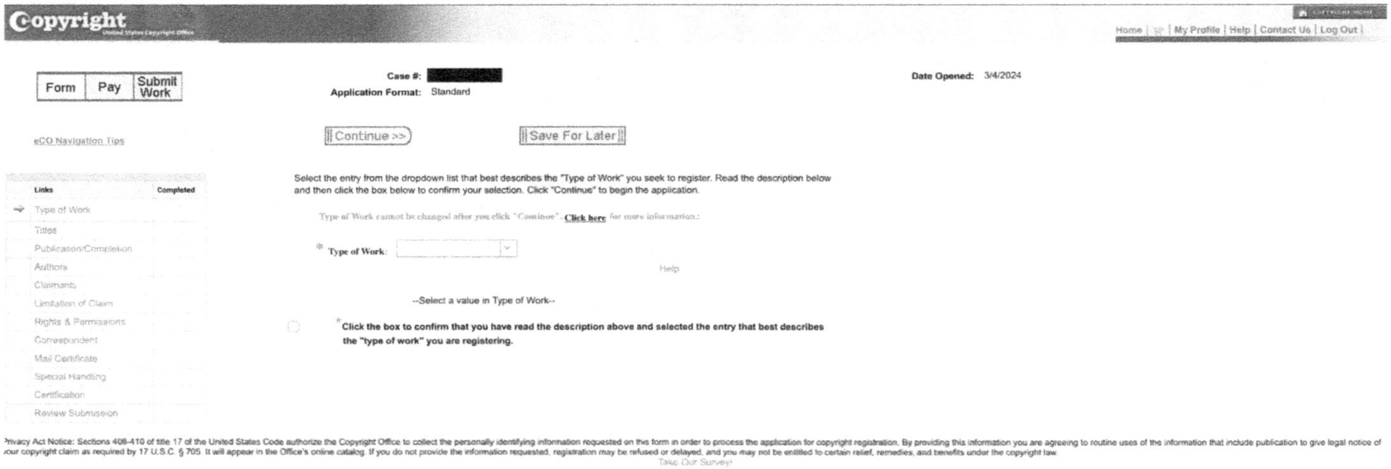

Figure 1-3   Page 1, online Copyright Reigstration Form PA, screenshot of: https://eservice.eco.loc.gov/siebel/app/eservice/enu?SWECmd=GotoView&SWEView=LC+Type+of+Work+Detail+View+(eService)&SWERF=1&SWEHo=&SWEBU=1&SWEApplet0=LC+Type+of+Work+Detail+Applet+(eService)&SWERowId0=1-6JCFT3H

Form PA
For a Work of Performing Arts
UNITED STATES COPYRIGHT OFFICE

REGISTRATION NUMBER

PA   PAU

EFFECTIVE DATE OF REGISTRATION

Month   Day   Year

Privacy Act Notice: Sections 408-410 of title 17 of the *United States Code* authorize the Copyright Office to collect the personally identifying information requested on this form in order to process the application for copyright registration. By providing this information you are agreeing to routine uses of the information that include publication to give legal notice of your copyright claim as required by 17 U.S.C. §705. It will appear in the Office's online catalog. If you do not provide the information requested, registration may be refused or delayed, and you may not be entitled to certain relief, remedies, and benefits under the copyright law.

DO NOT WRITE ABOVE THIS LINE. IF YOU NEED MORE SPACE, USE A SEPARATE CONTINUATION SHEET.

1

TITLE OF THIS WORK ▼

PREVIOUS OR ALTERNATIVE TITLES ▼

NATURE OF THIS WORK ▼ See instructions

2 a

NAME OF AUTHOR ▼

DATES OF BIRTH AND DEATH
Year Born ▼   Year Died ▼

Was this contribution to the work a "work made for hire"?
❑ Yes
❑ No

AUTHOR'S NATIONALITY OR DOMICILE
Name of Country
OR { Citizen of ______
Domiciled in ______

WAS THIS AUTHOR'S CONTRIBUTION TO THE WORK
Anonymous? ❑ Yes ❑ No
Pseudonymous? ❑ Yes ❑ No

If the answer to either of these questions is "Yes," see detailed instructions.

NATURE OF AUTHORSHIP Briefly describe nature of material created by this author in which copyright is claimed. ▼

NOTE
Under the law, the "author" of a "work made for hire" is generally the employer, not the employee (see instructions). For any part of this work that was "made for hire" check "Yes" in the space provided, give the employer (or other person for whom the work was prepared) as "Author" of that part, and leave the space for dates of birth and death blank.

b

NAME OF AUTHOR ▼

DATES OF BIRTH AND DEATH
Year Born ▼   Year Died ▼

Was this contribution to the work a "work made for hire"?
❑ Yes
❑ No

AUTHOR'S NATIONALITY OR DOMICILE
Name of Country
OR { Citizen of ______
Domiciled in ______

WAS THIS AUTHOR'S CONTRIBUTION TO THE WORK
Anonymous? ❑ Yes ❑ No
Pseudonymous? ❑ Yes ❑ No

If the answer to either of these questions is "Yes," see detailed instructions.

NATURE OF AUTHORSHIP Briefly describe nature of material created by this author in which copyright is claimed. ▼

c

NAME OF AUTHOR ▼

DATES OF BIRTH AND DEATH
Year Born ▼   Year Died ▼

Was this contribution to the work a "work made for hire"?
❑ Yes
❑ No

AUTHOR'S NATIONALITY OR DOMICILE
Name of Country
OR { Citizen of ______
Domiciled in ______

WAS THIS AUTHOR'S CONTRIBUTION TO THE WORK
Anonymous? ❑ Yes ❑ No
Pseudonymous? ❑ Yes ❑ No

If the answer to either of these questions is "Yes," see detailed instructions.

NATURE OF AUTHORSHIP Briefly describe nature of material created by this author in which copyright is claimed. ▼

3 a

YEAR IN WHICH CREATION OF THIS WORK WAS COMPLETED
This information must be given in all cases.
______ Year

b DATE AND NATION OF FIRST PUBLICATION OF THIS PARTICULAR WORK
Complete this information ONLY if this work has been published.
Month ______ Day ______ Year ______
Nation ______

4

See instructions before completing this space.

COPYRIGHT CLAIMANT(S) Name and address must be given even if the claimant is the same as the author given in space 2. ▼

TRANSFER If the claimant(s) named here in space 4 is (are) different from the author(s) named in space 2, give a brief statement of how the claimant(s) obtained ownership of the copyright. ▼

DO NOT WRITE HERE
OFFICE USE ONLY

APPLICATION RECEIVED

ONE DEPOSIT RECEIVED

TWO DEPOSITS RECEIVED

FUNDS RECEIVED

MORE ON BACK ▶ • Complete all applicable spaces (numbers 5-9) on the reverse side of this page.
• See detailed instructions.   • Sign the form at line 8.

DO NOT WRITE HERE
Page 1 of ______ pages

Figure 1-4 Page 1, online Copyright Registration Form PA, screenshot of first page of Form PA (NOT the instructions), https://www.copyright.gov/forms/formpa.pdf

(Writing original music "for hire" is rare in classical music, although arranging someone else's music can be one example.)

* Be clear and simple when filling out the "Nature of Authorship" portion. Descriptions like "Music," "Music and Lyrics," "String Quartet," "Symphony," and so on are fine.

* This next bit is tricky. Section 2 (or the online equivalent) asks for information about the creators of the work. Presumably that's only you, using your own name, but there can be other possibilities. If you use a pseudonym, you can leave the author's portion blank or give the pseudonym and identify it as such ("Fake Name, pseudonym" for example). Or you can give your real name along with the pseudonym while making clear which is which ("John Smith, whose pseudonym is Fake Name"). In all cases the citizenship or domicile (residence) of the author is required, as are the author's date of birth and, depending on the situation, the year of death. If you have collaborated with someone, say a lyricist, provide that person's data as well. (Obviously, if you're the author filling out the form, you're not dead yet, but your collaborator might be.) You also need to provide the "fullest form" of each author's name, as well as their contributions to the work.

* The next section (Section 3 on the paper form) makes a distinction between the year the work was created and, if applicable, the date (and nation!) of the work's first publication. If the work is unpublished, leave the publication information area blank.

* The next item in the application asks for the name and address of the person, persons, or entity claiming the copyright, "even if the claimant is the same as the author given in space 2." It may seem redundant to list yourself as both the author and copyright claimant, but it isn't. Remember that the author of the work, that is you the composer, is not necessarily the one claiming the copyright. If a publisher agrees to publish your work, for example, it will usually take over the copyright claim, by filing a new application indicating a *transfer* of the copyright assuming you've already registered the work in its unpublished form. To complete this section as an unpublished work, give your own name and address. If you have collaborators, list their names and addresses as well.

* The last page of the paper Form PA registration application, shown in Figure 1-5, and its online equivalent has five more sections. First is "Previous Registration," which only applies if you have already submitted a registration for the same work. If that is the case, you'll need to explain here why you're submitting a new registration. There are three general reasons to do so:

1. to register the first published edition of a work previously registered as unpublished;

EXAMINED BY	FORM PA
CHECKED BY	
CORRESPONDENCE Yes	FOR COPYRIGHT OFFICE USE ONLY

DO NOT WRITE ABOVE THIS LINE. IF YOU NEED MORE SPACE, USE A SEPARATE CONTINUATION SHEET.

PREVIOUS REGISTRATION Has registration for this work, or for an earlier version of this work, already been made in the Copyright Office?

❏ Yes ❏ No If your answer is "Yes," why is another registration being sought? (Check appropriate box.) ▼ If your answer is No, do **not** check box A, B, or C.

a. ❏ This is the first published edition of a work previously registered in unpublished form.

b. ❏ This is the first application submitted by this author as copyright claimant.

c. ❏ This is a changed version of the work, as shown by space 6 on this application.

If your answer is "Yes," give **Previous Registration Number** ▼   **Year of Registration** ▼

5

DERIVATIVE WORK OR COMPILATION Complete both space 6a and 6b for a derivative work; complete only 6b for a compilation.

Preexisting Material Identify any preexisting work or works that this work is based on or incorporates. ▼

a **6**

See instructions before completing this space.

Material Added to This Work Give a brief, general statement of the material that has been added to this work and in which copyright is claimed. ▼

b

DEPOSIT ACCOUNT If the registration fee is to be charged to a Deposit Account established in the Copyright Office, give name and number of Account.

Name ▼   **Account Number** ▼

a **7**

CORRESPONDENCE Give name and address to which correspondence about this application should be sent. Name / Address / Apt / City / State / Zip ▼

b

Area code and daytime telephone number   (   )   Fax number   (   )

Email

CERTIFICATION* I, the undersigned, hereby certify that I am the

Check only one ▶
❏ author
❏ other copyright claimant
❏ owner of exclusive right(s)
❏ authorized agent of _______________________

Name of author or other copyright claimant, or owner of exclusive right(s) ▲

8

of the work identified in this application and that the statements made by me in this application are correct to the best of my knowledge.

Typed or printed name and date ▼ If this application gives a date of publication in space 3, do not sign and submit it before that date.

____ Date _______________

Signature (X) ▼

X ____

Certificate will be mailed in window envelope to this address:	Name ▼	
	Number/Street/Apt ▼	
	City/State/Zip ▼	

YOU MUST:
· Complete all necessary spaces
· Sign your application in space 8

SEND ALL 3 ELEMENTS IN THE SAME PACKAGE:
1. Application form
2. Nonrefundable filing fee in check or money order payable to *U.S. Copyright Office*
3. Deposit material

MAIL TO:
Library of Congress
Copyright Office-PA
101 Independence Avenue SE
Washington, DC 20559-6000

9

*17 U.S.C. §506(e): Any person who knowingly makes a false representation of a material fact in the application for copyright registration provided for by section 409, or in any written statement filed in connection with the application, shall be fined not more than $2,500.

Form PA - Full Printed: 06/2019 Printed on recycled paper

Figure 1-5   Page 2, online Copyright Registration Form PA, screenshot of second page of Form PA (NOT the instructions), https://www.copyright.gov/forms/formpa.pdf

2. to submit yourself (the author) as the copyright claimant (which implies someone or some entity had done so previously); or
3. to register a work that has been changed in some manner, usually with revisions or additions.

* The sixth section, "Derivative Work or Compilation," is for works based in some way on preexisting material. This usually does not apply for composers of original concert music, but it comes in handy when dealing with arrangements, sets of variations, etc. The Copyright Office defines a *derivative work* as "a work based on one or more preexisting works." *Derivative* works can be arrangements, abridgements, or "any other form in which a work may be recast, transformed, or adapted." They can also include "editorial revisions, annotations, or other modifications," but only if the changes embody an original work of authorship. A *compilation* is a single work comprised of preexisting materials that are "selected, coordinated, or arranged in such a way that the resulting work . . . constitutes an original work of authorship." If your work is considered derivative you will need to provide information on the preexisting material itself and the material added to the work. Remember that a *collection* is not the same as a *group* when it comes to copyright. (See Step 1 above.) Most importantly, if you're utilizing preexisting material in your work, make sure you have legal permission to use it if it is already protected by copyright, or that the material is Public Domain. (More on Public Domain works below.)

* The next item, "Deposit Account," is for composers and publishers who maintain an account balance with the Copyright Office. Such accounts allow the Copyright Office to draw funds to pay registration fees without having a copyright claimant send a physical check or pay by credit card online each time a registration is submitted. It's more likely publishers will have deposit accounts than composers, but it's good to know they're available. Assuming you don't have a deposit account just leave this section blank and follow the rest of the instructions.

* Section 8, "Certification," is where you provide the date and your signature (or the electronic equivalent online) as the author of the work, or a different copyright claimant, or the owner of the exclusive right(s) to the work, or the duly authorized agent, claimant, or owner of the exclusive right(s) to the work. It seems redundant considering the information you will have already provided, but this is where you are confirming that you are doing this legally.

* The last and probably most important section is where you provide the "Address for Return of Certificate." This is where you want your (physical!) copyright registration certificate to be sent. *Be sure to complete this section.*

COPYRIGHTING NON-NOTATED MUSIC

Most concert music is notated, but certainly not all. Sometimes the only fixed form possible for a work is a sound recording of some kind. Such recordings can be registered for the music itself—what the Copyright Office calls "the underlying musical composition" or for the recording of that music, or both. Each, be it the underlying composition or the recording of it, requires its own copyright registration. (The paper Form PA and its online equivalent covers the underlying composition, while paper Form SR and its equivalent is for registering the copyright on recordings.) If your music only exists in recorded form, such as music with improvisational elements, you should register the copyright both ways. The registration process for sound recordings is very similar to that of compositions.

Whatever the fixed form of your work is being submitted, be sure to submit only a *copy* of your score or recording and not the original. This is easy when filing online, as you're only sending copies of files, but it's of utmost importance when submitting physical materials with paper forms.

A WORD ABOUT TITLES

As mentioned in Step Three, titles, names, short phrases, variations on established elements *cannot* be copyrighted. This is why there are so many works called "Symphony" or "Sonata." According to the Copyright Office, copyright protects the *expression* of ideas, and never the "ideas, procedures, methods, systems, processes, concepts, principles, or discoveries" themselves. It's all about the music you compose, no matter what you call it or how you went about writing it. That said, try to not use "Untitled" or any other overly generic term as a title unless it's absolutely necessary. It's not a legal issue, but it does make things *very* difficult for the folks at the Copyright Office (or anyone else doing music research) in finding specific works if the need arises.

PUBLIC DOMAIN

There are times when we composers are compelled or commissioned to write a work based on preexisting music. Using music that is in the Public Domain is, legally, the safest way to work. Works in the Public Domain (PD) are not or no longer protected by copyright laws or other intellectual property laws such as trademark and patent laws. There are several reasons why a work can be PD.

* The duration of the original copyright has expired.
(Music by Beethoven is considered Public Domain, for example.)
* The work was produced by the U.S. federal government.
(The pages from Form PA reproduced above are Public Domain.)
* The work is not in tangible "fixed form."
* The work was not given a proper copyright notice.
(This applies to works created before March 1, 1989.)
* The work has no original author.
(For music this usually means folk songs and other "traditional" tunes.)

As of 2024, any work published in the United States *prior* to 1929 is considered to be in the Public Domain. The "prior to" date changes annually. In 2025 any work published before 1930 will be PD, and so on. There's more information below, but here are two things to be aware of:

* Folk music and other "traditional" music by their nature have been handed down over generations and are prone to changes along the way. This has led many musicians to copyright their own versions of these tunes, with a slight change of melody here or a new lyric there. *Make sure the version you use is actually* Public Domain *and not someone's rewrite of it.*

* Copyright law in the United States is extremely complicated. So are the copyright laws of every other country that offers such protections. The United States has treaties with many of these other nations, the main agreement being the Berne Convention for the Protection of Literary and Artistic Works. The Berne Convention dates back to the late 1800s with the intent that creators of literature and arts of all kinds should be afforded the same (or similar) protections in all of its participating countries. There can be subtle or major differences in just how copyright laws operate from one Convention country to the next though. One has to do with when copyrights expire and the works covered become Public Domain. A work in the United States may be considered PD but might still be protected in Canada, for example. Or an instrumental tune that is PD everywhere may have had lyrics added later that are still under copyright. *Just make sure the music you use is actually in the* Public Domain *where you are and that there are no conflicts with other countries' copyright laws.*

USING OTHERS' MATERIALS

Be warned: This will probably make your head ache. Better you learn about it here though than the hard way in a courtroom where you're being sued for infringement or plagiarism. Besides, the following information can be useful when you go to register your copyrights.

The idea of quoting or otherwise incorporating other works in music has been around since humans began making music. Concert music composers still do it today. But when and why would composers, presumably with good ethical standards, use another composer's work as a source for their own? One reason is to create a series of variations. Writing variations on a theme or tune by another composer is a time-honored tradition. For example, Anton Diabelli, a music publisher in the early- to mid-1800s had the idea to ask the finest composers of the day to each write a variation on a waltz he himself wrote, which he would then publish as a collection. One of the composers he sent his tune to was none other than Ludwig van Beethoven, who decided one variation wasn't enough and, besides, he wasn't too fond of the tune. Being, well, Beethoven, he went all out: instead of just one variation, he wrote a set of thirty-three!

Sometimes a composer alludes to other works for extramusical reasons, such as Tchaikovsky's use of the hymn to the Russian czar and the French national anthem "La Marseillaise" in his *1812 Overture*. And of course, there's always the possibility of incorporating a well-known tune as as joke, such as when Debussy incorporated a tune from Wagner's "Tristan and Isolde" in his own "Golliwog's Cakewalk."

• *Permissions*. There is little to worry about if you're utilizing a Public Domain work in your own, although for ethical and practical reasons you shouldn't try to pass it off as your own, certainly not without transforming it to a significant extent. (Make sure the music actually is PD.) The same applies to any popular songs that are Public Domain if you're writing arrangements. But if you want to use music currently covered by copyright laws it will require getting permission at least, and more likely by obtaining a license for the use. When you quote or allude to another piece in your own work, credit the original composer whenever possible.

Some folks try to use a small number of notes or a very short phrase—a sample—and claim it's within the bounds of *fair use*. This is probably the least understood concept in copyright law and the most poorly defined by the law. The idea behind fair use is to allow a portion of music otherwise protected by copyright to be used for certain reasons under particular circumstances. Usually this means using excerpts for educational purposes, like when a music theory textbook quotes a couple of measures of something to show a cadence. But in those (literally) textbook examples, the quoted material, if not PD, has been licensed or has had permission granted just for that case. If you want to go the "fair use" route anyway, ask yourself these questions: (1) Are you using the music you want to use for profit? (If yes, you can't claim "fair use," so you would have to get permission or a license.); (2) how much of the original music are you using? (This is a gray area that gets darker the more of the original work you incorporate. Get permission or a license to ensure you don't get sued for infringement.); and lastly, (3) will incorporating the music have a significant impact on the original's ability to generate income for its creator or publisher? If you have questions as to what music you can use, how much you can use it, and how you can utilize it in your own work, the Copyright Office has a handy Fair Use Index on its website.[6]

Now that you've been scared into obtaining licenses for incorporating others' music into your own, let's pull back a bit and discuss permissions again. Sometimes, admittedly rarely, you will come across a situation that can be resolved with a relatively simple request for permission to use the material. For the second movement of my own *Quadtych* for cello and piano, I needed to utilize music by the composer J. F. Peter (1746–1813) and transform it compositionally. One look at the composer's dates makes you think "Oh, it's Public Domain, right?" Wrong. This work was edited, copyrighted, and published by the Moravian Music Foundation, and it wasn't available anywhere else. I requested and obtained permission to use the material, with the stipulation that I add the following text on the bottom of the first page of music in which Peter's music appears: "Musical themes and ideas from String Quintet No. 3, Movement 2, of J. F. Peter (1746–1813) quoted in this movement are used with the express written consent of the Moravian Music Foundation, Inc., Winston-Salem, NC, copyright-holders of the Six String Quintets." Sure, it's a long disclaimer and I had to put the text in a small point size so it didn't overwhelm the score or part, but it was worth it, especially since I didn't have to pay for it.

• *Licenses*. Licensing others' works to use in your own can be, make that *always is*, difficult. After all, the creators of those works or their estates, or their publishers, want to protect that music to the same extent you want to protect yours. For the purposes of this chapter, *you* are the one requesting a license, but as a composer you're going to be on the other side of the equation. It's good to know what happens from both points of view. We will discuss licenses further in the next chapter, but for now here is an overview. A *license* in this case is a formal agreement between you as the one wanting the license (the *licensee*) and the person or entity with the authority to issue that license (the *licensor*). Such a license will most likely cost money to be paid to the licensor; the amount is determined on a case-by-case and mostly arbitrary basis. The phrase "what the market will bear" comes to mind. Remember here we're only talking about licensing for the purpose of incorporating another composer's copyrighted work into your own. Things are less capricious and more predictable when it comes to other kinds of licenses (print, mechanical rights, etc.).

• *Sampling*. Hip-hop has been around for more than half a century and elements of it have made their way into concert music over that time. One aspect of the genre is the use of others' recorded music, of *sampling* those works.

Sometimes it's just a drumbeat, other times a short melodic or harmonic phrase. If you use sampling in your concert music you will need to deal with the following: (1) if it's a recording, is the *recording* Public Domain? (It can be if its old enough, but you have to do your homework to find out.); (2) is the *music* on the recording PD? If the answer is "no" to either or both you will need to obtain a license for whichever is protected by copyright. This will come up again, so it deserves emphasis: using a recording of someone else's music requires you to deal with both the recording *and* the music it contains.

Some final words about copyright. Register your works not only to protect your creation, but to protect yourself from having to deal with lawsuits whether you initiate them or someone else sues you. It's well worth the time, effort, and, yes, the money. Have questions about copyright? The Copyright Office has answers for just about anything that comes up on their website *and* you can contact them directly if you can't find what you need. It's your tax dollars at work and readily available for your use.

NOTES

1. The U.S. Copyright Office provides a variety of information on its website, www.copyright.gov, both online and as downloadable pamphlets called "Circulars." Circular 1, "Copyright Basics," gives a good overall view of what copyright is and how it works. You can download it here: **https://www.copyright.gov/circs/circ01.pdf.**

2. Circular 1 provides some information on copyright durations, but you can find more details in Circular 15A, "Duration of Copyright." You can download it here: **https://www.copyright.gov/circs/circ15a.pdf**.

3. Circular 38A, "International Copyright Relations of the United States," is a list of countries with whom the United States has agreements regarding copyright, as well as other related information. You can download it here: **https://www.copyright.gov/circs/circ38a.pdf.**

4. Circular 1, "Copyright Basics," *op. cit.* See definition of *fixed work* in the first paragraph.

5. Because the nature of and need for copyright notices have changed over the years, there may be different rules as to when and how they are to be used. For more detailed information, see Circular 3, "Copyright Notice," available for download here: **https://www.copyright.gov/circs/circ03.pdf.**

6. The index is updated regularly, about once a year. You can access it here: **https://www.copyright.gov/fair-use/.**

Chapter 2

INCOME STREAMS

DEFINITIONS AND EXPLANATIONS

Believe me, my sole purpose is to make as much money as possible; for after good health it is the best thing to have.

—Wolfgang Amadeus Mozart

"USE" VERSUS "PERFORMANCE"

This warrants repetition: more often than not, *you can't make a living as a concert music composer.* But your music can, and should, be able to earn income. So where does the money come from? In the most general sense, the music you write can generate money in one of two ways, through *performance* and *use.* Below is a basic chart showing different income sources or streams, starting with your composition and followed by the two basic income possibilities, but first let's define some terms.

Performance is the act of presenting your composition to be heard. We tend to think of a "performance" solely as "live," that is presented in front of an audience in person by the musicians involved. It's not always the case. Much if not most of the music we hear these days is streamed, downloaded, or aired on television and, still hanging in there, radio. Those performances may feature live musicians presenting music as it happens, or they may have been recorded and then disseminated. Hearing the music, whether that performance is live or recorded, is what makes it a performance.

Anything that requires your music but is actually not a performance is a *use* of it. For example, if someone wants to record your music, then they will need permission to use it. When the resulting recording is heard, the music is then considered a performance. If someone buys the sheet music, that is

19

considered a *use* as well. Synchronization (or "Synch") licenses are for the *use* of your music in audiovisual media. In fact, any sort of license to utilize your work that doesn't directly involve performance is a use.[1] Figure 2-1 shows, in general terms, different ways a single composition could generate income.

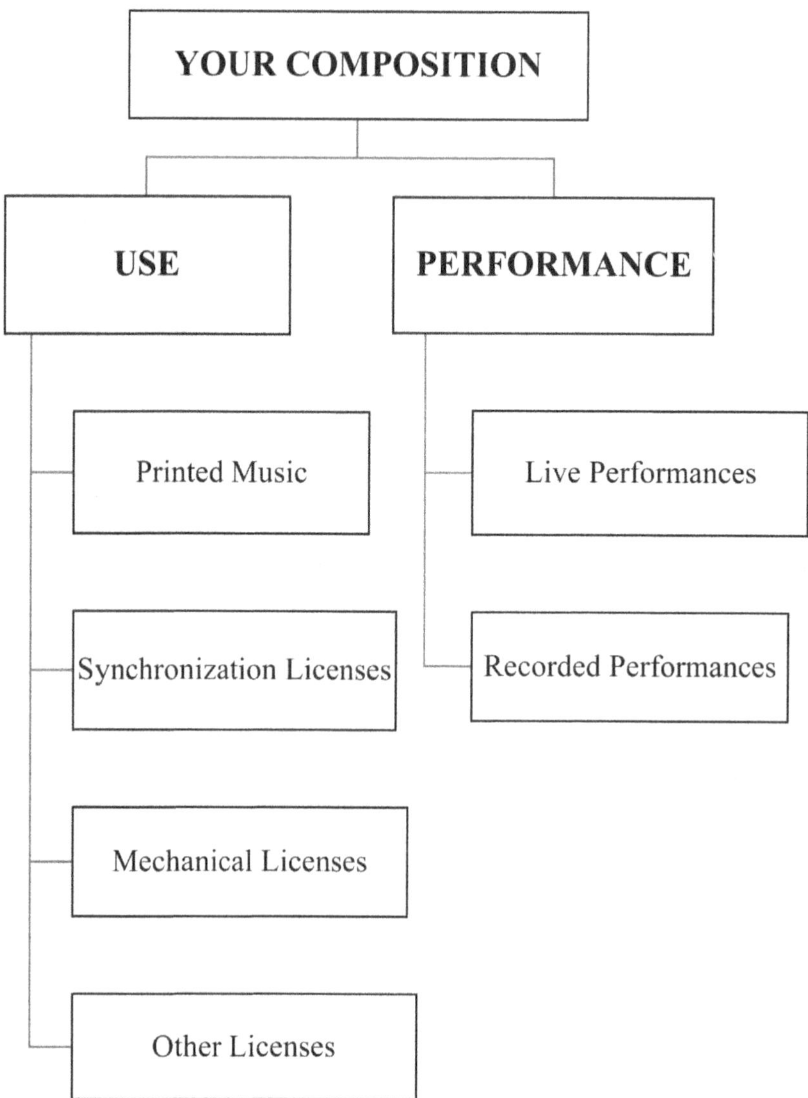

Figure 2-1   Possible Income Streams for One Composition, author created

Here's a hypothetical example in which one work could generate income. You've received a paid commission from the Second Tier String Quartet to write a new work. The result, your Third String Quartet, *aka* "Rosins," goes over well with the performers and the premiere's audience. Your Performing Rights Organization (PRO), which collects and distributes monies to its members based on performances of their music, is notified of the performance and arranges for you to be paid a performance royalty later in the year. Meanwhile, Second Tier has decided to record "Rosins," so they work out a license with you (or your publisher) to allow that to happen.

Since we're being hypothetical though, let's make the Second-Tier recording of "Rosins" a hit; sales and downloads are through the metaphorical roof, and it's even getting a lot of play across the nation via terrestrial radio. The "plays" you get are performances. Your PRO tracks those performances too, so more royalties are forthcoming. Your publisher has been on the ball as well, making sure the sheet music is prepared and available for sale to other musicians. You get royalties for each printed copy sold, and every new performance of that music generates more performance royalties. The publisher also arranges for a synch license with the producers of the next blockbuster movie in a series in a major science-fiction multiverse. But wait, as the old ads would say, there's more. That movie is a hit too, so naturally a soundtrack album is needed; that means yet another license is needed for your composition, and you get paid again. Also necessary are additional licenses to use the original recording from the Second Tier and you. And, if the movie is later shown on a cable station or internet streaming service, you've earned more performance royalty credits.

Those are a lot of possibilities from just one piece of music, right? Truthfully, the probability of *all* of that happening is slim. But the more you know about those possibilities, the more likely it is that you can help make them happen. Let's do a quick review of the hypothetical income sources, or streams:

POSSIBLE USE INCOME

* Commissioning fee (paid to have you compose the work)
* Recording license ("mechanical license" to record the work and disseminate it for profit)
* Print royalties (earned from sales of the work's sheet music)
* Synch license (to use the music in an audiovisual work)
* Mechanical license #2 (to use your music in the soundtrack album from the audiovisual work)

POSSIBLE PERFORMANCE INCOME

* Performance royalty (earned from the live premiere)

* Performance royalties (earned from radio play, etc., of the original recording)
* More performance royalties (earned from play of the movie in which the music appears)

COMPETITIONS, GRANTS, COMMISSIONS, AND COMPOSITION AND ARRANGING JOBS

Not all of the money composers can earn fits easily into either the "use" or "performance" categories, more so when you're at the actual writing stage of a new work. Winning competitions or contests, receiving grants, or getting commissions to write could be considered "use," although that's probably pushing the limits of the definitions we've been using. But contests, grants and, perhaps especially, commissions are an important aspect of our careers as composers and should be discussed.

As a composer I think of writing music as, well, a biological function. It's something I *must* do. But if I'm going to do it there are certain things I want in return: performances of my creations, hopefully positive reactions from those who perform or hear them, and, last but not at all least, compensation for the time and effort I put into the act of creation. That brings up the age-old question of "how do I support myself while I'm writing my music?" There are inevitable non-composing music jobs like performing and teaching, and they're important. So are jobs outside the music business. But any job, while supporting you so you can write, can often take time away from the act of writing. Unless, as composer Virgil Thompson once pointed out, you've inherited wealth or married into it, you need to bring in income somehow. And while getting prize money from a contest, grant, or commission may not pay the rent or put food on the table, it can help take up some of the financial slack if you get it.

Composition competitions, contests, and certain "calls for scores" all have several things in common. In general, they ask for new works, usually written within specific instrumentation requirements. Those specifics vary, but many competitions may also have restrictions in the composer's age ("composers under the age of 35") or location ("must reside within a 100-mile radius of . . ."), or other demographics. There can be musical restraints like the performed duration of the submitted works, or things like "must be unpublished" or "no more than one prior performance."

  * *Competitions and contests.* Some competitions ask to see scores without identifying information (i.e., your name). This is to help keep the judges of the competitions as honest and unbiased as possible. It's not foolproof, but it does help. Just make sure you've registered the copyright before sending the material. You can even leave "© [year]" on the first page of score if you

wish but take your name off. In addition to a score, competitions and contests sometimes want a recording that is either a live performance or an audio mockup, perhaps a one-page version of your biography and even a history of the work's performances. Competitions will at times also ask for an entry fee.

Some contests and competitions require you turn over all of your rights to the work you've submitted. (Did warning bells ring out just now? Did a mechanical voice yell, "Warning! Warning! Danger!"?) Let's say it plainly: NO competition, contest, or call for scores should ever get ownership of your music. Ever. Consider this yet another reason to register the copyright on your music.

What do you get, and what can you get, by entering one of your compositions in a competition? That depends on the competition itself: how long it has been in operation, its overall budget, and how much respect it has earned in the music world. Submitting a work to a competition could get you any or all of the following:

- The challenge of writing for a specific instrumentation or situation. It could be for an odd instrumentation, but more contests ask for works for more traditional ensembles or solo instruments. If you haven't already written for those, then this would be an opportunity to do so. Even if you're asked to submit a work for a strange instrument or combination of instruments, you can always rescore it later for more traditional forces.
- You could win prize money. The prestige of winning is nice, but the prestige of winning *and* having the satisfaction of receiving a check is even nicer. You've seen or heard the joke about the club or restaurant owner who tells a musician to "come play at my place for free; you'll get a lot of exposure," to which the musician replies, "that's great; my rent just went up 800 exposures per month." Most composers, unless they're rich to begin with, would prefer both the prestige and a check.
- A promise of at least one live performance by the musician(s) involved can be important to composers regardless of where they are in their careers. Even if a prize isn't offered, live performances are always welcome. Music doesn't really "live" until it's performed and heard. Besides, when your music is performed you can still earn money through your PRO.
- A promise of a commercial recording can be a career booster too. And, once again, you would be earning money through mechanical licenses and performances when the recording is played.
- Increased name recognition overall and within the musical community has no monetary value you can place on it. It is, in effect, priceless. Few living concert music composers have name recognition outside of the immediate musical community, so any chance your name can be "out there" in the world is good.

- You can gain increased credibility as a professional composer, which is particularly beneficial at the beginning of one's career. Having "winner of the XYZ Prize" in your bio can be pretty impressive to other musicians, audiences, grant givers, etc.
- Increased interest in, and respect for, your music overall and the submitted work in particular, from other musicians who could perform it can be reason enough to submit your work. Most composers have found that as exceedingly difficult as it is to get a work premiered, it's even more challenging to get a second performance, so winning a competition may help.

But there are potential downsides to entering contests as well.

- Any competition or contest that requires you to turn over your ownership, including that of copyright, of your music, should be avoided completely. It would essentially, and most likely legally, make your music a "work for hire." Works for hire are controlled by the ones who do the hiring. You could lose any and all rights and there would be nothing you could do about it without bringing a lawsuit, and even then you might lose the case. Financially you'd be stuck as well, as whatever monies you might have received as a "prize" could be considered onetime compensation.
- Entering any contest requiring a fee should be considered carefully. If the charge is nominal, say enough to cover shipping and handling for returning physical materials, it can be considered reasonable and acceptable. But some competitions ask for fees that are much higher. In those cases, there is a likelihood those fees contribute to the prize itself. To put it bluntly, you could be funding your own or someone's prize. Some composers never enter any contest with a fee more than the cost of two cups of coffee at their favorite high-end coffee shop. Other composers, like me, never enter any with any fee at all. My reasoning is simple. It's my music; if you like it, you give *me* money, or a performance, or a recording or, preferably, all three. My advice to you? Be wary.

Thanks to internet search engines, it's easy to find out about contests, competitions, and calls for scores you can enter. Entering "composer competitions [this year]" into search engines will bring up thousands of hits. There will be duplications of course, but those remaining will be lists of contests as well as links to individual ones. You can refine your search by adding terms like "young composers," or specific instrumentation like "band," or just about anything you can imagine. You could also join a composer's organization like The Society of Composers, Inc., or The American Composers Forum, or perhaps a local one. Most of these groups offer always-updated lists of competitions, contests, and calls for scores, as well as other opportunities its membership might otherwise miss.

    * *Scholarships.* While the *fellowship, scholarship,* and *grant* are often treated as interchangeable, they're not. A *scholarship* is money given to students who are either currently enrolled or just entering a specific program in a college, university, or conservatory. Scholarships are monies awarded solely to support the student's education and they are considered on the basis of the student's academic record or other achievements. The application process for a scholarship is similar to that for grants, but the specifics depend on the source. Scholarships can come from a school itself, or from a third-party person or organization. Some are subject specific, while others are more general in nature, and still others are based on criteria such as age, race, nationality, and so on. Some scholarships are given based on an essay. Scholarship money is given only to support the student's education; no work is required in return other than to maintain good grades in most cases. If you're in or about to enter school to study composition, look into a variety of scholarships.

    A *grant*, as described in more detail below, is money given based on the applicant's track record and/or potential for success in their work. A *fellowship*, for our purposes, is money and/or other considerations given to a student for a fixed period in exchange for teaching services or research. There are also medical fellowships, which operate on a different basis.

    * *Calls for scores.* A call for scores is just what it sounds like: musicians are asking to look at works by living composers with an eye to possible performance. Many of these calls don't require a fee, and those that do usually charge a token amount to cover their costs. But some charge a lot more. If a fee is requested learn as much as you can: what it costs, what the fee covers, what you can get out of it, and what you *don't* get for your hard-earned money. A large submission fee, like those for certain contests, is a way for the performers to fund the performances they're offering. By all means respond to calls for scores but be as cautious when it comes to fees as you should with contests.

    * *Grants.* So far, we've considered different ways of earning money mostly from the compositions we've written. What about earning some money *while* we compose, or to help keep us solvent so we can write? Getting a grant is one way to do this. A grant is money given outright to those shown to have professional level potential or have a proven track record as composers, but who do not have the financial resources to do their work without help. Grants come from a variety of sources, including music organizations; federal, state, or local government agencies, universities, fraternal organizations. Even corporations have been known to offer them. Grant money can vary in the amounts given, and grantors vary in how often they make grants available. As with competitions, you must apply for grants.

One rare exception is the MacArthur Fellowship, which is given to "individuals who show exceptional creativity in their work and the prospect for still more in the future," according to their website.[2] The awarded fellowship, known more familiarly as "the genius grant," is given with "no strings attached"—the recipient can do literally anything with the money, although the assumption is that the composing or other creative act will continue. The awarded amount, set as of 2024 at \$800,000, is extraordinary, even with it being paid out over five years in quarterly installments. But you cannot apply directly; you must be nominated, and the nomination and selection processes are largely kept private.

Grants offered by governmental agencies at any level will almost always focus on projects that can benefit society in some way. Some grants are co-sponsored by a government agency in conjunction with a national or local business, or a nongovernment charity.

Internet search engines are your friend when looking to apply for grants; entering "composer grants" will generate several *million* hits, and using any criteria relevant to you will help narrow that number down considerably. Most websites with information about grants will also provide instructions on how to apply for them. Read them carefully and follow those instructions precisely. With so many composers applying for the same grants, one item not filled out correctly could easily get it kicked out in the first round of screenings.

* *Commissions.* Commissions are often the first thing composers think of when it comes to earning money by writing music, but what exactly is a commission? The simplest explanation is that a commission is a formal request from someone or some entity to have you compose a piece of music with the expectation that it will be performed. Why do people commission new music?

- To add quality music to the repertoire for a specific instrument, instrumentation, level of technique, etc., that is otherwise lacking.
- To help support a local composer by giving the composer's music more exposure to audiences.
- To give musicians an opportunity to have music written expressly for them, to help bolster their own sense of worth, give "bragging rights," and so on. (This is very important for younger and/or less experienced musicians.)
- To commemorate an event, celebrate a holiday, or honor or memorialize an individual.

While you don't need a commission to start writing music, having someone ask you to write is motivating. But why write for a commission anyway? What can you get out of it?

- Money, usually and preferably. This is only to have you *write* the music. With very rare exception—again, preferably—we keep all of the rights to the music too, which allows us to potentially earn even more through performance royalties, and so on.[3]
- A chance (or excuse) to write in general, and perhaps to write something we don't normally get to do. Having more opportunities to express yourself musically is always a good thing.
- An almost guaranteed performance. I say "almost" because stuff happens, but in theory the commissioning party is promising to perform your work in asking you to write it. In formal agreements you'll spell such things out.
- A chance to write for specific performers or special event. Sometimes we'll accept a commission because the circumstances involve a cause we believe in and support.

In virtually all cases, you deserve to be paid for the act of composing, and if not paid outright you should be compensated in some fashion. But that concept scares people who might commission you. For most commissioning parties, be they individuals, ensembles, or organizations, the question that comes up first is *always* a variation of "what do you charge?" But what *do* you charge for your creative work? What factors enter into the equation? Unless you are a world-famous, already successful composer and can hard-set a rate—and most of us don't qualify, to be honest—"What do you charge?" is the wrong question. I suggest you tell whomever it is "before I answer you, let me ask *you* some questions." And then ask the following:

- *Who will be performing it?* Is it for professional musicians, community groups or other amateur performers, or students?
- *What are the instrumental and/or vocal forces involved?* Will it be a solo piece, a chamber work, or something for a larger ensemble?
- *How long is the desired piece?* Do you need a short piece, say three to five minutes, or something much longer?
- *When are you planning on performing the work?* Do you need it "yesterday," or in six weeks, or in six months, or for next year?
- *Why do you want the piece?* Is it for a special occasion, a particular holiday, or to celebrate an individual?

The very *last* question to ask a potential commissioner is about their budget. What can they actually afford? By this point, you will have an idea of what it is they want and need from you and what they are able to provide you as compensation. They in turn will have a much clearer concept of what goes into commissioning a work from you and what your time might be worth as a result. If everything is to your mutual satisfaction move on to the next step, which is formalizing an agreement. Depending on the people involved and the specific situation "formalizing" can be anything from a multi-paged written agreement to a "handshake deal." Unless the commission is from really good friends, I recommend getting things down in written form whenever possible, so all parties (1) know what is expected of them, (2) what to expect of the other party, and (3) the specific timing of events. There is a more detailed discussion on commissioning agreements in Chapter 8, "Contract (Agreement) Basics," but for now here are some suggestions to keep in mind.

- *Factor your estimated composition time into your negotiations.* You know your own composing process, and the amount of time you need to produce something in which you can feel pride. Say it takes you six months on average to write the type of piece they're asking you to compose but they want it in four months, or you already have other music on your desktop that needs to be completed. You can then decide whether to say "no" to the project (you *can* say that, you know), or increase your fee to accommodate the extra effort you'll be putting in. Also, add in a little extra composition time, if you can. A little "wiggle room" is always good.
- *Create a timeline for the commission.* It's best to work backward from the premiere date, in this order: premiere, deliver the parts (if any), deliver the score. Again, make sure you build in some flexibility. If you know it would take you a week to generate the parts, ask for two, and so on. Also be sure to give the musicians enough time to rehearse as well.
- *Include a payment schedule in the timeline.* Payments can be made in any number of ways: full payment up front, full payment when all of the materials have been delivered, or split payments. For large commission fees, I prefer building the payment schedule into the formal agreement. I usually ask for half of the fee on both parties signing the agreement, with the other half paid on delivery of the score. Any parts are delivered within an agreed-upon amount of time after that. Also included is the stipulation that, if for any reason the project is cancelled after the agreement is signed and while I'm in throes of composition, the first payment is then considered a "kill fee" that is non-refundable and non-recoupable. So far no one has questioned this even if they want to negotiate the amount for the first payment,

because they realize it would be fair compensation for the work I've already put into the project.

- *Maintain the rights to your work.* Unless you choose to accept otherwise, you own the work you're writing for the commission. That covers all of your rights, including and especially that of copyright. When commissioned, make sure the other party knows they are being given certain exclusive rights as part of the agreement but not anything beyond them and with certain limitations. You can offer the exclusive right to premiere the work within a given time frame for example, and/or their name in a dedication in the score, but the music is *yours.*

Figuring out what to charge for your work is nerve-racking, frankly. You want to find a balance between what you *know* your music is worth and, in business terms, "what the market will bear." Some composers have a strict set of guidelines for commissioning fees based on the instrumentation and type of work (orchestra, chamber, band, etc.), the technical level of the music (professionals, amateurs, school musicians *et al.*), the desired length of the work. This works well for many established composers, who are generally busy enough to be able to say "no" to a project because the fee can't be met. For others it's more important to write the music no matter the financial situation. Finding out what the commissioning party's budget is like is a simple and direct way to help you determine if you should do the gig.

You've no doubt noticed there have been no specific commissioning amounts mentioned so far. The simple reason is that rates or averages vary wildly and never stay the same; everything changes frequently and, just as often, drastically. *Any specific amount of money I tell you* ("you'll earn $162.23 per . . .") *will be wrong by the time this book has been printed, if not much sooner.* You'll have to do some research beyond this book to find out the currently going rates for whatever it is you want to do. There are of course resources available that can give you an idea.

There is a fascinating and mostly useful tool available on the New Music USA website called the Commissioning Fees Calculator.[4] You start by narrowing down the genre of music you write. Once you've selected the genre— for our purposes it's "Concert Music"—you're then asked to select the instrumentation of the piece, starting with the number of musicians ranging from "Solo or Duo" to "(22–40 players)." Adjust your selections according to what you know you need. The last prompt is for the estimated duration of the work, going from "under 10'" to "over 25'." It then gives you a range of what you could/should charge for commissioned work of that type, that duration, and so on.

There is also a PDF booklet covering the same information available on the same website, which might be better to have handy as a reference. What is interesting is that as of this writing, the monetary amounts given in both the booklet and the calculator haven't been updated since 2009, yet the ranges of money given seem high even after more than a decade. Unless it's revised, the amounts will seem less formidable as inflation, etc., affects the economy. The calculator assumes you will be commissioned by top-tier musicians or organizations who can afford to pay your exact worth. The suggested fees are likely to be fine when you're writing for world-famous musicians and organizations, but they seem out of reach for both most commissioning parties and composers.

In the best of all possible worlds—my apologies to philosopher Gottfried Leibniz, and later, Voltaire—composers would be paid what they're worth. But no matter how much potential commissioning parties want to have you write music for them, funding is all too often an issue. Available money can be severely limited. Professional and large community ensembles are more likely to apply for funding through grants and other resources but you can assume their own budgets don't cover commissions. Smaller community and religious institution ensembles will also have limited budgets, and funding for school music programs is dependent on the school's location, the community's tax base, and so much more. One way composers and the musicians interested in commissioning new works have developed to work around limited funding is through consortium commissions.

* *Consortium commissions.* A consortium commission is one in which a group of similar musicians or ensembles agree upon an amount they *each* can afford to pay so that the composer receives a total that is appropriate for the work done. That total amount would otherwise be difficult to get from any single commissioner. An increasing number of composers, me included, have taken to initiating consortium commissions because of the mutual benefits assuming all goes well.

- If the consortium meets its goal of having a certain number of participants, composers can receive the amount they would expect from one source to write the piece. If the consortium is open-ended but goes over the break-even point—the amount the composer determines is appropriate—it can mean even more money for the composer.
- The participants pay less, often a lot less, for a work written expressly for their needs.
- The composer can receive as many performances as there are participants in the consortium. Depending on the situation, participants might give multiple performances once they've given their premiere.
- Participants get bragging rights—"*we* commissioned this," and "the composer wrote this for *us*"—are powerful reasons to boast.

- With multiple performances comes multiple performance royalties from the composer's PRO.
- And with multiple performances, the work stands to be considered by other musicians, by music publishers, and so on, because it has already been proven to be a viable piece of music. It has been given a track record.

Commissioning agreements for consortium situations are much the same as for individual commissions. The only difference, as you will read in Chapter 8, is that certain information will vary from one consortium participant's contract to another. Each will consider premiere dates, the sizes of the commissioning fees, and so on.

** Arranging.* Arranging, as I like to tell my composition students, is composing with someone else's ideas. But that concept is a little simplistic. Is an orchestral version of a solo piano work an arrangement, a transcription, an orchestration, or some amalgam of all three? A transcription is an adaptation, taking a work written for one medium and rendering it for a different one. If it's a literal transcription, instruments will be assigned lines that adhere as closely to the original ones as possible, with little added creatively except timbre. A string orchestra transcription of a chorale harmonized by J. S. Bach is an example familiar to anyone who has taken an orchestration class in college. But if a more creative approach is taken and certain liberties are taken with range, instrumentation, and so on, I would call it an orchestration. But an arrangement goes beyond a transcription or orchestration. When something is arranged, even if for the same forces as the original, it implies significant changes have been made. The changes can be structural, by adding or rearranging sections. The music can be reharmonized. Altered or new countermelodies can be introduced. The style (or feel or groove) of a work can be altered as well. Jazz composers and arrangers do this sort of thing all the time.

At what point is an arrangement, or a transcription, considered a composition? There is no clear answer. Mussorgsky's piano work "Pictures at an Exhibition" is a fantastic work in its own right, but more people know the orchestral version written by Maurice Ravel. It's a transcription, yes, but it's also an orchestral *tour de force*. As such, when it's performed by an orchestra both composers get credit. Stravinsky, on the other hand, took music by Pergolesi and completely transformed it—made it his own—when he wrote *Pulcinella.* Stravinsky didn't just transcribe the music, he also made changes in the harmonies, the structure, and other ways music theorists still explore.

You will probably arrange as well as compose music at various points in your career to earn some money, so here are two suggestions. First: unless you have prior permission or a license, or if you're hired by the copyright owner to do it, do *not* write arrangements or transcriptions of copyright protected material. That would be infringement. Second, if you're creating a transcription be as faithful to the original as you can. Audiences will hear it with certain expectations. But if you're writing an arrangement, you can be as creative as you want with the original music. It's "composing with someone else's ideas" after all. Again, remember to keep enough of the original present so folks will recognize it *and* what you've done with it.

When your work is arranging PD material, you can claim complete ownership, including copyright. Give credit to the original composer, if known because, well, people will know. In all other respects you can treat it as if it's one of your own original works. If you get the work published, you can earn the full writer's royalty on sales of the sheet music, and performances will earn you full credit from your PRO.

Writing an arrangement of copyrighted material is an entirely different matter. Early in my career I wrote arrangements of popular tunes for major music publishers. I did it to get something with my name on it "out there," to develop some credibility as a writer of music, to earn money so I could compose my own works and, frankly, to stretch my abilities and learn more about my craft. I only wrote arrangements of songs the publisher owned or controlled. No other publisher could legally publish them anyway because they didn't own the rights. And because it was almost always pop music, the publishers of the time had the idea that it was all somewhat disposable. (They still do this.) They would only print a limited number of copies of arrangements of the latest hits, and that would be it; they would let it go out of print. By the time sales would inevitably dwindle the publishers were onto the next hit song. Having to pay royalties on sales of the sheet music for arrangements of pop music didn't make sense to the publishers because of the lack of "shelf life," nor to me as the arranger because of the intentional limitations on the number of copies printed. Instead, I accepted being paid a single "flat" fee for each arrangement, the amount varying with the type of arrangement. Big publishers are still around and still put out a lot of arrangements of the latest hits, so there are possible opportunities to get work as an arranger. Most pay a single fee and your arrangement is considered a "work for hire." It should be said that the odds of getting arranging work of this type are slim. And the pay per arrangement isn't really much better than it was decades ago when I started out either. But hey, it's work, it's writing (someone else's) music, and it's a way for people to get to know your name.

You can arrange music for any number of situations and performers. I've been commissioned to write arrangements of Christmas music for bassoon and cello duet, and traditional Irish songs for soprano and concert band. Your name goes on the arrangements, performers remember you (especially if the arrangements are good!), and your work does your networking for you.

You can earn money arranging and orchestrating for staged musicals, and for films as well. These can be lucrative, especially film work, but both are exceedingly difficult work to obtain and, once you get the jobs, you don't get to own your work. You might not even get credit. Another thing to consider is that work in either field can offer you opportunities to make connections, develop a good reputation, and put you in the right place at the right time to get in on the actual composition end of things.

One more thing: if you're under thirty-five years of age, very fit, and honestly patriotic, you can try for one of the rare salaried jobs as a writer of music—being an arranger for one of the U.S. military bands. Many a famous composer and/or arranger have started out that way, including film composer John Williams and big-band composer-arranger Sammy Nestico, just to name two. Be aware that military funding goes in cycles or pendulum swings, so such positions may not be available when you're looking.

PUBLICATION (SHEET MUSIC)

A source of possible income from your music can be the sales of it in sheet music form, whether it's as physical printed product or as digital downloads, and through traditional publishers, self-publishing, or some hybrid of the two. There are upsides to having sheet music of your work available in print:

* You get an opportunity to disseminate your work to a larger number of musicians.

* The chances of having more performances as a result of sales of sheet music increase.

* You stand to make some money with each sale.

* Most performances of the music purchased will result in performance royalties.

When a copy of your music is sold by a publisher or by you acting as your own publisher, as either a physical copy or digital download for the consumer to print out, you earn a print royalty. A *print royalty* is a percentage of the retail selling price set by the publisher (or by you). In Chapter 6, there is more detailed discussion of how this works and even some basic figures with which to work, but for now know the following:

* The amount of money a traditional publisher earns net (after expenses) on the sale of a copy of your music is a *lot* less than you think.

* Some publishers will offer a percentage of the *wholesale* price, which is the price they sell the music-to-music dealerships for sale to the consumer. If the publisher suggests a retail price of, for sake of this discussion, ten dollars, they are selling it to the dealership for about five dollars. It always works better to get a percentage of the full retail selling price.

* If you're self-publishing keep in mind that you will be paying all of the expenses that a traditional publisher has to shell out. Some of those expenses will be relatively smaller than a big publisher simply because you are dealing with a smaller catalog, a much smaller staff, and a smaller base of operations and its costs, but you will have them.

* Going with an established publisher *versus* self-publishing is ultimately a personal choice based on a number of factors which are discussed in Chapter 6.

"LIVE" AND "RECORDED" PERFORMANCES

If music is presented for entertainment or enrichment, or the education of listeners, then it is a performance. But a "performance" can have several meanings when it comes to it potentially generating income. We think of a "live performance" as one in which there are performers and an audience together in one place, and that's certainly true. We also tend to think of a "recorded performance" as something done in a recording studio, and that is true as well. But possibilities branch out from there. A broadcast of a performance in progress over radio or television or having it on something like YouTube is now an additional form of "live performance." Broadcasting a recording of that live event is also considered a performance, as is doing the same with something recorded in a studio. And if a work is performed live and recorded for commercial release, and that commercial release is then presented over some sort of media, they are also considered not one performance but two.

Putting things into perspective, let's use the hypothetical example from the beginning of this chapter. The first performance is the Second String Quartet having played your work "Rosins" before a live audience. They have also paid for a mechanical license to record the performance for commercial release, and later release the recording for sale, downloading, etc. The recording of your work is now played over various media, and those plays are also considered performances. Your PRO will be busy on your behalf. We'll get to PROs in a bit.

STREAMING AND DOWNLOADING MUSIC

"Streaming" and "downloading" are related terms in that both are methods for hearing audio files and watching audiovisual files from the internet on your device (computer, phone, etc.). Both became available in the 1990s but didn't take off in popularity for another decade or so. There are plenty of music streaming and downloading services, and the same for videos; many of these services provide both.

Streaming is the delivery of media—audio files, for our purposes—over the internet instantly, but not permanently, for the consumer. Files are broken down into small data packets to be read by a device's streaming application (app); the app reads and plays each packet as it comes in, discarding it as the next one arrives. Nothing of the file is retained or saved.

Downloading conveys media much the same way, except the files are retained on the consumer's computer, phone, etc. Whether it's as streaming or downloading, the files are kept on a large-capacity computer system, or server, to be transmitted to a consumer's device.

Even broken down into data packets, sound files are usually too large to effectively transmit, receive, and process. (Audiovisual files are even larger.) Raw, that is unaltered, files would overwhelm the internet, so streaming services process the files using a coder-decoder program, or codec. Codecs compress the data at the sending end of a transmission and decompress them on the receiving end. Some files lose data we don't often notice when they're decompressed, like frequencies outside of normal human hearing. These are known as "lossy" files. The sound is decent enough and the files are comparatively small. Other codecs create files that are considered "lossless" but those files are larger. Currently, the best-known sound file types are mp3 and AAC (lossy), and Apple Lossless Audio Codec. These are very different from uncompressed formats like AIFF and wav files, which you'll more likely find in recording apps and offer higher-quality sounds.

Streaming and downloading are used much more for popular music than for concert music, but earning income this way is possible. Any digital service provider (DSP) wanting to provide downloads or streaming of your music needs a mechanical license, just as anyone making a physical recording needs one. Your publisher, or you if your music isn't with a traditional publisher, will collect and share equally with you, those mechanical royalties. And any time that music is streamed (performed), it generates a performance royalty which your Performing Rights Organization will collect and distribute. An important distinction to remember is that streaming is a performance, but downloading is a use and requires a mechanical license.

PERFORMANCE ROYALTIES

To paraphrase a poem by the poet and author Gertrude Stein, a performance is a performance is a performance, whether the music is presented in person or through an electronic or digital medium, or if the musicians are performing "live" in real time or recorded and the recording is played back. If music is presented and meant to be heard, it is performed. And we've established that performances should generate income for its creators. But how?

Performing Rights Organizations (PROs) track performances, issue and maintain performance licenses, collect fees for those licenses, and distribute monies—performance royalties—to their writer and publisher members.

PROs are informed of performances in different ways depending on the medium as well as the type of music presented. Concert composers are most often their own reporters, letting their PROs know when something of theirs will be or has been performed. PROs collect fees from the presenters and distribute those fees to their members in as fair a manner as possible. We will go into more detail about PROs and what they do in the next chapter, but here's an overview.

The United States have three PROs: ASCAP, BMI, and SESAC. Writers (composers and lyricists) can only belong to one PRO at a time. It's okay if a work is created by a team consisting of members of each, such as a composer being a member of ASCAP and a lyricist belonging to BMI. Any performance revenue generated for that team would by necessity be divided between the two PROs and, therefore, each of the writers. Say you're the composer of a choral work and you belong to BMI, but your collaborator, the lyricist, belongs to SESAC. You get a major performance of your work, with a sold-out audience, that is reported to both of your PROs. BMI will process only your part of that performance and issue you a performance royalty accordingly. SESAC will only process your collaborator's portion and issue the lyricist's performance royalty appropriately as well.

PROs only handle performances of *non-theatrical*, that is *non-dramatic*, musical works. Performances presented on television, radio, in restaurants and, especially, in concert and recital halls, are all covered by PROs, as long as they are considered non-theatrical. Each PROs negotiates and issues what's called "blanket licenses," which allow a venue or station or other performance venue to use any of the PRO's catalog of music. As near as can be figured, all three organizations are fair in their methodology for collecting performance data and in their distribution of performance royalties.[5]

MECHANICAL LICENSES

Any time you transfer some of the rights to your music while retaining others including the copyright, you are issuing a license. You are, by definition, the *licensor* and the person or entity to whom you are issuing the license is the *licensee*. In almost all circumstances a license is granted in exchange for some form of financial compensation. There are many types of licenses and many variations on each one; there are no true standard licenses save for *compulsory mechanical licenses*, which we will discuss in a bit, and even then, there can be differences. Yet there are commonalities among licenses that are used to determine what is charged:

* The music itself being licensed is the first factor considered. When prose is licensed, there are often restrictions dealing with *moral rights*, which essentially protect the work owner's ability to control the work's fate. Moral rights are defined by the Berne Convention as the right "to claim authorship of the work and to object to any distortion, mutilation or other modification of, or other derogatory action in relation to, the said work, which would be prejudicial to his honor or reputation." Similar concerns are often addressed when licensing music as well.

* A second factor in determining licenses is the duration. For music licenses "duration" has two meanings. The first is the duration of the music itself and how much of that is used. The second meaning is for the duration of the license itself, which can take different forms depending on the type of license.

* A third factor is determining where the music will be used. Music license for local use, say for a single radio commercial or a local production of a Broadway musical, may be less than for something intended to be used worldwide.

* Additional factors can include how the music is to be used—the context in which it is placed—and the manner in which it is presented.

* Finally, licenses can be issued as exclusive or non-exclusive. Non-exclusive licenses, which allow copyright owners to issue similar licenses to others, are more prevalent.

A *mechanical license* is granted to make recorded performances that can be reproduced and distributed in some way. These days this refers to sound recordings for distribution as streams, downloads, vinyl records, CDs, etc., but the term dates back to the beginning of the twentieth century, when player pianos were in vogue. Player pianos utilized rolls of paper punched with holes, called piano rolls, that corresponded to a musical work's notes; the mechanism inside the piano would "read" the data and would "play" the music. It's not that far a stretch to compare it to the "piano roll" view of many music sequencing programs today.[6] Before 1909 piano roll makers did so without compensating composers and publishers. In 1908 a court case that went all the way up to the Supreme Court determined that piano rolls weren't considered sheet music which would require royalty payments.

Naturally this made creative folks and their publishers irate, and they successfully lobbied Congress to do something about it. The 1909 Copyright Act formally declared that a license must be purchased to reproduce a musical work by mechanical means and set a statutory rate of two cents ($0.02) per item manufactured. Surprisingly that rate stuck for decades, not keeping up with inflation at all. That changed with the 1976 Copyright Act, which not only reset the rate but how it is determined. A compulsory mechanical license (the "mechanical" part of the term had since stuck) would be based on the number of what would be called "phonorecords" being both manufactured and distributed. The rate itself was raised to a whopping $0.0275 or $0.005 per minute, or fraction thereof, whichever is larger. Overall, it was a tiny change but recording companies still fought it the metaphorical "tooth and nail." Say your solo flute piece that has a duration of 1 minute is recorded for distribution on vinyl. You or your publisher would receive $0.0275 per record manufactured and distributed. But say your thirty-minute orchestral work is recorded, also for physical records. In that case you or your publisher would get a mechanical royalty of $0.15 per record. If we were to assume a year's sales of the flute recording were 1,000 units, you'd earn $27.50. The orchestral work selling the same number of units would generate $150.00. (If published by a traditional music publisher the monies earned in both cases would be collected by the publisher and share equally with you. You'd receive $13.75 in flute recording mechanical royalties, and $75.00 for the orchestra work.)

One of the more positive changes made over the years was the creation of the Copyright Royalty Board (CRB), which is a panel of three copyright royalty judges. The panel sets rates for five-year periods known as "Phonorecords I," "Phonorecords II," and so on. As of this writing (2024) we are in the "Phonorecords IV" period, and the current "per unit" statutory rate for physical media and digital downloads are up to 12.4 cents per recording or 2.38 cents per minute or fraction thereof, whichever is larger. The rates will no doubt change, and probably increase.[7]

Remember there are always two types of copyright for sound recordings, the copyright for the recording of the music and the copyright for the music itself. Mechanical licenses only apply to making a recording. Some changes—or arrangements—can be made if the specific license allows it to suit a performer's style, but anyone making the recording can never claim a copyright on the music itself if it doesn't already belong to them.

There are not only two types of copyrights involved with sound recordings, but also two different mechanical licenses entailed as well. You should know about these two licensing entities: The Harry Fox Agency and The Mechanical Licensing Collective (The MLC). The Harry Fox Agency (HFA) was established in 1927 to license music for mechanical reproduction—by piano rolls, records, and basically any and all *physical* products containing or utilizing music. HFA negotiates licenses, collects the resulting royalties, and distributes the monies to the publishers or composers involved. Long an independent organization, HFA was acquired by SESAC in 2015. And while they are owned by SESAC, there seems to be no discernable bias in its favor when it comes to dealing with mechanical licenses.[8]

The MLC is a separate, nonprofit organization created under the auspices of the U.S. Copyright Office as a result of the Music Modernization Act of 2018. The MLC's mission picks up where HFA leaves off, dealing with *digital reproduction* of music. According to its website The MLC strives "to ensure songwriters, composers, lyricists, and music publishers receive their mechanical royalties from streaming and download services in the U.S. accurately and on time."[9] Although separate, HFA is a vendor to The MLC and shares its musical works data with it and even helps with matching the data and with royalty processing.

If your music is not with a traditional publisher and you need to issue mechanical licenses for your work, find out how the music will be distributed, whether it will be just for physical media, for digital streaming and downloads, or both. Contact both HFA and The MLC as necessary but consider working with the Harry Fox Agency first as it may save you some time due to their vendor status with the Collective. Check both websites for more information before you do anything though, especially since operating procedures and laws may change by the time you read this book.

One side note: There are instances when a mechanical license is needed for situations you wouldn't normally associate with "sound recordings." These include, but aren't limited to, music boxes and things like greeting cards with embedded sound chips. Yes, music boxes are similar to player pianos in how they operate, and they are still made and sold. Physical greeting cards may not have the sales they used to but they, too, are still produced, and some play a recording of some sort when they are opened. Both of these items require mechanical licenses and, if the greeting card's sound chip is using a specific recording, an additional license is needed for that recording. These are all considered "use" of the music.

COMPOSING AND SYNCHRONIZATION FOR VISUAL MEDIA (TELEVISION, VIDEO GAMES, FILM, ETC.)

While *The Concert Composer's Business Handbook* is for those of us who primarily write music for the concert and recital hall, many of us write, or want to write, for visual media. There are books and other resources available that can give you a wealth of information on the musical, technical, and business aspects of this part of the music business, but a brief discussion here may be helpful. If you plan on getting heavily involved in media scoring you're going to need the following:

* Beyond your training/education as a composer, you'll need to learn how visual media are made with attention to how music and other sounds are added, produced, edited, etc.

* A basic understanding of the media industry itself, both overall and its various subsets (movies, television, video games et al.).

* You'll also need a résumé and a portfolio of your work. That of course begs the question, "How do I put together a portfolio if I haven't done anything yet?" See the next portion.

* Gaining experience is imperative, yes. Getting work with the big-league directors and producers requires having a track record. Putting together those all-important resumés and portfolios is impossible without the experience. So to gain the experience, build up your résumé, and have a portfolio to show potential clients, here are some suggestions. (1) You can start in several ways. You can take courses (even earn a degree) in film and media scoring at many universities, colleges, and other institutions of higher learning; or you can work with student filmmakers, creating scores for their short film assignments for a nominal fee. You can find the students at many of the same schools that have film scoring programs or, if you're in an area without any such programs, you can find them on social media. (2) Your portfolio should be a short "reel" (video, really), with a three-to-five-minute total duration, with clips demonstrating your basic compositional skills as well as a variety of musical styles with which you feel comfortable. The music should demonstrate how it can be used in different ways—as scoring for title sequences or end credits, as underscoring for emotional or action scenes, and so on. (3) As for musical advice, be *you* in your writing, not a clone of someone more established/famous. (4) That said, if a director says to you, "Can you write me something like [famous film composer's name here] did for [movie the composer is known for]?" answer truthfully, well, mostly. If you *know* you can do it, say so. If you *think* you can but you're entirely not sure, say "yes" with confidence and do your homework later to work out how to get the sound the director wants. But if the musical style is so completely alien to you, however, there is no shame in saying so. You won't get *that* gig, but your honesty might work in your favor for a later project with that director.

* Networking is important too; all you need is that one person to say to a director or producer, "I know someone who would be perfect for your project." It doesn't happen all that often, but it does happen. Social media is wonderful for networking, and some forms have specific forums for filmmakers that you can tap and make your presence known.

Composing for visual media is different from writing for the concert hall in many, but not all, ways. The idea for both is to communicate musical ideas through our choices of melody, harmony, rhythm, dynamics, structure, orchestration, and so on. The main difference is that media composers do so at the service of what is being presented on the screen; the music can support emotions or negate them, or help set a scene in time and place, or it can set the overall tone. Even then, there's an element of being deferential to the drama presented when we write operas, ballets and, of course, musical theater, but other factors also come into play. Writing music for media, particularly for television shows and movies, is usually within tight budgets and even tighter time frames. (There are always exceptions, of course, like full orchestras used for certain science-fiction movies.)

Another way music for media can differ from concert music is while concert works are created with a sense of overall musical structure in mind, music for media is often thought of and treated as a series of cues. A *cue* in cinematic terms is a piece of music that is to be heard from beginning to end of a sequence or scene. (The word comes from theater, where a cue is an indication for an actor to start. Sometimes, it's a bit of a dialogue line given to a stage actor surreptitiously who has forgotten it.)

Because of the lack of time—music is almost always added last to any visual medium project, most composers now use a variety of computer programs and sound libraries to create at least a reasonable mockup of a performance of the score. Sometimes it becomes the score or an element of it, especially if the sounds are meant to be otherworldly in some way. Once that is done the rest of the team—even if it's just one other person—finishes the work by completing the orchestration, then the parts for any musicians who may record the score. If there is a recording session and the composer isn't doing it, a conductor (which could be the orchestrator) will be brought in to lead. Everything is done as quickly and in as few takes as possible for each cue.

Before going further, a word of caution: *Don't do any large-scale media scoring project without first consulting with an attorney and/or agent (if you have one).* As you will see, writing music for media can be very rewarding, but negotiating for the work is not for the faint of heart.[10]

We briefly discussed cue sheets in reporting the use of music in media earlier, but what wasn't stressed is that cue sheets list *all* of the music used in a film or television program. That not only includes the music written for the project itself—underscoring, title and end credit sequences and, rarely, music heard/performed by the characters themselves—but also any pre-existing music licensed for the program or movie. Either way, the music supports the actions and emotions presented or, as in title and end credits, helps us focus our own emotional responses to what we see. Underscoring cannot be heard by the characters onscreen (unless the character is "breaking the fourth wall" and acknowledging the audience) or it can be diegetic, that is heard or even performed by the characters. Cue sheets help keep track of all this information, making it easier for PROs and others to know how much money is owed to whom.

Preexisting music is often used in visual media in a variety of ways. (It happens much less so in video games, so we'll limit the discussion to television and movies.) The now-classic film *2001: A Space Odyssey* started with "temp tracks" of already recorded music selected as place holders to give the film's composer, Alex North, an idea of the types of music the director wanted. Through no fault of North's—his eventually unused score is powerful —director Stanley Kubrick chose to use the temp tracks as is and drop North's score altogether. (North still got paid.) As a result Kubrick had to get synchronization licenses to use recordings of Richard Strauss's symphonic tone poem *Also sprach Zarathustra* (*Thus Spoke Zarathustra*), as well as two works by György Ligeti, and even Johann Strauss II's *An der schönen blauen Donau* (*The Blue Danube*) waltz. For the music itself that was still under copyright, Kubrick had to secure synch licenses for both the recording of the music *and* the underlying music, that is the music featured in the recording.

When is film scoring *not* film scoring? When it's one song written expressly for the title portion or end credits of a movie. There are plenty of examples. Paul McCartney's "Live and Let Die" for the James Bond picture of that name; Christopher Cross's "Arthur's Theme (Best That You Can Do)" for the movie *Arthur*; and Sufjan Stevens "Mystery of Love" for the film *Call Me by Your Name* are just a few. For a songwriter as well as a concert composer, one of your songs at either end of a movie has the equivalent of prime real estate. Your music *will* be heard, and you can earn some serious money whether it is being licensed or newly written for the occasion. Music publishers currently charge synchronization fees in the low-to-mid-five-figure range to use an existing song or other piece of copyrighted music (which they will split with you). It can be less if the project's budget is small or of perceived lesser importance (student films, etc.), but it can also be higher if the music is heard more than once in the film or if it's important to the script. This is in addition to the licenses negotiated by the record company that owns the recording of the music. (A film producer *could*, conceivably, pay to have a new recording of the music made, but that rarely turns out to be cost effective, let alone musically satisfying.)[11]

So, how much do you get paid to write scores for film, or a television show. The answer is necessarily vague: it depends on a number of considerations. The primary factor is, always, the project's overall budget. A short student film will not have nearly the same size budget as a film produced by a major movie studio. Your stature as a composer is another important consideration. Are you well known in the industry? Are you well known as a concert composer? If you're already a film composer, what is your track record? Other factors come into play after that, many of which are important negotiating points. Let's look at the sorts of things that get covered in a typical film composing contract:

* What the composer is expected to do. This most often includes all aspects of the music's creation and production for the film until it's handed over to the project's music editor: composing, arranging and orchestrating as necessary (or hiring people to do it to save the composer time), hiring musicians as necessary and as the budget allows), *and* the amount of time in which the composer has to do all of this.

* Transportation and living expenses. With a compressed and stressful period of time usually imposed on such projects, these expenses are not considered unusual. This is especially true in cases where the composer lives in another state (or country!) from where the production and/or music recording is taking place.

* Screen credit and credit in advertising. In 99.99 percent of the movies and television shows produced you will see the composer of the music get credit on screen. How long the name stays on screen, where in the title or end credit sequences it appears, and how prominently (how large is the font in relation to the screen), are all negotiating points.

* Copyright ownership. It may be surprising to learn that media scores are usually treated as works for hire. Composers relinquish all rights to the scores they compose for media projects, especially if those programs or movies are produced by a major studio. Still, an indie producer working with a smaller budget may negotiate to allow a composer to retain the music's ownership including copyright, and to treat the situation as more of a commission and/or synchronization license.

* Royalties outside of the project. These could come from any soundtrack albums or other use.

Notice there is no specific mention of a synch license in these considerations; hiring a composer to score a program or film assumes the inclusion of synchronization. Composers need to keep in mind the first factor mentioned, that is what they are expected to do. This results in the composing fee, any service fees, royalties from performance, potential mechanical royalties, sheet music, and more, all depending on the specific agreement between the composer and the producers. This bears repeating: don't do any large-scale media scoring project without first consulting with an attorney and/or agent (if you have one).

Ultimately there are no standard composing fees in the media industry because every situation is unique and things change—up or down—as time passes. Giving you hard figures for composing fees is close to impossible. But based on the considerations we've just discussed and assuming you're going after one of the big studio projects, you can assume that the fees could range from the low-five figures (say, $20,000) to as much as a million dollars or possibly more for the well-known composer working on a major blockbuster with a huge budget. Drop your expectations, though, for independent films or even big-studio small-scale movies or programs and drop them *much* further for student films (perhaps zero dollars if you just want the experience and/ or for your demo reel). Composing fees, by the way, are not always paid at once. It depends on the agreement you negotiate. One common possibility is to receive one third on signing your agreement, or when you first work the production team (director, producer, music editor *et al.*) to determine where music belongs. (The term used for making those decisions is *spotting*.) You would receive the next third of your composing fee when recording the score begins. This assumes hiring musicians, etc., and not you working at home or at your own studio. The last payment would be made when you have completed all of your agreed-upon services and have delivered the master recording of the score to the producer in a timely manner *and* the producer has deemed it acceptable.

Most of this discussion has been about writing original music, or providing already-written music, for television programs and movies. Music for video games functions much the same way but there are differences that are more technical than musical. In a movie or television program the music is presented sequentially, once, as the story progresses. In a video game, each scene is a different level of the game. The action *and the music* in a scene continue as long as it takes the player to either move on to the next level or lose the round or game. Since there is no way to know just how much music will be needed until the scene or level change is triggered, the music cues are written as loops. A *loop* is, literally, a chunk of music that repeats as long as necessary. In their earliest incarnations video games didn't have any music. The next generation of games used very simple computer sequencing and sounds that never changed within a game level. Skip to today, and you'll find highly sophisticated soundtracks, sometimes recorded with full symphony orchestras, on many a game. But they're still using loops. How do they keep you from getting bored with the music?

The trick is a combination of computer shrewdness and orchestrational flair. The music is written and recorded using *stems*, that is different tracks of the same recording each containing a different combination of instruments. The result is that while the music itself may not change the orchestration changes over time according to whatever the programmers have arranged; the music changes dynamically with the play of the game.[12] When a certain set of moves has been achieved it triggers the move to the next level and music cue complete with its own set of stems, or the screen and music that says "you've lost."

Getting to write music for video games and other situations in which facility with looping composition aren't in the scope of this book, but if you're interested:

* Get to know people in the gaming industry, the people who make the games, especially anyone who has been in the business for a long time.

* Learn whatever you can about creating music for games. Some universities have courses, even majors, in doing it, and there are books available as well.[13]

* According to some sources, some 60 to 70 percent of music licensed for games is instrumental and if you're a concert music composer, writing instrumental music shouldn't be a stretch.

It's more likely to get work writing music for games than getting something already in existence licensed for them. Assuming you've made the necessary contacts and have demonstrated your abilities as a composer, how and how much do you get paid?

Most independent composers for games charge on a per-minute-of-music basis. These can range (in 2024 in terms of U.S. dollars) from fifty dollars ($50) to three hundred dollars ($300) per minute for a newer, less experienced composer, to anywhere from four hundred dollars ($400) to well over a thousand dollars ($1,000) per minute for more established composers, as of 2024. And by "established" we mean within the gaming industry. The amount of money will also, necessarily, be contingent on the project's budget. Depending on your experience, negotiating skills, and attorney or agent (if you have either), you could also wind up with ownership of the music tracks to release separately as commercially available soundtracks, as well as the publishing rights. More and more orchestras and concert bands are including music from video games in their concert programming, and this trend doesn't seem to be stopping.

As to how to deal with the director of the game's production, my best suggestion is simply to listen to what they say. Many directors (of any medium, really) don't know the jargon we use as musicians, or they'll speak in vague terms ("this scene is sad").[14]

A final word about negotiating to do a film, program, or game score: don't offer a quote without knowing, even as estimates, what is the overall budget for the project. I have lost or walked away from potential jobs because the producers refused to let me know what their budgets were up front. I'd say "I can't give you a quote without knowing what you can afford." They would respond with "Well, we can't do that without knowing what you would charge." Their response in those cases makes no logical sense. Answering with "my budget is" and giving a number, even if it's nowhere near correct, gives you a good sense of (1) whether they can afford your services and talents, and (2) whether you'd work on the project despite possibly getting a low fee, or because you'd be getting a higher fee than you'd expect, or if you need to turn it down altogether. Learn what their music budget is if at all possible.

GRAND RIGHTS

You, as the composer of a musical work and its owner, have certain exclusive rights. As we discussed in the previous chapter, you have the *exclusive* right to "copy, distribute, adapt, print, publish, perform, or record" the work, or to authorize others to do the same. Those rights, depending on the music you write, can be described as having either "small rights" or "grand rights." These aren't legal terms but ones that the music industry itself has developed. *Small rights* cover any *nondramatic* works that can be performed in an arena, concert hall, recital hall, classroom, bar, restaurant, and so on. *Grand rights* cover *dramatic* works with music intended for the stage, such as operas, operettas, musicals, oratorios, ballets and other dance performances, and other theatrical works. Any time such work is to be performed the production needs to acquire the grand rights to do it.

One important distinction is that small-rights works require a licensee pay a one-time fee for unlimited use, almost always through a PRO's blanket license. (The licensee is the venue in which the music is performed.) For works in the grand rights category, though, the licensee pays *per performance* directly negotiated with the owner of the work's copyright (either you or your publisher). Licenses for productions of complete works (operas, musicals, etc.) are customarily first based on a percentage of ticket sales, although choreographic works are more likely to be done on a flat-fee basis.

How the fees are determined, as you expect, are also based on the size of the venue and number of audience seats. "Off-off-Broadway" seating is anything under 100 people; "off-Broadway" seats between 100 and 499; and "Broadway" theaters hold 500 seats or more. Other considerations can include whether the production is to be a limited run or open-ended, and if the production is to be kept in one location or done as a "bus and truck" tour.

If you are interested in writing musical theater specifically you should know a bit about how composers and lyricists get paid. The creators of a musical used to get a percentage of the *gross* ticket sales per performance, that is a percentage of sales before any other expenses are deducted. Typically the percentage would start at about 4.5 percent and rise to 6 percent once the production had recouped its investment, and that percentage would be split among the writers. If each job was done by a different person and the percentage was 6 percent, the composer would get 2 percent of the gross, the lyricist another 2 percent, and the librettist the last 2 percent. In cases where one person did two jobs, such as Stephen Sondheim writing both music and lyrics but another person writing the script, Sondheim would earn 4 percent and the librettist the remaining 2 percent.

Over the last two decades or so productions of musicals have moved to a "profit pool" system. In this case the writers weekly receive a percentage of the *profit* (not the gross!), if the show is earning above its costs, or a small guarantee if no profit has been made, whichever amount is larger. Although the writers don't get a larger amount up front, they're helping a production that may be struggling at first to continue its run because the costs of running the show are being dealt with first. If the show then turns out to be a hit, the gains for the creative team can be greater.

The percentages and other factors change, but a look at what was the norm even twenty years ago can give you an idea of what to expect. The Dramatists Guild,[15] which looks after the rights of its author, lyricist, and composer membership, has developed standardized contracts for new productions and grand rights. For a new work, according to the Guild, writers should be earning at least ±15 percent of the profit before the show has recouped its expenses, and at least ±17% after it has recouped them. The writers then split the monies accordingly.

The reason for the change to the profit pool system is costs. Decades ago a show could survive on Broadway if it ran at 50 percent seating capacity until it recouped its expenses. These days a show needs to run at least 75 percent capacity.

To review: producers of your work, whether your work is for the opera house or Broadway, have to do the following in order to put your work "on the boards":

* Obtain the grand rights for the work to be produced. These rights are negotiated with the copyright owner (you or your publisher). PROs do not handle grand rights. If, however, excerpts from a dramatic work are done in concert form (presented without costumes or story telling), PROs will collect the data and pay performance royalties.

* Purchase or, more likely, rent the materials to use for the production. These can include scores, vocal scores, orchestral parts, scripts, etc., and are acquired through the copyright owner.

* Obtain any licenses needed to promote the performances, such as mechanical licenses, through HFA and/or The Mechanical License Collective.

NON-PERFORMANCE LICENSES

The likelihood of concert music being used without the intent to perform it might seem doubtful, but you never know. There are men's ties with a Mozart piano sonata prominently displayed, and tea towels inscribed with the sheet music of the classic song "Tea for Two" by Victor Youmans (composer) and Irving Caesar (lyrics). The tie doesn't need a license from a copyright owner to feature Mozart because the sonata is PD, but the tea towel with the copyrighted song does. If you can think of a way to put music on something to sell it, you can bet it has been done or soon will be.

When your music is published in the traditional manner, your publisher has obtained the right to print and sell your music on your behalf. You in turn receive a print royalty for each copy of the music sold. The publisher can also negotiate licenses with third parties to reproduce the sheet music on tee shirts, umbrellas, etc. For those non-performance licenses you may get the same royalty rate as for printed music, or you may get a fifty-fifty split with the publisher. The latter is more likely. Will you see your music on a coffee mug any time soon? Who knows? But if you do, it will be because your or your publisher has successfully negotiated a license for it.

NOTES

1. Lawyers and other legal advisors, and accountants and other financial consultants, are there to advise you and work for your own best interests. If your music is with a traditional publisher, they too work to maximize your income as it's in their own best interest. This is why they handle things like licenses on your behalf. Still, it helps to know as much as you can. One hefty tome on the subject music licensing may prove of use in this regard: *Kohn on Music Licensing, 4th Edition (with CD-ROM)* by Al Kohn and Bob Kohn, 4th edition, 2009, Aspen Publishers. As of this writing there is no 5th edition, but the general information the book contains is very useful.

2. The URL for the MacArthur Foundation and information about the Fellowship can be found here: **https://www.macfound.org/programs/awards/fellows/faq.**

3. In Chapter 5, "The Gig," we discuss how to know when to say "yes" to composing work and, more importantly, when to say "no."

4. You can find it here: **https://newmusicusa.org/nmbx/commissioning-fees -calculator/.**

5. See Chapter 3, "Performing Rights Organizations (PROs)" for more detailed information.

6. There are player pianos today, made by Yamaha and other companies, that utilize digital files instead of paper rolls. These have the capability of playing with more nuances that real pianists would incorporate into their playing (*rubato* and so on) and have much larger capacity to hold and play music. (Paper rolls are limited, literally, by the amount of paper that could fit on the roll and in the piano's mechanism. Digital files are only limited by the mechanism's data storage.)

7. For up-to-date information on mechanical royalty rates and other information see the Copyright Royalty Board's website: **www.crb.gov.**

8. Here is the Harry Fox Agency's URL: **https://www.harryfox.com.**

9. This is the Mechanical Licensing Collective's URL: **https://www.themlc.com.**

10. There are many books to check out about writing for movies and television programs, and visual media in general, but here is a good place to start: *Complete Guide to Film Scoring: The Art and Business of Writing Music for Movies and TV* by Richard Davis, 2nd edition 2010. Berklee Press/Hal Leonard.

11. The 2019 film *Yesterday* takes as its premise the idea that a struggling musician suddenly finds himself to be the only who remembers the Beatles and their music. The musician spends most of the film passing off the Beatles' songs as his own. A total of sixteen songs by the team of John Lennon and McCartney, and by George Harrison, were used in the film; sixteen licenses had to be negotiated. The film's producers reportedly paid about ten million dollars to license the songs.

12. Electronic Dance Music (EDM) works in a somewhat similar way, with the same four, eight, or sixteen bars of music repeated throughout with only the orchestration changing to indicate new sections. EDM is musically more static than music written for video games, but it is great to dance to.

13. Some suggestions for books on writing music for games:

- *The Theory and Practice of Writing Music for Games* by Steve Horowitz and Scott R. Looney, 2024, CRC Press/Taylor and Francis Group.
- *A Composer's Guide to Game Music* by Winifred Phillips, 2017, MIT Press.

14. The Game Developer site, aimed at the creators of the games themselves, offers some useful insights for composers too. Here's a link to a discussion on hiring a composer: **https://www.gamedeveloper.com/game-platforms/how-to-commission -music-for-your-game#close-modal.**

15. The Dramatists Guild website makes much information available without having to be a member, but if you write musical theater, you should considering joining. Here is their webpage on writers' rights: **https://www.dramatistsguild.com/rights.**

Chapter 3

PERFORMING RIGHTS ORGANIZATIONS (PROS)

The amount of money one needs is terrifying.

—Ludwig van Beethoven

WHAT PROS ARE, WHAT THEY DO AND DON'T DO, AND WHY YOU SHOULD JOIN ONE

Performing Rights Organizations (PROs) exist to protect your interests in obtaining and distributing performance royalties. PROs are owned either by a corporation or other business with memberships or "affiliates," or by the members themselves. They track performances, whether occurring in live performance venues or on various terrestrial or satellite or digital media, and issue and maintain performance licenses. "Live performance venues" include concert and recital halls, restaurants and bars that feature music, as well as television and radio stations (broadcast, cable, satellite, etc.), airlines, amusement parks, websites, and much more. After calculating the performance income generated over a regular period of time, the PRO determines how to fairly distribute those funds.

PROs are not music publishers, although they represent them as they represent composers and lyricists when it comes to tracking performances and distributing monies. They do not negotiate any aspect of a composer's work except for the license to perform it. They do *not* negotiate or issue mechanical licenses, synchronization licenses, or grand rights, etc. Some PROs do what they can, in addition to dealing with performance licenses, to promote and develop their members' careers through educational programs, networking events, and more.

The reason for joining a PRO is clear: you deserve to be compensated when your music is performed and heard (and, presumably, enjoyed). PROs exist to make sure that happens legally and fairly. A PRO will collect and analyze performance data and determine how much you can get paid, in a much more efficient manner than you could on your own.

ASCAP, BMI, AND SESAC

We have three PROs in the United States: the American Society for Composers, Authors, and Publishers (ASCAP); Broadcast Music, Inc. (BMI); and the Society of European Stage Authors and Composers (SESAC). All three are known today primarily by their acronyms. In other countries, there is usually just one PRO and often they are government run: Britain has the Performing Rights Society (PRS); Germany has the Society for Musical Performance and Mechanical Reproduction Rights (*Gesellschaft für musikalische Aufführungs-und mechanische Vervielfältigungsrechte* in German, or GEMA); and so on. How did the United States wind up with three PROs anyway?

ASCAP was first; it was created in 1914 by nine composers and lyricists led by operetta composer Victor Herbert, two music publishers, and a copyright attorney, all with the express mission of protecting the copyrighted compositions of its members from exploitation without proper compensation.[1] ASCAP's concert composer membership presently includes the Pulitzer Prize winners Julia Wolfe and Michael Abels.

In 1940, ASCAP decided to double its licensing fees, and radio broadcasters—radio being the only commercial broadcast medium at the time—rebelled. They boycotted ASCAP, and no music under the PRO's umbrella was broadcast on the major radio networks. Instead those stations played music that had been rejected by ASCAP (country music, etc.). The situation escalated and wound up in the courts; ASCAP settled by reducing its rates, but the broadcasters saw an opportunity. They formed their own PRO, Broadcast Music, Inc. (BMI), as a response to what they considered ASCAP's stranglehold. Today BMI's concert music composers include Joan Tower, Steve Reich, and John Adams.

The Society of European Stage Authors and Composers (SESAC) was founded in 1931 by Paul Heinecke; it's the second-oldest PRO in the United States. SESAC's original repertory focused on works published by European companies, but it has since branched out to include church music, film and television scores, and pop music. Current members ("affiliates") include Adele, Ariana Grande, Bob Dylan, and Zac Brown. There seem to be no concert music composer members *per se*. Both ASCAP and BMI allow anyone to join as a composer and/or lyricist, publisher, or all three.

SESAC is unique in that potential members or "affiliates" must be invited to join. Their website says, "SESAC is an invitation-only company, so the best route is to have your representative(s) (lawyer, manager, agent, etc.) contact us on your behalf. We're sorry, but SESAC does not accept unsolicited submissions." One onetime advantage to this approach is that if you're invited to join, there is no application or initiation fee.

Joining BMI as a songwriter or a classical music composer, according to the BMI website, requires "a valid email address" and a payment of a onetime affiliation fee paid by credit card or debit card. The fee is, as of 2024, seventy-five dollars ($75); presumably you recoup that cost when you begin earning performance royalties. Enrolling as a classical music composer is a little more than joining as a songwriter though. BMI says, "It is only necessary to affiliate through BMI's classical area only if your works will be primarily performed under BMI's symphonic, chamber music and other classical licenses. For classical composers we ask that you send us a copy of your resume and a list of works with information on performances and venues. This may come via e-mail if that is easier. Once we have this, we will mail you an application." In other words, you can't just say you're a composer of concert music; you have to be vetted and proven as such. Whether as a songwriter or as a classical composer, you sign a two-year agreement if and when you are accepted to BMI.

Of the three PROs, ASCAP seems to be the easiest to join. Writers, and writers who are also publishers, can join for free, and publishers who are not also writers pay a non-refundable fee, as of 2024, of fifty dollars ($50). Writers need to supply their legal name, mailing address, an e-mail address, and their Social Security Number (SSN) or ITIN (which is the business equivalent of an SSN), and must be eighteen or older to apply online. (There is a procedure for minors to join as well.)

The BMI and ASCAP each ask you to fill out forms that will give them insight into your work and allow them to function on your behalf in performance information collection and performance royalty distributions. SESAC will likely obtain the same sort of information once you've been invited and have accepted the invitation.[2]

The ASCAP has a membership roster of "more than 975,000 songwriters, composers and music publishers" as of 2024. BMI boasts of having even more, "more than 1.4 million songwriters, composers, and music publishers." Although growing, SESAC is the smallest of the three PROs, with some 30,000 members as of 2024. If you don't already belong to a PRO, consider joining as soon as you can. But first, here is some important information:

1. All three PROs work essentially the same way once you're a member or affiliate when it comes to collecting performance information and

fees and the distribution of the monies earned. After you do your "due diligence" and have learned as much as you can about the one(s) in which you're interested, you can choose which PRO to join based on your personal preferences.

2. You cannot belong to more than one PRO; anything else is considered "double dipping" and could be considered fraud on some legal level. (Unwritten "rule": It does not seem wise, helpful, or even legal, to join as a writer member of one PRO and as a publisher of a different one. If you're a composer and a self-publisher, just join one PRO for both.)

3. BMI and SESAC are owned by corporate entities and are run "for profit," while ASCAP has been owned by its membership since its inception in 1914. Both systems have worked well for a long time, so deciding which to join is still based on your personal preferences.

4. Expect a time lag between a domestic performance of your music and when you receive a royalty payment from your PRO; royalty payments are never instantaneous. Currently SESAC pays out the fastest, in around three months after the quarter in which your music has been played and reported has ended. BMI presently takes about five and a half months to pay out, and ASCAP takes around six months. Pay out schedules are always being adjusted. Foreign performances can take a lot longer to make their way to US PROs, so pay outs also take longer. Some performances don't get reported to PROs in a timely manner, so those may not be reflected in a royalty statement for some time.

HOW PERFORMANCE ROYALTIES ARE COLLECTED AND DISTRIBUTED

The first step in the collection process is actually the composer's. Once you are granted membership in a PRO you need to register your works in its database. Each PRO has a system in place for you to do so, and also accepts cue sheets from film and television production companies. BMI uses a song registration form (formerly called a "clearance form") that is strictly for songs, media scores, Broadway and off-Broadway shows, or infomercials. Concert composers, on the other hand, are instructed to contact BMI's Classical Department for its own registration form. ASCAP uses its proprietary "Work Registration system" on its website, which you can use as a composer member or that your publisher can if you have one. As of this writing, SESAC's information on registering works into their database doesn't seem to be available to the public, except to say that cue sheets can be e-mailed to a specific address.

The next step in the procedure is for the PRO to negotiate with, issue to, and maintain performance licenses, called "blanket" licenses. These allow the licensee—concert and recital halls, bars and restaurants, television and radio stations, etc.—to use any of the music contained in the PRO's catalog for an unlimited number of times within the term of the license. This is different from grand rights for theatrical works, which requires payment per performance. With three PROs each having huge numbers of members—easily tens of thousands—and by extension mind-boggling numbers of musical works covered, you can begin to imagine how difficult it could be to keep track of performances and performance royalties. Each PRO has its own way of dealing with the situation, although all are similar in nature.

Blanket licensing fees are based on the type and size of the venue or medium. Based on the information derived from various collection methods, performance royalties are then calculated and distributed to the PRO's writers and publishers. That information is gathered and analyzed through sophisticated and robust collection system and is followed by an equally vigorous and rigorous method to determine distribution.

Take streaming for example. DSPs like Apple Music, Pandora, and Spotify, who are signed on with PROs provide quarterly play counts. Metadata (song titles, recording artists, etc.) are matched up with the titles provided. Any music with "a significant number of performances" will warrant manual research and identification if the metadata doesn't find a match. Interestingly, each DSP has its own threshold criteria for payment, but they all base it on the number of plays, the licensing fees, and more, *and* those thresholds change each quarter.

For film and television, PROs rely in part of cue sheets provided by a program or film's production company. Cue sheets include detailed information like the name of the music, the writers and publishers of the music used, the length of the performance of the music, and how it was used (is it featured, or used as a theme, and so on).

When possible PROs use census surveys, that is as complete a survey of performances as possible is done for a given type of performance. When that is not practical, which is more the case in the twenty-first century than before, they utilize sample surveys. The surveys are designed, as ASCAP puts it, "to be a statistically accurate representation of performances in a medium." These surveys cover every part of the United States, all types and sizes of radio and TV stations, etc.; all are represented even if they're not covered in as much detail as they would individually in a census survey. And as PROs blanket licenses differ in price depending on the performance source, so do the frequency with which they are sampled.

This is wonderful for those of us who write music for media or have pop songs on the charts, but for those of us focusing on classical music the bulk of our performances will be live in concert and recital halls, and in educational situations. PROs have licensing agreements with those types of venues, but mostly depend on printed programs and other notifications from performers or the composers themselves. Yes, we need to notify our PROs ourselves (or ask performers and/or venues to do so) whenever possible.

The next step is to determine royalties. All three PROs do it in similar ways. Here, for example, is ASCAP's general formula for calculating amounts as shown on their website:

Use Weight

x

Licensee Weight

x

"Follow the Dollar" Factor

x

Time of Day Weight

+

Premium Credits

=

Credits

"Use Weight" is a value associated with each type of performance covered by ASCAP. "Licensee Weight," or "hook-up weight" "reflecting the number of stations carry a broadcast," is based on the license fee paid by the licensee. For symphonic and chamber concerts, airlines, circuses, and so on, "weights" are also assigned based on the license fees paid. The "Follow the Dollar Factor" is a term used by both ASCAP and BMI. ASCAP describes it as a way to ensure that "license fees that ASCAP receives from any medium are paid to writers and publishers for performances on that medium." Although not explained in detail, this appears to mean that performances in one medium that would otherwise generate a higher royalty will not get lumped in with performances that pay a lower rate (and *vice versa*). It's an interesting and fair approach. BMI's approach is similar. (SESAC currently provides very little information for writers on its website regarding how royalties are calculated, but what is provided indicates very similar procedures.) The "Time of Day Weight" is factored in if it's applicable, meaning if the music is broadcast. Radio and any sort of television, be it network, cable, or satellite, draw different numbers of listeners or viewership at different times of day. Those industries still use the expression "prime time" to indicate the period of time when the audience is the largest.

Continuing our look at ASCAP's methodology as an example, the first four factors are multiplied, and then any "Premium Credits" are added to the results. ASCAP refers to "Audio Feature Premium (AFP) Credits" (for works meeting a certain threshold of performances on radio, satellite, and streaming services within a quarter); "Classic Song Bonus Credits" (in which *songs* earning over 300,000 performance credits since their registration receive additional credits if they hit a predetermined mark in a single quarter); and "Audiovisual Premium (AVP) Credits" (which apply to "performances only on TV and certain over-the-top [OTT] audiovisual services, where applicable"). Mind you, this is only the first stage. The second stage in ASCAP's calculations is getting from "credits" to "royalties." ASCAP thoughtfully provides a formula for that as well:

Credits

x

Share

x

Credit Value

=

$ Royalty

ASCAP's explanation: "After establishing the number of credits generated by a performance, the next step is to allocate these credits among all of the writers and publishers of the work based on the SHARE each should receive. ASCAP is advised of the correct shares to be paid when members submit Title Registrations. For example, if two co-writers of a song share royalties equally, each will receive 50 percent of the total credits. The final step is to multiply credits by the appropriate CREDIT VALUE to arrive at the ROYALTY payment. The credit value accounts for financial income (investment income and other non-license fee income); all members share in financial income in proportion to their credits for surveyed performances."[3] As of this writing in 2024 the "credit value" is pegged just above eight dollars ($8.00). It's interesting to note that not all of the money ASCAP brings in is from licensing fees; a portion also comes from investments. What is *more* interesting is that the "extra" money earned isn't to make a profit—the organization is, after all, a not-for-profit business—but specifically for passing on to its membership and help pay operating costs. Presumably, BMI and SESAC also invest but with an eye toward profit.

ASCAP's explanations of how royalties are calculated, which are all available on its website, are the most detailed of the three PROs. The organization's transparency is, in fact, one of its points of pride and most likely due to its ownership by its members. BMI and SESAC, owned by for profit corporations, are not required to be as open about how royalties are computed.

Like most private businesses, they are reluctant to disclose their financial processes. This is of course legal and right for them.

BMI's website says of royalties for classical music that it pays for "original classical works performed at live classical concerts in the U.S. that are presented by entities licensed by BMI under classical and symphonic licenses." In other words, if the venue is licensed and your music gets performed there, you're likely to receive royalties. They also say that payment is based on "a census of all eligible concert programs received from these licensees. The rates are determined annually based upon the fees received from classical licensing and the total number of BMI works performed." The BMI website also points out that "if a local commercial radio feature performance is of a classical work [covered by BMI], each performance will be paid at the *minimum* rate of 32 cents per minute for total participants."[4] The rate will of course change, but let's use it hypothetically. Say a twenty-five-minute symphony written by a BMI composer is featured on a commercial radio station. That would earn a total of eight dollars ($8) in performance royalties, to be split fifty-fifty between the composer and the publisher.

SESAC is the most tight-lipped of the three PROs; there is nothing currently on its website regarding just how performance royalties are determined. Again, it is a for-profit business and as such is not required to make this information public. It is likely that invited members can access the information once they have joined. But like both ASCAP and BMI, SESAC also evenly splits royalty payments between the writers and the publishers of a work.

To repeat though, all three U.S. PROs operate essentially the same way, whether its licensing music users or paying out performance royalties at approximately the same rates and similar schedules.

All of the PROs, it should be said, focus primarily on pop music of all types and tend to marginalize other musical styles, especially classical music. SESAC, for example, rightly boasts of representing "a significant amount of music in every musical genre . . . with a diversified repertory including Top 40, Pop, Hip-Hop, R&B, Rock, Country, Spanish (Pop, Regional Mexican, Tropical, Rhythmic), Blues, Jazz, Big Band, Folk, Contemporary Christian, Gospel and many others."[5] It's interesting to note that the SESAC website also includes film and television show scores and composers; even more interesting for our purposes is the seemingly complete lack of any concert/classical composers or music. Of course pop, hip-hop, etc., earn the most money, so that focus is understandable and even necessary. But this has no bearing on your ability to earn performance royalties in any way. In short, find the PRO that is best suited to your needs and *join*.

NOTES

1. The founders of ASCAP were composers Victor Herbert, George Botsford, Silvio Hein, Irving Berlin, Louis Hirsch, John Raymond Hubbell, Gustave Kerker, and Jean Schwartz; lyricist Glen MacDonough; publishers George Maxwell and Jay Witmark; and copyright attorney Nathan Burkan. Interesting note: ASCAP's original rules made composers who could not read and write musical notation ineligible for membership, but an exception was made to admit Irving Berlin (who was one of the most popular composers of the time).

2. Not being either a writer member or an employee of SESAC has made research into their operations on behalf of their membership very difficult. Whatever information I have gotten is mostly through the SESAC website.

3. Here is the URL for ASCAP's discussion of how royalties are calculated: **https://www.ascap.com/help/royalties-and-payment/payment/royalties#:~:text =CREDITS%20X%20SHARE%20X%20CREDIT%20VALUE%20%3D%20 %24%20ROYALTY&text=For%20example%2C%20if%20two%20co,arrive %20at%20the%20ROYALTY%20payment.**

4. **https://www.bmi.com/creators/royalty/live_concert_royalties.**

5. **https://www.sesac.com/frequently-asked-questions/.**

Chapter 4

PRESENTING AND PROMOTING YOURSELF AS A COMPOSER

(PREPARING TO GET LUCKY)

Beware of missing chances; otherwise, it may be altogether too late someday.

—Franz Liszt

Over the years teaching composition at New York University, I have frequently met with incoming music majors in their Freshman Orientation classes at the beginning of the academic year. The classes would always be a mix of those studying instrumental and vocal performance, composition, music education, music technology, music therapy, and more. The discussions have always been interesting and diverse, but there are certain things I always wind up having to say. One is that anyone interested in composing at all, and anyone who will perform in a professional or educational setting, needs to make friends *now*, while everyone in the room is at the beginning of their studies. The friendships and connections you make at this stage, I would tell them, can be mutually rewarding throughout your careers. Basically, I introduced them to the concept of *networking*.

NETWORKING AND FINDING OPPORTUNITIES

Originally a "network" described links between machines that allowed them to interact more efficiently. In the 1930s and 1940s radio stations across the United States owned by the same companies were referred to as networks, and television adopted the term in a similar fashion soon after that. Computer networks came next, and it became inevitable that the social sciences would adapt the term to mean a group of, or relationship between, people. Since the late 1960s people have used the word *networking* to mean the action of connecting and interacting with others specifically to develop social or business contacts, or simply to exchange or acquire information. An example of this could be when you go to a concert to hear a friend play in an orchestra; afterward your friend introduces you to the conductor as "a fine composer." You've made a connection through your friend, expanding your own network.

Networking isn't, and shouldn't be, only about connecting with someone because of what they may be able to do for you; it's about interpersonal relationships. Human beings are social animals, and to varying degrees we *need* other people in our lives. We all look to make connections on social and emotional levels. Some members of your circle of people in and out of your compositional career—your network—will be friends only. They can't do anything for you besides being your friends. That is always a good thing. With others your relationships could be less personal and more about your connections through your business, in this case, making music. Everyone else will fall somewhere in the middle, and again, this is good. This is *not* to say you need to define people in your circle as "useful to me" or "not useful to me." If someone in your network realizes that you only associate with them because they're convenient, you *will* lose that person in your life. What is better is to be interested (not just show interest) in what *they* do. Other people are as a rule at least as interesting as you think you are, and oftentimes more so. You might learn some things.

Networking can help you find collaborators. "Collaborators" can be another way of saying finding conductors, instrumentalists, and singers who are supportive of your work enough to help you get it performed. And of course having a collaborator could be literal, as in having someone to write the libretto for an opera or song cycle you want to compose. Networking may also result in your finding a mentor, someone in the same business as you but with more experience and expertise in the non-musical aspects of being a composer, someone who can advise you about certain situations in which you may find yourself along the way. It can also help you find opportunities you wouldn't normally come across otherwise.

What is an opportunity, anyway? It comes down to recognizing a situation that could lead to you writing music, or having music featured that you've already composed, that will be performed, or published, or recorded, or some combination of those. Say you're attending a chamber music concert featuring an ensemble of clarinet, bass clarinet, horn, and accordion. You've enjoyed the performers very much. Afterward you get to speak briefly with the performers and compliment them on a job well done. Then you say goodnight and are ready to leave, right? Very often, yes. But if in the course of the conversation they mention that they wish they had more music for their exact instrumentation, you've just been handed an opportunity to explore.

Opportunities don't only arise from networking. But how do you find them, or at least recognize opportunities when they arise? One way to find an opportunity is to attend concerts, especially local ones. Be a repeat customer/audience member. Get to know the musicians with whom you want to work. If or when performers look for music by a living composer they tend to go in two directions, either for a famous name or a local composer. You could be that "local composer" if you're not one of the famous ones. Going to local concerts can get you on a familiar basis with the performers. Once people know you as a person and that you're supportive and approachable, you've made it more possible for your music to be performed. (If you're shy and awkward in social situations there are some recommendations below that may help.)

You can also find opportunities by attending conferences, workshops, and other events where potentially useful people might attend. By attending these you can meet people in person with whom you may already have an online relationship, or meet people whom you haven't yet met but want to meet, or meet someone entirely unexpected who can provide that boost your career needs. (This is where making a good first impression comes handy. Sometimes you get to meet someone who is already a fan of your music, and you never know to whom they may introduce you). Perhaps even more importantly, you can make new friends this way too. Giving a lecture, demonstration, or workshop at a conference on a topic with which you're knowledgeable is another way to connect with people. I've given sessions on copyright and commissioning works, and other topics. Most of these have resulted in commissions, guest conducting work, and giving master classes in composition. Whatever your strengths are can be of interest to someone.

Another way to find opportunities is to belong to composer groups, particularly national ones like the Society of Composers, Inc., and the American Composers Forum. But state or local groups can also help. Such groups are very beneficial for independent composers who aren't affiliated with universities, colleges, or conservatories. The larger groups offer some opportunities themselves, but mostly disseminate information about contests, reading sessions, and prospective performances from around the country (and sometimes the world). Local groups will often put on their own concerts featuring works by members. And if you're involved in teaching at any level, consider joining music education organizations like your state's chapter of the National Association for Music Education (NAfME), or the American String Teachers Association (ASTA), or any number of band-focused educational groups. Do your research first to determine which of these are best suited to your needs. You don't have to belong to everything.

If you're a performer as well as a composer, you can perform your own music in concert. Composers have done this for hundreds of years, to generate income from the performances themselves, promote their works, and expand their audience (or fan base). Steve Reich built his career in part by forming his own ensemble to perform his works, as did Philip Glass, Laurie Anderson, and many others. Performing your own works will help build the public's awareness of you and your work, your fan base, as well as your credibility in the classical music world.

These days you might not have to do much of that though. Using Facebook or other social media is an immediate and often effective way to get your music and name "out there." Joining social media platforms and signing up with any number of groups that focus on your interests is easy enough and usually doesn't cost anything. You don't have to join every group out there; be selective. Focus more on groups for performers than other composers. Read the posts; find out what people are interested in and what their problems are. Musicians at all career levels are on social media, and being involved in these groups can make networking a lot easier than it is in person. You can join groups for composers to compare experiences if you like, but they may not be as useful over time.

Whether it's in person, by e-mail (or physical mail), or on social media, remember that the first time you connect with someone you're making a first impression, and first impressions don't get "do-overs." Some folks instinctively know how to make a good first impression, while others—most of us composers, probably—feel uncomfortable in those situations.

MAKING A FIRST IMPRESSION AND COMMUNICATING WHO YOU ARE AND WHAT YOU DO

How do you want to be perceived? The first thing you need to think about is your *attitude* when meeting someone. People are generally hesitant and feel awkward when meeting someone new; this is normal. One way to combat those counterproductive feelings is to prepare for the possibility if you can. If you know who it is you're going to meet ahead of time, do some research. Get a sense of who they are and why you're meeting with them. Are they conductors with a favorable preference for new music? Did you go to the same school or have something else in common? Anything you learn can be helpful.

Your attitude will be on display the moment you meet. Show attentiveness, interest in the other person, and a balanced ego just by asking questions and listening, really *listening*, to what the other person has to say. You also learn a lot about your new acquaintance that way too. Asking a question, especially one based on what you know or have learned from your research, can also impart a sense of your intelligence, dedication, or seriousness as a potential colleague.

Your attitude should also project a balanced sense of self-assurance; too little confidence and you'll seem too "hungry," while too much will spill over into egoism. You need to know *yourself* for this. Do you consider yourself as lacking confidence? Listening to the other person gives you time to learn and assess things and to mentally prepare yourself for seeming more poised than you feel. Do you hold a very high opinion of yourself? That is much harder to recognize in oneself than a lack of self-confidence, but you need to be aware of it. If you are overly self-possessed, that, too, will come across clearly, and the other person is likely to retreat quickly, not wanting to deal with you. It's not always easy to do, but finding a balance is key.

Body language helps project the right attitude. We respond to body language at least as much as we do to what is being said. Look people in the eye (without staring!) when speaking or listening; stand straight without being stiff. Posture and eye contact work no matter your gender or that of the person with whom you're speaking. If shaking hands, make sure your hands are dry (some folks get damp hands when nervous) and that you give a firm, but not too firm, handshake.

Since COVID-19 first hit, it has become acceptable not to shake hands. You can keep your hands at your sides, or show your palms together or place one of your hands on your chest, and give a little nod or bow (all of these are traditional gestures of peace).

Another factor in making a good impression is how we physically appear to others. This isn't so important when you're on social media, where the photos we post usually don't do us justice. That goes for everyone else on social media too, though, so it's unlikely you will be judged on your online appearance. Meeting someone in person, or in an online video chat, is another story entirely though. In Shakespeare's play *Hamlet*, Polonius says that "apparel oft proclaims the man." The idea that people tend to judge us based on the clothes we wear was around before Shakespeare put pen to paper and still has impact today. Sure, you don't have to go around dressed in your Sunday best or for a black-tie affair every day of the week. But if you're in a social situation where you might meet or expect to meet someone of importance to you, you should always look "presentable." Be clean yourself and wear clean clothes (yes, that needs to be said) that are appropriate to both you and the situation. "Appropriate" in this case means to wear what you consider your style but be aware of social norms for the particular occasion. Look the best version of yourself. There's a side benefit to this too. Dressing your best helps bolster your self-esteem, which improves your attitude and, ultimately, aids you in making a good first impression. (If you know someone in the military, any branch, watch their posture and attitude when they're in uniform and when they're in civilian clothes. The differences can be startling.)

Try not coming off as too "hungry" or desperate. When we're less experienced most of us come off as over-eager, and we usually learn the hard way how to mitigate it. Here are some ways to not come off as desperate:

1. *Don't* start a conversation with someone new by saying "I'm a composer and you should play my music," or anything of the sort. That is *the* fastest way to get shut down by the other person. Unless someone else is making the introductions, introduce yourself ("Hi, I'm [insert your name here]. It's a pleasure to meet you."). It's okay to make "small talk." Ask a question and *listen.* Be attentive; be more interested in the other person than trying to have them be interested in you. It's a bit of a cliché that the less you say the smarter and more approachable people think you are, but there is an element of truth in it.

2. *Don't* carry scores or recordings (on thumb drives, CDs, *etc.*) with you to social events where you expect to meet someone important, but if you do, definitely *do not* hand that important person those items to them *unless they actually ask for them.* This is the second fastest way to lose an opportunity. And don't expect them to ask for scores there and then in any case.

3. But once the other person asks, *be prepared.* You can say whether you have some music they would be interested in checking out. If you do, mention the piece(s) and offer to provide perusal scores or links to those and/or recordings. If you don't already have music that would be appropriate, say so, but temper it with something like "I've never had the opportunity to write for that, but I'd love to do it."

4. Even with the proliferation and pervasiveness of social media, the very old-school approach of having *physical business cards* to offer still works. Keep it simple: your name, your contact information (e-mail, social media links, phone numbers, and physical address if you desire), and what you do ("Composer, Arranger, Conductor," that sort of thing). These are especially useful in situations when you shouldn't have scores, *etc.*, with you on meeting someone for the first time. You can offer a card and say something like "the link to samples of my work is on my website" or "please send me an e-mail and I will provide you with perusal scores," and so on. If they don't want to take your card, offer to send them an e-mail and take down their address.

Your appearance and attitude aren't the only things that need to make a good first impression. Your music has to present itself in the best possible light as well. Whether you're providing physical scores or PDFs, they should look as professional as possible. If your music is published by a traditional publisher you have little to nothing to worry about in this regard. Publishers want to put out the best edition possible of your music and they go to great lengths to make sure that happens. If you're self-publishing (or not publishing your music at all) you get to do all of the work.

Scores, be they for solo instrument or symphony orchestra, should be clear and have consistent notation. For example, when you have the same rhythm in two different measures, don't have four eighth notes beamed together in one and broken into two two-note beams in another. Most notation programs (Finale, Sibelius, Dorico *et al.*) are helpful in this regard by having default layouts and other preferences, but they're not always optimum. Set your preferences before notating ("engraving") your score. Chapter 7, "Presenting Your Music," goes into details about making your music look its best, but again it comes down to *clarity, consistency*, and *performability.*

Making a good first impression comes down to paying attention to details without obsessing over them. These are the details about the people you meet, about yourself physically and emotionally, and about your music. The more you know ahead of time, the more you're prepared, the less awkward you will feel in making initial contact, and the more likely it will go successfully.

OPTIMIZING OPPORTUNITIES AND FOLLOWING UP

Making a good first impression is one way to optimize an opportunity. There are other things you can do to carry it further. If you're talking to someone whose work you admire—Why else would you want to work with them?—you can express that. But don't go overboard. Be appreciative, not a "fan." Don't make it a big deal, but an acknowledgment that you know their worth.

But improving your chances with an opportunity isn't always about making a good first impression. There are occasions when you may be asked to write something you'd rather not do, perhaps because it's not important enough or because it's too "small," or it doesn't pay enough. But taking on something less important to you could lead to something bigger/better/more important later. Take the gig unless it's completely wrong for you. Here are some aphorisms to think about:

* *Carpe diem* —Latin saying for "seize the day."
* *"Put yourself into a position to 'get lucky,' but be prepared for when you do."* —Me

That second quote, something I wind up telling almost all of my composition students at some point, is worth considering. Opportunities do not always present themselves; instead of being *reactive* pursuing existing opportunities you should consider being *proactive* and creating them. I'll give a personal example:

The first time I successfully created and optimized an opportunity was long ago when the New York Philharmonic held fundraisers called "Radiothons." These were weekend-long live radio broadcasts over the classical music radio station WQXR.[1] Famous classical musicians, many drawn from the orchestra itself, would come on-air to chat with the radio station's hosts, some music would be played either live or via recordings, and, most importantly, solicitations for donations to the orchestra would be made. In exchange for donations, the Philharmonic would offer gifts, the type depending on the level of donation. I was *very* early into my compositional career and feeling stymied by my lack of advancement. WQXR was constantly advertising the upcoming Radiothon. I made a mental connection at some point and got the idea to *donate* my services as a composer to the New York Philharmonic. I contacted the folks handling the gifts end of the donation process about it, and they liked what I had to say.

I donated a commission for "a three-to-five-minute work for any instrument, with or without accompaniment" in exchange for a donation to the orchestra of four hundred dollars ($400). I was interviewed for at least a half hour during the broadcast, and I got to chat, nay *schmooze*, with the likes of orchestra members and the conductor, Zubin Mehta (with whom I traded quips in Yiddish!). Best of all, someone made the $400 donation and asked me to write a work for piano.[2] I followed up by doing the same sort of thing for two more years. It never resulted in a commission from the orchestra, but the second work done for the Radiothon was for its principal oboist at the time, Joseph Robinson. He premiered it on air the third time I did the fundraiser. As a result of those efforts I wound up with three good chamber works, one of which was premiered not only by a top-tier musician, but on a major radio broadcast. My status as a composer increased, and it helped working toward my next project.

Besides having scores accessible (not always with you but ready to go as needed), it's good to have recordings of your works available as well. If you can't get a good live recording of your work, MIDI demos (*aka* audio mockups) are suitable. All the major music notation programs can generate audio files to varying degrees of listenability on their own, but there are add-on programs and sound libraries that can improve on them significantly. No MIDI demo can replace the sound of live musicians, but the recordings you provide are demonstrations of your work and should suffice.

There are many ways we can succeed. Sometimes it's the small things we do that help. One way is to make sure to follow up on an opportunity, first meeting, and so on. See Chapter 9 on "Follow Up" for a more detailed discussion, but let's start here with some basics. If you've met someone you think might be helpful to your career in some way, don't just hand them your business card and leave. Keep the lines of communication open without badgering the other person. Send a short e-mail, text, or even a physical note a day or two later saying that you enjoyed meeting them. Maybe mention what you discussed, or perhaps provide some information they've asked about. Then be very patient. Don't expect an answer right away or even at all. But just the fact that you followed up, that you treated the other person with respect, will likely stay in that person's mind in a positive way.

THE INTERNET AS A TOOL

We've discussed social media in some depth, and most readers here are probably knee-deep in that aspect of the internet already. But the internet can be a useful tool in other ways. The primary way to use the internet is as a research tool. Whether it's Google, Bing, DuckDuckGo, Edge, or any other search engine, you can find just about any information or resource you need. For example:

* Instrument ranges, transpositions, and other information you might need to write for particular instruments or combinations of instruments.[3]
* Composer-oriented organizations.[4]
* Information on PROs, copyright, and other legal and financial matters.
* Composition competitions, grants, calls for scores, etc.
* Instrumentalists, singers, conductors, ensembles.

Of course, the internet is also useful for streaming, or downloading for later appreciation, other people's music. You can find and download (for free or for purchase) sound libraries that you can use in your compositions. You can make music online too, collaborating with other musicians by using such programs (as of 2024) as Soundtrap, Bandlab, Albeton Link, Splice, and dozens more. These collaborating platforms all currently have some built-in time-lag issues, but they can make for some wonderful musicmaking, especially in genres that are improvisation-based.

You can also promote your compositions online, usually by having your own website. The site can range from bare bones—your photo, a bio, a list of works (and how to get them), and maybe some external links to recordings, scores, and so on—to a complete package including a "store" for people to purchase to download or stream your music directly. Some folks just maintain a social medium page and provide links there. No matter how you do it, an internet presence has become the norm for composers who wish to get their music known and performed.

Getting your own website set up can run from free (the bare bones version of a website) to very expensive (the more elaborate type of site), but all require a domain name and a website host. Some hosts provide a domain name from a list of possibilities you create (i.e., "www.composer.com") as part of their package offerings; otherwise, you need to secure a web domain from a separate provider. Search "web site providers" and "web domain providers" for current lists. Once you have a domain and a host you will need to actually build your site. Many site providers make it relatively easy by supplying a selection of formats. There are books on how to build your own website available; a quick search will turn up at least a half dozen at the top of the results.

BIOS AND WORK LISTS

You can never go wrong having a short (one to two pages) biography, or "bio." If you have a composer website a dedicated page for your bio is a necessity, and if you are sending out a press release or information to a prospective publisher or commissioner you may want to include one. A *bio*, for our purposes, is a concise introduction to who we are, our backgrounds (educational, career, etc.), and any accomplishments we've made. In general terms, composer bios should include:

* Your name.

* Your job(s) in the briefest possible terms. You probably don't make your entire living as a composer; most composers have several jobs at one time. It's okay to say what else you do (unless it's embarrassing for you or illegal).[5]

* Your hometown and/or current place of residence. For privacy's sake you can generalize it—you can say something like "[your name] lives in Maryland" instead of "[your name] lives in Bethesda," for example—or omit it entirely.

* Quotes from reviews, if you have any *and* they're positive, with the name of the source (newspaper name, television show, etc.).

* The most current and/or relevant names of musicians who have performed your music. I like to start my list with the largest ensemble and continue down to solo artists, but that's a personal preference.

* Education information, especially as it relates to your work as a composer. You don't need to go into details. Just the degree or certification and where you earned it suffices. (This isn't for a nine-to-five-type job, so you don't need to put in the years you received your education.)

* Optionally, you can expand on your job list a bit here. You can also say who publishes your music and on what recording labels your music has been released if you have that.

* Many composers, me included, like to give a very short list of our most current compositions and, perhaps, a mention of what could be considered other important works in our catalog.

* Lastly, you can mention some tangentially related but non-composition achievements, like writing books or articles on musical subjects, or any awards, grants, residencies, *etc.*

As with press releases (see Chapter 9, "Follow Up"), bios should end with an indicator at the bottom after the text and, optionally, a word count for the text. The reason for this is to allow the bio to be used in multiple ways, such as part of program notes or for interviews and reports. Skip a line after the last paragraph, then put in "###" centered to indicate the end of the text. On the next line, also centered, you can put in the number of words used in the body of the bio ("480 words," for example). Bios should be updated on a regular basis. Depending on how active your career is going, you could be revising it anywhere from two to twelve times a year.

Have an organized list of your compositions and arrangements at hand as well, and keep that up to date. It's a catalog or survey of everything you've ever written. It can be useful for you personally and help you determine what to write next. ("What haven't I written lately?" or, "What have I written a lot of lately?" are questions that can come to mind.) It can be useful when presenting yourself to potential performers, conductors, commissioners, or reviewers too.

The hardest part of putting together such a list, especially if you've been writing music for a long time, is the organization of the information. If you have a database program on your computer it makes things easier, but determining *what* data needs to go in is the question. Here are some possibilities:

* Title of the work.
* Subtitle of the work, if any.
* Genre and/or ensemble.
* Instrumentation specifics.
* Duration.
* Publisher, if any. Also, if published but "POP," or "permanently out of print."
* Year of composition or arrangement.
* Grade level, if relevant.
* Additional information: commissioning, premiere, or other important facts.

Once you have this information in a database you can organize it any way you want, *and* you can extract specialized lists on request.

WHAT ARE COMPOSERS' AGENTS AND WHEN ARE THEY NECESSARY?

Any agent in the arts works on your behalf to help you get work, and to negotiate to get you the best possible deal in the process. Because of the time and effort that they expend in doing so, agents' rosters are usually limited. There are a large number of classical music management firms; most will have a large roster that focuses on singers, instrumentalists, and conductors, but there will be few composers listed. Even those few are commonly there as conductors and/or performers first. There are also many agents for composers specializing in visual media, but they rarely mention concert music unless the composers do both.

The reality is that it's easier to sell—and yes, "sell" is the proper verb here—an instrumentalist, singer, or conductor than it ever is to sell a classical composer. The results for performers are tangible; they can get a concert with this or that orchestra, and everybody gets paid. What can an agent or manager get by selling a composer? Securing a commission, even a big one, is more ephemeral, and the payoff comes later than with performances. Recording projects happen rarely. Unless composers have huge followings or a fan base for performing skills that fill concert and recital halls, there's little incentive for an agent to take them on. In short, management agencies will only be interested in you when your career is big enough to show up on their radar. Even then their interest might be mild.

As a side note, this may be why many composers have traditionally retreated to academia. Teaching is a steady and rewarding gig in its own right and, in theory at least, leaves one time to compose. Also, with an educational connection you have more opportunities for performances from faculty and students at your own school and other institutions of learning. This is not to denigrate composers who teach, as it works and allows for a creative freedom that allows one's work to prosper.

To put it briefly, don't bother chasing down a composer agent or management company. Let them find you. It's odd to think of it this way, but if your career is at the point where you don't really need an agent, that's the most likely time you will be approached about having management. That is, unless you're more interested in creating scores for visual media. Then it's a matter of making sure you have a good résumé and a great portfolio of work already done before you can approach such an agent.

More often than not, we must function as our own agents. This is another reason to do what we can to present ourselves in the best way possible, and that we follow through on situations in a professional and effective manner. You don't have to be a full-out extrovert, but you do have to interact with others in a way that works in your favor. It may take some time and effort, but it's worth it.

NOTES

1. They were patterned after the then-long-running muscular dystrophy telethons hosted by the comedian/actor/director Jerry Lewis.

2. *Philharmonic Preludes*, published by Music-Print Productions.

3. **https://www.orchestralibrary.com/reftables/rang.html**, for example.

4. **http://www.societyofcomposers.org**, for one.

5. When asked what I do as a musician, I sometimes joke about having "seventeen jobs at any given time." Of course that's not true. It's more like nine, and yes, they're all legal.

Chapter 5

THE GIG

The barriers are not erected which can say to aspiring talents and industry, "Thus far and no farther."

—Ludwig van Beethoven

I am one of those who will go on doing till all doings are at an end.

—Wolfgang Amadeus Mozart

In our hearts composing is a calling, a mission. We compose because we cannot *not* do it. We spend time at the piano, or the guitar, or some other instrument, or at the computer, or we sing, and we create . . . something. Music. Art. We express the inexpressible. The philosopher Friedrich Nietzsche said that without music, "life would be a mistake." Hopefully, what we create will be performed, heard, and appreciated by others. But composing is also an occupation; it's a job, a way to earn a living, a gig. And such a weird and wonderful gig it is, too. But we should never have to do it for free, unless we *choose* to do so. *The gig* begins when you decide or are compelled to sit down and write something, or when you've been commissioned to compose a work.

We start out as composers still learning our craft. I tell composition students I can't teach them *how* to compose; that's up to them to figure out on their own. But I also say I *can* teach them the craft and some of the "tricks of the trade" of composition. Having composition lessons in a college or conservatory is a bit like learning to drive; the lessons are the equivalent of driver's education, and graduation is like earning your driver's license. Only after you've received that license do you first learn to drive in real situations, and only after you've earned your degree in composition do you really learn how to compose. In both cases you move from safe and protected environments to the real world, where your actions as a driver has consequences and your work as a composer is judged, fairly or not, by your musician peers, audiences, and critics. This usually results in a self-imposed sense of pressure to produce works of Great Importance, and to take on every composing opportunity that comes your way. There's also the self-imposed pressure to build your portfolio of works as quickly as possible.

It doesn't always matter to new composers if the opportunity is the right one for their compositional style, or if they have the knowledge and experience to handle the project, or if the work is worth their time and effort. The hardest thing for a less-experienced composer to do is say "no" to a possible composing job. If you're a less-experienced composer presented with an opportunity, please consider taking a moment before saying "yes" to ask yourself some basic questions.

WHEN TO SAY "YES" AND WHEN TO SAY "NO"

There are no rules for determining when to say "yes" or "no" to a composing opportunity. Every situation, and every composer, is different. We have individual needs and abilities, strengths and weaknesses. Yet there are ways we can address those needs and accommodate our abilities. Figuring out whether to say "yes" or "no" comes down to answering questions that only you can answer, such as:

* *Will the style or genre of music be a good fit?* Will the project play to your strengths? Are you strictly a classical composer with no knowledge of jazz but have been asked to write for a big band, for example?[1] If not, would it be a good "stretch"?

* *Will the music be for instruments or voices you've written for before?* Do you want to write for them again? Frederic Chopin wrote almost exclusively for solo piano and had no issue with it. Leonard Bernstein, on the other hand, wrote for orchestra, chamber ensembles, musical theater, and more, and had no issues with that either. Do you want the challenge of composing for brand-new forces?[2]

* *What is the technical level of the performers?* Are they professionals, talented amateurs, or beginners? What can musicians do at those levels?

* *What would you get out of it?* In other words, what about the project would motivate you to take it on? Motivators could be money, prestige, the challenge of the specific situation, or perhaps an opportunity to do something beneficial to a community. Perhaps it could be some combination of those possibilities.

* *Do you have enough time to write this?* How much work do you already have pending? Would the new work be more important or of lesser importance?

No doubt you can ask yourself more questions, but the above questions come up most often. Start with these and you're likely to figure out if you should do the gig. As for when to say a hard "no," consider:

* *Would you have to give up your rights to your work?* No situation should ask you to give up your copyright or moral rights, with the possible exception of writing for audiovisual projects. Say no.

* *Do you have to pay to write the work?* It happens rarely. When it does someone or some entity will ask you to cover the costs of performance or pay for other reasons. Like certain "calls for scores," this is a "pay to play" ploy, and composers should avoid it.

* *Does the work and/or time involved completely outweigh any benefits?* After determining if you have the time to do the work, you need to decide if it's worth it.

Saying "no" is almost always difficult, especially at the early stages of your career. If you must, be polite, respectful, and business-like. Thank the people with whom you're communicating for thinking of you. Then you can explain why you're turning down the opportunity, perhaps saying something nonspecific and noncommittal. You could say, for example, "I'm sorry, I don't have the time right now to take on a project of this scope." If the situation warrants it you can be more direct. For instance, you could say "I cannot take on work that requires my giving up the rights to my music." Whatever your approach you can end with something courteous that lets the reader know you would be open to future opportunities. Even something simple like "I hope to work with you in the near future" would be appropriate.

It might seem counterintuitive, but when turning down a commission you can recommend another composer you feel is suited to the gig and/or who you know could use the opportunity. It's a sign of professionalism for one thing. People asking about your availability will remember your willingness to help even if you couldn't take on the work. Helping another composer is a good thing to do as well.

WHEN TO DO A "FREEBIE"

The *Handbook* is all about earning income on the music you write. So why discuss writing for free? The answer is because the benefits of accepting a commission are not always income-related. Being paid what you and your music are worth is important, of course, but some of the more intangible benefits can be "priceless." There are few reasons for taking on a "freebie" project, but they can be pretty powerful and convincing.

* *You can earn prestige and respect.* You could be presented with an opportunity to write for a musician or ensemble that would elevate your status

immediately, immensely, and noticeably. Your credibility as a composer can be enhanced to other musicians and the public at large.

* *You can give back to society.* A few years ago I was asked to write an easy work for full orchestra, for a middle school ensemble with *no* budget. Not a small budget. *None.* These were students playing on school instruments lent to them by the school. The instruments were not the best by any means. The students had only classroom time to learn to play them. But the orchestra director wanted "his kids" to have a positive musical experience. There was little to no music for the exact instrumentation he had. Could I help? The short answer was "yes." The students not only got to perform as an ensemble for the first time, but with a work written expressly for *them.* This boosted their morale immensely, and it gave the school administrators something positive and important to consider. The following year the orchestra received its first (small) budget in years. The feeling you get when you've helped someone, with no expectation of something in return, can be wonderful.

* *Other types of compensation.* Altruism is good, but sometimes you can be compensated in other ways. Compensation doesn't always have to be monetary. It could be an invitation to guest-conduct the ensemble for which you've written. The commissioning party could arrange for you to be inter-viewed on local media. Maybe you'll get a great recording of the work out of it that you can use later on. These and other possibilities should be considered should the circumstances arise.

When you compose something for free, you shouldn't expect anything in return. But you can still earn income from the music later. Subsequent performances by other musicians can generate performance royalties. The music could also be published, generating print royalties on sales as well as performance royalties, and so on.

SCHEDULES

Chapter 2's brief discussion on how to schedule a composing project applied to projects with set premiere dates. If you're writing for yourself "just because," any scheduling will be self-imposed. But for projects where dead-lines are involved, it's worth having a scheduling process to help keep you on track. It's all in the details.

* *Make sure you have enough time to write the work in the first place.* This means you need to know how quickly or slowly you usually compose, and then judge accordingly.

* *Work backward from the deadline.* This will help you determine when certain stages of the project need to be done. Again, this requires your know-ing how long it takes for you to do things. Working out a schedule in reverse

chronology is an effective method for maintaining control over your time and energy. Say you've been commissioned in October for a work for small orchestra, and the premiere is set for May 1. The orchestra is a community ensemble and will have six rehearsals including a dress rehearsal once a week. Right there you have enough information to set your schedule. The reverse chronology could be:

- Premiere: May 1.
- Parts delivered: March 11 (about seven weeks before the concert).
- Score delivered: February 19 (about three weeks before the parts are delivered).

Depending on how quickly you work, October through the first two weeks of February could be enough time to compose the score and to get it into shape for the conductor. Generating parts is a necessary but often annoying process no matter how it's done, but it doesn't take a lot of time thanks to current music notation programs. Most programs let you extract parts from the score's file, and then edit the individual parts. Following the sample timeline, you'd have about three weeks to get the parts in good order. And if you finish the score early that gives you extra time to work on the parts.

* *Build in reasonable amounts of extra time into the schedule.* This will allow for almost inevitable unforeseen circumstances that often crop up. Your computer might crash, or you might get another gig with a shorter timeline that is even more important, or you may want to include time off for a vacation. Having that cushion of time built-in takes some of the mental pressure off too. One extra benefit to building in a cushion of time is if you finish early your commissioning party will be amazed and pleased when you hand over the score to your new work before the deadline!

For determining the composing part of the schedule consider how much research you'll need to do before putting any notes down. If you're writing for an instrument that's new to you, you'll undoubtedly want to know as much as you can about it. Similarly, if you're writing for a standard instrument but for a specific performer, you may want to learn as much as possible about what that performer can do—what their strengths and weaknesses are, and perhaps what extended techniques they can do.[3]

If you're interested in writing something for a publisher to consider—something that's covered in more detail in the next chapter—you will need to find out the publisher's schedule. When do they start looking at submissions? Many look at possible new works in the spring, but starting and ending dates vary widely between companies and from year to year. Some will post such information on their websites or on social media. Once you have that information you can create your own reverse chronological schedule, such as:

- Submission within publisher's date range.
- Recording of work (if any), either done with live musicians or an audio mockup.
- Score preparation.
- Composing.

There are two good opportunities during this process for a little shameless, but effective, self-promotion in the form of press releases. A *press release* is a statement provided to news media that gives information about an upcoming event or on a significant matter. Depending on the circumstances a press release could lead to pre-concert coverage, a review, or an interview with you or the performers.

The first time you can write and send out a press release is when you've signed a significant contract, such as an exclusive publishing deal, or for a major commission. The second opportunity would be to announce a premiere or other noteworthy performance of your work. There's an in-depth discussion about it in Chapter 9 on "Follow Up," but start thinking about it here.

Lastly, here is one strong recommendation: don't try to multitask and compose more than one work at a time. Yes, it can be done and yes, people do it. But it's rare to turn out two works of high quality that way. One or both works might suffer.[4] If you must, for some reason, work on more than one piece at a time, try to overlap their schedules rather than trying to write them simultaneously. Try to switch between projects infrequently. Give each enough time within your schedule constraints, and give a bit more time to the earlier project during the overlapped portions. This allows you to keep the two works separate in your mind, and the music will sound more distinct from piece to piece. Think of your scheduling as shown in Figure 5-1.

Do your best to adhere to your schedules and to meet your deadlines. Schedules and deadlines can easily get the better of us, so whatever you can do to be more effective will help. It may seem counterintuitive, but also be sure to take break now and then. It will help you keep your focus and allow you work things out to some extent subconsciously. You can even build the breaks into your day-to-day schedule. Sticking with composing schedules, as with scheduled meetings, can make you seem more professional. There's a saying that can apply here: Early is on time, on time is late, and late is (usually) unacceptable.

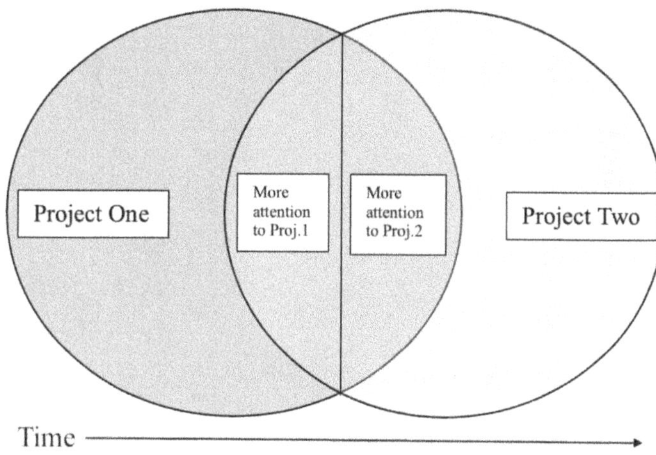

Figure 5-1   Diagram of Overlapping Project Schedules, author created

NOTES

1. This has actually happened. In 1945, clarinetist Benny Goodman commissioned Igor Stravinsky to write for Goodman's big band with himself as soloist. Stravinsky's *Ebony Concerto* was the resulting work.

2. I mostly compose for traditional forces—string orchestra, full orchestra, band, chorus, chamber ensembles, solo works, and so on—but I also enjoy the occasional challenge of writing for an unusual instrument or an unusual combination of instruments. I've written, for example, a concerto for Baroque lute, a work for four harps (*For the Gipsy in My Soul*), and, perhaps even stranger, a piece for three alphorns, harp, and double bass (*Other Side of the Mountain*). Each work presented its specific difficulties, but I felt rewarded by how it turned out.

3. Some decades ago I was commissioned to write a work for alto saxophone and piano by the exceptional classical alto saxophonist Gary Louie. I went down to Maryland and spent a few days with Louie to learn everything I could about his specific abilities, strengths, and weaknesses. For the record, he didn't have *any* weaknesses. He has extraordinary control over dynamics and mulitphonics, both of which I wound up incorporating into my work *The Ides*.

4. The idea that "multitasking" is more myth than reality isn't just my opinion. A study by the Cleveland Clinic has shown that just 2.5 percent of people are able to effectively multitask. According to their report "when our brain is constantly switching gears to bounce back and forth between tasks . . . we become <u>less efficient</u> and more likely to make a mistake" (**https://health.clevelandclinic.org/science-clear -multitasking-doesnt-work**). But if anyone is capable of multitasking, it would be parents of two or more small children, or conductors.

Chapter 6

PUBLISHING YOUR MUSIC

Dearest friend, I am only too thankful that you are not parsimonious to me and are so willing to publish my works. But this is nothing new, I have always appreciated your large-hearted liberality. Merci, merci, merci*!*

—Pyotr Ilyich Tchaikovsky, in a letter to
music publisher Pyotr I. Jurgenson

In Chapter 2, "Income Streams: Definitions and Explanations," you read some reasons for making your music available for purchase or rent. Those reasons can be generally stated as: (1) it makes your music available to the people you want to have perform it, and (2) it helps generate income from both the sale (or rental) of the music itself and through its subsequent performance. Music publishing as a business can be traced back to the early days of printing, certainly as far back as 1501, when Ottaviano Petrucci (1466–1539) produced the collection *Harmonice Musices Odhecaton*.[1] Self-publishing music likely started not long after that; one significant early self-publisher was Georg Philipp Telemann (1681–1767).

PUBLISHING COMPANIES VERSUS SELF-PUBLISHING SHEET MUSIC

Your music can be published in two basic ways: by an already-established business or by publishing it yourself. There are upsides and downsides to each. The benefits of a traditional publisher handling your music are clear.

 * *Longtime publishers are already known.* Customers and potential customers have come to know, respect, and trust established publishers and

83

expect them to offer high quality music. To put it another way, they have high credibility.

** Many publishing houses are known for being the sole source for music by certain prominent composers.* Boosey and Hawkes, for example, is known for publishing the works of Leonard Bernstein, Aaron Copland, Eric Whitacre, and others. If a publisher of that stature adds your works to its catalog, it can bolster your credibility by associating you with the other composers.

** Traditional publishers have distribution outlets in place.* There is no need to start from the beginning in developing relationships with music stores and sheet music distributors. The publisher does all of the "heavy lifting."

** Longtime publishers have developed standards for their production processes.* Their standards cover editing, engraving, and proofreading the music, as well as the printing itself. There really is a "professional look" in sheet music, and it includes everything from the formatting of a page to the type of paper used. Even digital-only publishers aim for that level of quality. Sheet music from certain publishers will have a consistent "look" that signifies high quality to the consumer. Self-publishers can achieve this level of quality too, but it takes work at the beginning. See Chapter 7, "Presenting Your Music," for ways to give your music a more professionally produced look.

** Traditional publishers do all the work.* They edit, engrave, and prepare the music for printing; they get it printed, collated, packaged, and ready for sale. They also do the promotion and handle the sales. Lastly, they maintain all of the financial records and regularly provide sales and royalty reports to you, and give you statements of sales and any accompanying royalties earned from those sales.

** Established music publishers have marketing and advertising budgets, not to mention the necessary staff to promote their publications.* Self-publishers seldom have the financial or human resources to do that work with the same efficiency.

** Publishers have the flexibility to offer composers an exclusive contract or right of first refusal agreement.* An *exclusive contract* is one in which the publisher promises to publish any music you provide. A *right of first refusal* is what sounds like: you agree to submit your work to the publisher first, and if they turn it down you can then submit it to other publishers for consideration.

This doesn't negate self-publishing by any means. The sheer number of composers in the United States—the PRO BMI currently claims over a million and its counterpart ASCAP just under that number—can lower your chances of getting a traditional publisher to take on your work. Self-publishing is a way to get your music before performers. There are other, more positive reasons to go with self-publishing:

** You have complete control of all aspects of your work, creatively and business-wise.* No one can tell you what to do. That includes the production of the sheet music from editing to printing, the distribution and sales, marketing, and so on. You can promote your music in the way you want it promoted.

** As a composer and a publisher you get to earn 100 percent of the print and performance royalties earned from your work.* If your music is with a traditional publisher, you would have to share any income earned.

** You don't have to go hunting for a publisher.* Self-publishing eliminates the need to find a publisher that is appropriate for your music, as well as the need to negotiate terms once you've found the publisher of your choice.

** You, too, can produce "publication-quality" sheet music.* With the improvements in music notation and printing technologies over the past two decades, it has become relatively easy, effective, and inexpensive to produce professional-looking music. Anyone with the right equipment and programs, and a bit of knowledge about printing, can learn to publish their own music that rivals most traditional publishers' output.

As you can see, traditional publishing and self-publishing each has its good points. But there are down sides to each as well. Some limitations of traditional publishing are apparent.

** You have less control over your music.* Your music is edited and formatted to match a publisher's established norms. Even covers are usually out of your hands. Think, for one example, how the covers of most of the music published by G. Schirmer are a distinctive yellow with a green border and all text in green as well. Those covers effectively act as Schirmer's trademark. Or, a publisher might tell you the title of your work "won't sell" and it needs to be changed. If their agreement with you allows for it, they will change the title.

** The submission process can take a long time.* Remember, you're not the only composer submitting works. Some publishers receive, literally, hundreds of submissions each year. When they go through those submissions they have to determine if a work (1) is good, (2) will sell, (3) doesn't oversaturate their catalog with similar works, and (4) will sell. Yes, I repeated "will sell." Even in concert music, sales are a priority.

** Your royalty rate on sales with a traditional will seem low.* You might think that you could make more money by self-publishing. As you will see later in this chapter, however, the income you would earn can be offset by the expenses you incur in the publication process.

** Some bigger publishers hold on to their (that is, your) copyrights tenaciously.* This is true even if they let a work go out of print. There are ways, according to the copyright laws, to have a copyright revert to you, but it's a highly complicated and long-term process that those same publishers know how to manipulate to their benefit.[2]

Exclusive contracts, by intent, prevent you from taking your music elsewhere. If you have an exclusive agreement with one publisher, you can't make a better deal with another without breaking your contract. That would likely result in your publisher suing you.

Right of first refusal agreements are less restrictive but still have a downside. You can't look for another publisher if you're unhappy with the way your current one treats your work. In the meantime, you're obligated to submit your work to them first.

The downsides of self-publishing can also be daunting.

Your distribution network is a lot smaller. Even if you have your own website for digital sales, your music won't be as available for purchase as you wish.

You have to do your own promotional work. Promotional work is difficult to begin with, and self-promotion is even more so. Many composers feel emotionally uncomfortable promoting their music, let alone themselves.

You're likely to have little to no track record or credibility as a publisher. This is true, even if you have an excellent reputation as a composer.

Quality control is difficult to maintain. Setting standards and sticking to them is more difficult for self-publishers, even with others' help.

Your royalties seem higher than with a traditional publisher, but your costs will be higher. You can be working out of a spare room, basement, attic, or garage, but you will still have expenses. These expenses can include utilities, rent or mortgages, property and personal insurance, the costs of paper to print, the printing machines and their supplies (anything from laser toner to staplers), shipping supplies, and much more. If you hire someone, say, to help pack boxes for shipping, you have to pay that person wages, unemployment insurance, taxes, and so on. Even if you work solely in the digital realm, you'll still need printed reference copies, file maintenance for copyright, legal, and financial reasons, and your computers and such will need to be top of the line and have an abundance of backups. You'll need to have an accountant to handle the books because this sort of business is more complicated than just filing a Form W-2 or Form 1099 with the IRS, as well as an attorney for handling contracts, any legal disputes, and more.[3]

Many composers have taken to self-publishing despite any potential disadvantages. Most of the music I write gets published through established channels because I prefer to have a publisher handle the day-to-day stuff. The rest of my works are self-published, mostly because I believe in them, but they don't fit the catalogs of the publishers with whom I usually work.

A sort of hybrid of self-publishing and traditional publishing has developed over a decade prior to this book. In this hybrid a distributor or traditional publisher sells your music on your behalf while you keep your copyright. You supply all of the materials necessary for printing or downloading. The distributor or publisher in turn adds your work to their catalog, promotes it to some extent (you'd still need do your own advertising and marketing to make your enterprise more effective), sells the music, and, after taking out an agreed-upon amount, gives you a royalty statement and the appropriate amount of money. Not many publishers will do this, and as of this writing only one distributor, J. W. Pepper, is doing it in the United States in any major way. Their My Score program requires a onetime fee to join.[4]

There seems to be an inverse ratio between the size of a publishing concern and your importance to it. If you self-publish, you are not just the most important composer on the roster, you're the *only* one. The bigger the publishing operation, the less important you might feel. After all, your work(s) might be among hundreds of others, each work vying for purchases and performances, each composer (or composer's estate) competing for attention. That might be an erroneous perception though, so it's better to give those publishing concerns the benefit of the doubt. With a smaller business you may receive more attention, but there may be fewer resources at hand to promote your work.

One thing worth noting is that some publishers, especially those with primarily pop music in their catalogs, allow works go out of print once the initial print run has sold out. This can happen even if they have, or have moved to, printing on demand.[5] If a publisher expresses interest in taking on one of your works, ask if they use print on demand. Also ask if they keep things available in their catalog.

It helps to know what a traditional publisher does and what costs are involved in putting out a single piece of music. You can then work out what you will have to deal with if you decide to self-publish. Here's a simplified version of the process, along with some comments:

* *A publisher must decide what kind(s) of music, that is what product, it's going to sell.* Some publishers focus on music for the educational market (grade school through high school, and some on through college), while others lean heavily toward selling to professional concert musicians. Some try to provide the gamut of works from solo instrument pieces to full orchestral symphonies. Other publishers are pop music–oriented and more interested in publishing arrangements of those tunes than anything we might call "serious music." If you want to get your work released by a traditional publisher, get to know which ones are most appropriate for the music you write. Start by going through the scores in your own collection and see who publishes the sorts of works you write. Keep in mind that publishers go into, and out of,

business often, and many get gobbled up by bigger companies; you will probably have to do some digging into who owns whom.

** The next step is to select the repertoire.* Not every publisher wants to publish new works or are open to new composers, so again, do your research before submitting your music. Once you've done that and have submitted your work, the publisher's selection process begins. The bigger publishing companies will have a committee to determine if a submitted work is right for them; for smaller companies it's usually the owner or perhaps just a couple of people making the determination. Whomever is looking at your music, it's worth repeating something said earlier: You're not the only composer submitting works, and publishers have to determine if a work (1) is good, (2) will sell, (3) doesn't oversaturate their catalog with similar works, and (4) will sell.

Exclusive contracts were mentioned earlier too. Why would a publisher offer you one? First and foremost, their interest would be in the potential sales they could make. Finances aside, they could believe in your work from an artistic standpoint, or the prestige of having an important composer, or some combination of the three. If you get an exclusive agreement note that you will have just one place for people to find your work—"one-stop shopping" as it were—that makes it easier to promote it. Your royalty rate might be slightly higher depending on your negotiations. With an exclusive you can usually rest assured that you music *will* be published. (The number of living U.S. composers with exclusive agreements with publishers, as of this writing, is around two dozen.)

** Once your work is accepted for publication, several things then happen simultaneously.*

- The publishing company will start the legal process of obtaining the rights to your work. They will offer you a contract that promises you certain things, like sales statements and royalties if earned on a regular basis, in exchange for the copyright. You will retain your *moral rights* to your music for the most part, although that might not be spelled out in the agreement. The Berne Convention defines *moral rights* as the rights "to claim authorship of the work and to object to any distortion, mutilation or other modification of, or other derogatory action in relation to the said work. . . ." That said, your agreement may allow the publisher to make certain changes in your work, usually musically unessential ones, to bring it in line with the rest of the publisher's catalog. Titles, formatting of the score, and other aspects of the printed music might change. The agreement might also allow the publisher to produce other versions, arrangements, of your work. If so, they may ask you to do it yourself before hiring a third party to create it.
- The music will be made ready for printing. Even a great prose writer needs an editor. It helps to have another set of eyes to go over a manuscript for

mistakes, inconsistencies, and the like, as well as prepare it for the typographers. Composers also need an editor for similar reasons. Not only do music editors check for incorrect pitches, rhythms, and so on, they mark up the score and parts for formatting for the engraver.[6]

Formatting sheet music is something most musicians don't think about when it's done correctly, but we rant and rave when it's not. The editor's work involves making a score *look* right—that it's set for the properly sized paper in the correct proportions, and that it's neither too crowded on each page nor too sparsely laid out—as well as making sure the pitches, rhythms, etc., are not only correct but consistent in appearance. Individual parts too have to be edited, again not only for the look of the page and the consistent and correct notation, but also for page turns. Once edited the music needs to be engraved according to the standards prepared by the editor. Nowadays the editor often functions as the *de facto* engraver as well, but there are still those dedicated to the profession of music engraving who are on publishers' staffs or who work independently.

Once engraved, the music needs to be proofread. Most of the time a publisher allows the composer the chance to proofread the score and any parts, but sometimes (perhaps due to time constraints or just company policy) they don't. In any case, the publisher will have at least one person, likely the editor, go through the newly notated music for mistakes, deletions, additions, and so on. The music then goes back to the engraver to fix those items. If the editor is also the engraver of the music, someone else will be (or at least should be) asked to look over the engraved version of the music with the edited version of the manuscript. Once the corrections and other changes are done and the engraver returns the music to the editor or proofreader for a final okay, it's ready for printing. But not yet.

- Other departments or employees will be working on other aspects of production. The art department, or an independent artist hired for the purpose, will design the overall cover. Others will determine the catalog number and, based on the genre of music and the number of pages of music being printed and other factors, how much to charge the consumer for the final product.

In theory a publisher takes the following factors into account when determining the retail selling price: (1) the size and number of pages of music and the cost of its physical production (printing, folding and trimming, collating, etc.); (2) the genre; (3) whether it's only black ink/toner on white paper or there is full-color printing involved (for covers, etc.); (4) the publisher's overhead (utilities, mortgages or rents, and so on); (5) the composer's royalty rate; (6) the company's desired profit; (7) what percentage of the retail price should the publisher charge stores and distributors; and (8) the break-even point, that is how many copies at a particular price will have to be sold before actual profit begins. But that's theory. The reality is that pricing sheet music often comes down to two factors: (1) how much it costs *per copy* ("per unit") to print a predetermined number of copies, (2) what the going rate is for similar works. A publisher would then multiply the *pro rata* costs, anywhere from ten to twenty times the amount but typically around ten. The ratio varies widely among publishers. Say a publisher wants to print three hundred copies of something, and the *pro rata* cost of a single copy is $1.00. The going rate for similar works might be $8.00, or it might be $12.00. The publisher then might decide to set the retail sales price at $10.00. The publisher would have to determine—and here's a familiar phrase—what the market will bear and figure out if a $10.00 retail selling price works.

- An advertising and/or marketing department, which can consist of as few as one employee, will do their part to sell your music. Marketing is based on four principles: product, price, place, and promotion. Your music is the product, so that's taken care of. The price is too, presumably. Where marketing should shine is in placement and promotion, deciding to whom and how to sell your work. A good promotional team knows to *whom* they have to sell the music, *where* to find them, and their best guess—because there are never any guarantees—on *how* to sell it to them.

Assuming everyone has done their jobs, your work is ready for sale. The publisher has determined a *retail* price, that is the price the consumer pays. Let's say, hypothetically, that the price is $10.00 a copy. You should get most of that, right? No. The process of preparing your work for sale as just described is a costly one. Besides, in most cases a publisher will sell most of its product—your music—to a distributor or music store for sale to consumers in turn. Most stores or distributors pay publishers a *wholesale* price, which is usually about half of the retail price. Music dealers, stores, and distributors pay that amount because they have overhead too, and the difference between what they pay and what they charge the consumer has to pay for *their* overhead and earn a usually small profit. In short, the store or distributor in our scenario receives ten dollars from the consumer but has to pay the publisher half of that. What's left has to cover the store or distributor's costs before they can realize a bit of profit. Meanwhile the publisher has received the five dollars but must pay its own overhead, including your composer's print royalty, before considering any money left over as profit. So how do you fit into all of this?

Unless what you've written is a work for hire and you have received a one-time fee for it, you will receive a print royalty. A royalty, for our purposes, is a percentage of money earned through the sale, rental, or licensing of your music. Royalties for sheet music are most often calculated on the retail selling price, multiplied by the number of copies sold.

There are no industry standards for royalty percentages, but the average has been 10 percent since at least the mid-twentieth century. Using our hypothetical retail price of $10.00, one copy sold would earn you $1.00 in royalties. That may seem like small change, but the publisher is only getting about $5.00 out of which you get that buck. You're actually getting 20 percent of what the publisher earns. Succinctly put, you're getting a decent deal. If you have one of those exceedingly rare exclusive agreements with a publisher you *might* get a better royalty rate of as much as 12.5 percent on the retail price of your work. That would be 25 percent of the publisher's take. While any larger percentage is possible it would be highly unusual.

With self-publishing, your gross income could be higher. Your costs will also be higher though, as you'll be handling all of the nonmusical aspects of publishing in addition to the music itself. Your effective royalty, that is your net income after deducting your costs, could be lower, higher, or the same compared with having a traditional publisher sell your work. This disparity is most likely to occur at the beginning of your self-publishing enterprise, but with adjustments in expenditures and other aspects of your business you could maximize your earnings. If you plan on self-publishing do your best to consult your financial *and* legal advisors on how to go about it. One suggestion your financial advisor will probably recommend is that you have enough capital—enough money on hand—to run your business until it can turn a profit. Consult your attorney (CYA) and consult your financial advisor (CYFA).

WHEN AND HOW TO GRADE YOUR MUSIC FOR EDUCATIONAL USE

In Chapter 2, the discussion on ways to generate income from your music includes arranging and working in visual media. Another income source for composers is writing music for what's commonly referred to as "the educational market." Composers have long written works for students. Beethoven, Czerny, Debussy, Bartók, and even Stravinsky all wrote works for student pianists. Others have written music for students of other instruments with less experience. Despite the stereotype of beginning works being "meaningless kiddie music," pieces written for student musicians can be, and *should be*, treated as "real" music.[7] Ask any music teacher, and they will tell you there is a need for good music at all levels of performance. That goes for everything from solo instrumental works to pieces for full orchestra and concert band.

Admittedly, one thing that has kept the stereotype in the forefront of composers' minds is that for years most of the people writing for learning musicians have been music teachers first and writers second. These were good, even great, musicians. But until they perceived a need for repertoire for their students' needs, as well as the inability to find that music published, they hadn't given much thought to composing or arranging. Teachers know *exactly* what their students need, and they can write music to suit if they're motivated to do so. Things have changed considerably over the past few decades, and there are now more people who are equally dedicated to teaching and writing music. There are also more full-time composers who write for the learning musician.[8] There are also more professional composers who are aware of the needs of less experienced musicians—the Stravinskys among us—and are willing and even eager to write for them. Given the parameters ("limitations" being too negative a term), a composer will make every effort to write good music.

Music for the educational market is normally broken down into five or six levels of technique, depending on the instrument or voice, the ensemble, the number of years of study, the publisher, and basically with whomever it is you're speaking. In other words, it's rare to have a uniform agreement as to what student musicians can do at any given point in their education. We can, though, generalize to some extent.

* *Grade 1.* This is for the very beginners, the students learning how to read music, how to hold their instrument and produce a sound. Singers at this stage are young, preteens, and have narrow ranges and may not be able to do anything beyond a melody; harmonies usually need to be simple if used. The music is almost invariably tonal or mildly modal, although some "special effects" can be used for fun value. Singers can make noises, whisper, and more. Instrumentalists can do things like playing on the "wrong" side of the bridge of string instruments or playing just the mouthpiece of a clarinet.

In the instrumental world, grade 1 clarinetists don't play above "the break," of written B-flat mid-staff. Most grade 1 trombonists cannot physically play a B-natural in the staff; that note can only be played by pulling the slide all the way out, to the 7th position. Most students in elementary or early middle school simply can't reach 7th position because they don't yet have the physical reach.

* *Grade 2.* Considered for students who have played for a year, usually by junior high/middle school. More basic playing techniques are introduced, harmonies expand somewhat, and rhythms are slightly more complex and/ or varied.

* *Grade 3*. This grade level is acknowledged by most educators and music publishers as for high school level or other musicians with three years of experience. The music is more varied and can be challenging up to a point. Grade 3 works can be considered an overlap point with professional-level music. Although not labeled as such by the composers or their publishers, a large number of "real" compositions at this level are available, and they are often performed by community, and military and other professional orchestras and bands.

* *Grade 4*. University/professional-level music.

* *Grade 5*. Challenging works for university/professional players/singers.

* *Grade 6* (if used). The most difficult music to perform.

In music education there is an inverse ratio between the grade levels and how much music at those levels is needed. Grades 4, 5, and 6 works sell the least for student musicians, with grade 6 selling the least within those three. Professional-level musicians may well pick up the difference in those sales. Grades 1 and 2 sell the most. Grade 3 is very often considered the "sweet spot" by music publishers; this is where the grade level and demand for works at that level are pretty much equal. This goes for all instruments, voices, and ensemble types.

A word about what to write for when it comes to works for learning musicians. Just as there is an inverse proportion between grade level and demand, there seems to be a hierarchy in which ensembles need music. In the United States, band is king: whether it's concert band, marching band, brass band, or British-style brass band, works for band at all levels are the most popular. Music for choruses, at least as of 2024, is next in terms of demand, followed by works for string orchestra. Full orchestra gets the least demand because in school systems around the country it requires pulling winds, brass, and percussion players from the band to make up the whole ensemble, which can be difficult, and because there is already a wealth of orchestral repertoire dating back to the Baroque era that makes it possible to find things that work.

Here are some recommendations if you want to write for the educational market.

* *Decide for which instruments, voices, or ensembles you want to write (band, orchestra, chorus, etc.).* If you've written something on commission already, go to the next step.

* *Determine the grade of your work as best you can.*[9]

* *If the work was commissioned, try to get a recording of the premiere.* If you wrote it without a commission or promise of performance, you could offer ensembles the opportunity to perform it or at least read it down to make a recording. A recording can come in handy should you want to approach a traditional publisher. Counterintuitively, submitting a recording of actual students playing something even if it's a rough not-note-perfect performance is

often better than a really good, note-perfect, MIDI demo. Hearing the music as performed in real life gives the "powers that be" at most publishing businesses a sense of whether the music is good, if it works at the proposed level, where any pitfalls (aka "teachable moments") occur and if it's sellable. Still, you can always create a MIDI demo if a recording of a live performance is unavailable.

* Make a short list of publishers who are the most likely to be interested in the work if you're not going to self-publish.* You must do your "homework" for this and learn which publishers sell similar works for the same instrumentation or voices. Start with the largest, best-established publishers of course but don't ignore the smaller companies by any means. Go to the publishers' websites and find out (1) if they have their own grading system and where your work fits within it, (2) if they even accept unsolicited works for consideration, (3) what their submission processes are, and (4) what their stated turnaround time is from receipt of your work to when you're notified if they will accept it.

* It's okay to contact companies directly for information.* It's ultimately the easiest way to learn anything you can't discover from their websites or in their catalogs. And if you can get the name of the person in charge of submissions in the process, all the better.

* Follow the publisher's submission process to submit your work.* Then comes the hardest part. You'll need to wait for an answer, most likely longer —sometimes a lot longer—than their stated response times. You *could* drop a short note asking when you might hear from them, but I do *not* recommend it. They'll get to it when they get to it. However: if you're first told it will take two to three months, but you haven't heard in over, say, five, one of several things may have happened. One possibility is they never received the submission, although in these days of electronic submissions you'll know if they received your work. Another possibility is that they simply haven't gotten to your work yet for any number of reasons having nothing to do with your music. Be patient. The hardest part of this really is the waiting.

* Don't submit the same work to several publishers at once.* This "shotgun approach" can backfire if two (or more!) publishers decide they want the piece. Telling one publisher no because your work was picked up by another is not a good way to ingratiate yourself with the rejected publisher, who just might have wanted more of your music later on.

* Do not sign a publishing agreement without reading it all and asking questions about things you don't understand or with which you disagree.* If it's your first time dealing with such a contract try to get an attorney to look it over, preferably one who specializes in copyright and other intellectual property. Make sure you understand not only what a contract says, but what the ramifications are, *and* that you agree to it all. Some things are negotiable,

others are not, depending on the publisher. The next chapter goes into more detail about publishing contracts to give you an idea of what to expect.

** If the publisher rejects your work remember: IT'S NEVER BECAUSE YOU'RE A BAD COMPOSER.*[10] There are a myriad of reasons for a publisher to say "no" to a submission, including:

- The publisher has too many of the same type of work at the same grade level.
- The publisher doesn't handle this particular type of work. (This is why you should "do your homework" before submitting your music.)
- The work may be musically fine, and they may otherwise be interested in it, but it doesn't fit the grade level they need. (They *might* ask if you'd be willing to adjust things to fit the grade level they do need, though. Try to be open to that.)
- It just might not be one of your better works. Let's face it, it happens.
- Sometimes, for any number of reasons, the reviewers don't "get" what you're doing or they feel it's just not reaching its potential. Maybe they're right, or maybe one of them got the wrong coffee order that morning and it has made them feel "off" the whole day. Who knows?
- Another reason is that the publisher can only afford to publish a certain number of works each year, and if your work is the very next work after that number, it will not be selected no matter how good it is. (On the upside, it's possible that they may ask to hold the work for the following year's production lineup.)

** If one publisher rejects your work, do not allow yourself to get discouraged.* Go ahead and submit it to another appropriate publisher. This is yet another reason for doing your "homework" about potential publishers. It's always good to have a Plan B, or even a Plan C and Plan D. I once submitted a band arrangement of a great piano tune to one of my favorite publishers, but it was rejected as being just not what they wanted. Rather than wallow in self-pity, I submitted it to another publisher. The second publisher's response? "Why did [name of first publisher] reject this? This works. I can sell it!" Sometimes a piece can wind up going to several publishers in succession before one decides "This works!" and publishes it.

Writing for the educational market has a few downsides. For one, it's easy to get pigeonholed as a writer for a particular type of ensemble or within one genre. It can also be tricky getting the metaphorical foot in the door without some pedagogical background or without some name recognition as a concert composer in the professional world. Also, if you establish yourself as a composer for the educational market first, it may make it more difficult to break through into the professional world—that old stereotype of "meaningless kiddie music" rearing its ugly head again.

The upsides are more numerous. Getting professional orchestras and the best bands to perform your music even the first time, let alone more than once, is extremely difficult and rare to pull off. But if a work intended for the educational market is published you will likely receive multiple performances. Also, teachers often consult with each other about repertoire that works for them, and they can recommend your music.

RECORDINGS

This discussion is not about the pros and cons of having your music commercially recorded. In today's world of streaming and downloads, not to mention extremely shortened attention spans, it's difficult to know if having your music available in recorded form is even worth it. You've read about the differences between recording musicians versus making MIDI demos (*aka* audio mockups), and how useful either can be in getting another musician's attention or that of an educational music publisher. Let's leave that for now and concentrate on how recordings can help you get your music published generally, and even performed.

Folks are busy, and music publishers are always *very* busy no matter what type of music they publish. Many carve out a period of time, anywhere from a few days to a couple of weeks once a year, to dig through piles of submissions or their digital equivalents. When they review the submissions, they look for and are listening for works they not only think are good music but, more importantly to them, are sellable. The number of submissions each year can be in the hundreds. Based on their experiences and needs, publishers know what they're looking for to put in their catalogs. But they have to be won over in a short amount of time because of the other 199+ works waiting to be considered. Having been on the publishing side of the desk, I can tell you a publisher can make a fairly accurate judgment call on a work, one way or the other, literally within the first thirty seconds to a minute and a half of music. If the music makes it past that mark, and it works all the way through to the end, it's considered a "go" and will be considered publishable.

Great-looking scores help, as do details of numerous and/or important performances, but recordings can help most of all. It's a given that publishers' reviewing teams can read scores and hear the music "in their heads." Nevertheless, having recordings to listen to with the scores saves the reviewers time and gives a clear idea of how the music sounds, how it works, and that ineffable quality, how well it could sell. A recording of the work's premiere, or even a link to a video of that performance, could be extremely useful. And yes, even a MIDI demo can help, although some publishers bristle at the synthetic nature of them. Just warn them it's a MIDI demo when submitting your work.

Recordings can also come into play once a work is published. Professional-level concert music may not need a recording for promotional purposes as such, because publishers of such works can rely on the composer's name, or previous performances, or reviews of the music to promote sales. Educational music publishers, however, have long relied on "demo" recordings to help teachers select new works or even play for their students as guides to their own performances. Music teachers are busier than even music publishers, and anything that can help them sort through all of the new works they're inundated with from many publishers is welcome. Some publishers' demos will be professionally performed and recorded, while others will be a little more "homespun" using amateurs or students, and still others will make their own MIDI demos.[11] Deciding what gets recorded and how will depend on a publisher's marketing and advertising budget and production plans.

If you're communicating directly with performers about doing something of yours or selling them sheet music for a work, deciding whether to provide a recording can be tricky. This is particularly true when doing business with musicians at the professional level. Some musicians may welcome it as a listening aid, to get a better idea of what you're after musically. Others may take offense because *they know* how to read a score. Neither reaction is wrong, but you need to handle the circumstances carefully and respectfully. It's best not to just provide a recording in those situations, but to also ask the performers if they would want one along with the score.

NOTES

1. Literally "One Hundred Songs of Harmonic Music," this was a collection of polyphonic secular songs printed using movable type.

2. Apparently, their thinking is to let the work earn performance, mechanical, and other royalties without having to deal with all the messy stuff of keeping sheet music around.

3. More on these topics in Chapter 10, "Finances." Meanwhile, always, *always* have an accountant on your team if you're going to self-publish.

4. The mega-publisher Hal Leonard Corporation operates Arrange Me, which allows writers to arrange pop music and other works under its control and to sell those arrangements through the program. Arrange Me also allows original works to be published, but the main focus is on arrangements. Universal Edition, a music publisher based in Vienna, Austria, runs a program similar to MyScore called Scodo. Each work submitted to Scodo has to be reviewed by UE's Artistic Committee, which is clearly an effort to maintain high standards.

5. "Print on demand" should be understood literally. Any publisher, large or small, has the technological ability to receive an order for a specific piece of sheet music and have it ready for shipping within a short amount of time. This effectively can eliminate the need for printing multiple copies of works and storing them in a warehouse. For smaller publishers, music can be printed on home printers. Larger publishers may have larger, more sophisticated all-in-one units that print, collate, trim, and bind works quickly, using PDFs or proprietary files as the printing source.

6. Yes, the term *engrave* is archaic; it harkens back to the days when music was produced by etching it—literally engraving it—into metal plates for printing. (Producing sheet music using movable type came before that.) The term *engraving* stuck through all of the advancements in setting music for publication: plate engraving; lithography (which is similar to plate engraving, but the music is etched with a mild acid into limestone, the limestone cleaned, then ink is applied); ink stamping; stencils; dry transfers (*aka* "rub offs") like Notaset sheets; music typewriters; and then the whole evolution of computerized music notation. At times in the twentieth century and even now, all of the different methods of notation except typesetting have been used, depending on the publisher. One publisher, G. Henle Verlag, rightly boasts that the reason their publications look as good as they do—and they are beautiful to look at—is that they still use plate engraving and have strict standards to go with it. (There are videos of that process online if you're interested.) Still, the makers of Finale music notation software are doing quite well servicing music publishers large and small, as the output can be "publication quality" when handled correctly. Some publishers have developed proprietary notation programs for their publications too. The next chapter goes into a bit more detail, including events in August of 2024 surrounding the discontinuation of the Finale notation program and its recommendation to switch to one of its competitors, Dorico.

7. I personally see writing for less-experienced musicians as a challenge: How much music can I find, can I create, can I squeeze out of the given parameters?

8. In the world of classical orchestra music arranged for student players, one name has stood out: Merle Isaac. His arrangements are known for expert musical treatments with solid pedagogical backing. (He's also known for truncating famous works severely, but at least those arrangements get less-experienced musicians exposed to the main tunes.)

9. Bandworld.org has a very useful grading chart online that covers ranges, rhythms, keys, and much more. You can find it here: **https://www.bandworld.org/pdfs/gradingchart.pdf.**

For string orchestra, the American String Teachers Association also has a practical grading chart available: **https://stringorchestrasheetmusic.com/wp-content/uploads/2015/05/ASTA-GRADING-SYSTEM.pdf.**

10. This goes for any publisher of anything! For the record, I and every other composer I have known have had works rejected and still get rejected by publishers, even those of us with lots of music already published.

11. Making live demo recordings is both exhausting and fascinating. I've co-produced a number of these recordings over the years, sitting with colleagues and recording engineers in one room while a conductor and a band or orchestra reads

through dozens of works over just a couple of days. And by "read through" I mean the players get a moment or two to look over their parts for each work, with the conductor giving some tips on various passages, and then dive into recording. Most of the works are essentially recorded "one and done"—one full time through of the music, with only some of the rougher spots given a second or third "take." Later, the engineer will take the best bits and "comp" together—that is, make a composite recording of—the best possible representation of the music. That these recordings get done as well as they do in such a compressed amount of time is amazing, but then this is working with professionals, performers with well-known orchestras, military bands (on off hours), and those who regularly do studio gigs, all of whom have the training and experience to pull it off.

Chapter 7

PRESENTING YOUR MUSIC

Hide not your Talents, they for Use were made. What's a Sun-Dial in the shade!

—Benjamin Franklin, in *Poor Richard's Almanack* (1750)

It's not just you who needs to make a good first impression. Your music must as well. Any time an opportunity to introduce yourself and your work comes up it's the first impression that will get things moving . . . or not. Even if you haven't written a lot, whatever you want people to see needs to *look* right, that is, it needs to look professional.

MUSIC NOTATION

One of the most important aspects of giving your music a professional look is to be consistent. If a rhythm repeats, notate it the same way each time. Spell pitches consistently, too, unless there is a specific reason—say a change in tonal center—to give the enharmonic equivalent. Scores, whether for solo instrument, symphony orchestra or band, chorus, or any chamber ensemble, should be clear and consistent in notation.

Sheet music published these days has almost all been produced via music notation programs on computers. Not all publishers use the same programs or even the type of computers or their operating systems. Many publishers have used Finale as their standard (on PCs or Macs), while others use Sibelius, Dorico, other commercially available programs, or even proprietary notation programs designed for their specific needs. In August 2024—at this writing—MakeMusic, the company that has supported Finale, entered into an

101

agreement with Steinberg, the business that handles Dorico. It was announced somewhat abruptly; that generated a backlash from Finale users that resulted in some backpedaling and adjustments on the part of MakeMusic. The result is that Finale will no longer be updated or otherwise supported. Finale users will be forced to either switch to Dorico or another music notation program. The questions, issues, and chaos that ensued with the announcement should have been resolved by the time you read this. Some composers who, like me, have been using Finale for a long time—it has been around since 1988, first for the Mac, then for Windows—may have decided to keep using Finale for as long as they can. For that reason, any references to music notation programs here will treat the program as "current."

Most notation programs help keep things consistent by offering default layouts and other preset preferences, but they're not always optimum for your needs. Make sure to adjust things so your music appears the way you want, and that it resembles how commercially produced sheet music looks.[1]

Should you decide to go "old school" and hand-copy your music in this era of computer music notation, it should be for a *very* good reason. For example, some computer programs handle graphic music notation better than others, but usually not as well as what you could do with pens and ink on paper. Can Dorico, Sibelius, or Finale create scores that look like Penderecki's *Threnody for the Victims of Hiroshima* or some of George Crumb's or John Cage's works? They probably can, but with a lot of work; you may ultimately decide it would be easier to create graphic notation using good old pens, ink, rules, and so on. The only advice I can offer in this situation is to create the score in the size you want it printed (9x12, 8.5x11, *etc.*) and then have it scanned into PDF files.[2] Of course you could do the score in a very different size, but keep in mind how they will be reproduced.

When writing for more than one performer, instruments and voices should be listed top to bottom generally grouped by their type, and from highest pitched to lowest. The instrumentation for full orchestra varies widely depending on the composer's needs, but it usually breaks down to these groups:

- Winds
- Brass
- Percussion
- Other (if applicable)
- Solo Voices/Chorus
- Strings

This general ordering is considered standard in the Major Orchestra Librarians' Association's "Guidelines for Music Preparation."[3] Instrumental ordering for orchestral works break things down further. Note again that specific instrumentation and the number of players depend on the piece.

Winds:	Piccolo[4]
	Flute(s)
	Oboe(s)
	Clarinet(s)
	Bassoon(s)
Brass:	Horn(s)
	Trumpet(s)
	Trombone(s)
	Tuba
Percussion:	Timpani
	Other pitched percussion (bells, xylophone, *etc.*)
	Piano
Voices:	Solo singers (in descending order of soprano, alto, tenor, and bass)
	Chorus (also in descending order of soprano, alto, tenor, and bass)
Strings:	Violin 1 (section)
	Violin 2 (section)
	Viola (section)
	Violoncello (section)
	Double Bass (section)

In one of my own works, *The Inspector General: Overture*, shown as an excerpt in Figure 7-1, the piccolo is listed first. The phrase "Transposed Score" is used in the upper left corner because there are no key signatures, but the clarinets, horns, and trumpets are shown transposed.

This overall ordering—winds, brass, percussion, other, strings, each group high pitched to low—took years to become the norm. Even so, there are still only traditions and no hard and fast rules about it. Even Beethoven's Ninth Symphony, as shown in Figure 7-2, displays a very different ordering with the strings split into two groups: Violin 1, Violin 2, and Viola, followed by the solo and choral voices, then ending with the Cellos and Basses (on one line).

Modern score ordering scales down for most smaller ensemble works too. String orchestra uses the same ordering for those instruments, and string quartets (one on a part) will be Violin 1, Violin 2, Viola, and Cello. Brass quintets will usually be ordered Trumpet 1, Trumpet 2, Horn, Trombone (or Euphonium or Baritone Horn), and Tuba (or Bass Trombone). Wind quintets order the instruments: Flute, Oboe, Clarinet, Horn, and Bassoon.[5] Vocal or choral music will order the vocal ranges as shown within their grouping,

Figure 7-1   *The Inspector General: Overture,* © **2017 Steven L. Rosenhaus**, author created

Figure 7-2 **Ludwig v. Beethoven,** *Symphony No. 9, Movement 4*, screenshot of a work in the Public Domain.

with the piano part (if any) appearing below them. In orchestra score order the horns are listed before the trumpets, despite their ranges being lower. In music for concert band or wind ensemble, however, trumpets are listed ahead of the horns. Also, in band music there will be saxophones—usually two alto saxophones, one tenor, and one baritone—as well as a euphonium or baritone horn part, sometimes more. There may also be a double bass part, which will appear at the bottom of the score page after the percussion.

Winds:	Piccolo
	Flute(s)
	Oboe(s)
	Clarinet(s)
	Bassoon(s)
Saxophones:	Alto 1 & 2 (usually on one staff)
	Tenor
	Baritone
Brass:	Trumpet(s)
	Horn(s)
	Trombone(s)
	Euphonium(s) or Baritone Horn(s)
	Tuba
Percussion:	Timpani
	Other pitched percussion (bells, xylophone, *etc.*)
	Piano and/or Harp

Figuring out score order for band works that include voices can be just as tricky as for orchestra, as there are no specific rules or traditions. Some works have the vocal lines on top. (Jazz band charts with vocals will often do this.) Some band works will put vocals between the winds and brass, and still others show voices above the piano or harp part if there is one. You can see in the Figure 7-3 excerpt from my own *Ayshet Chayil (A Woman of Valor)* for baritone voice and band, the baritone's staff appears between the winds and brass.

For an arrangement of the traditional Irish song "Danny Boy" I wrote for soprano and band, I put the vocal line toward the bottom, above the piano part. You can see this in the excerpt in Figure 7-4. This ordering was, frankly, more for my own convenience, as it made it easier to create a piano reduction score later.

Chamber music scores, which include piano, will have the keyboard part on the bottom. The other parts will be in the usual score order. Here are examples in Figures 7-5 and 7-6:

Figure 7-3 *Ayshet Chayil (A Woman of Valor)*, © 2014 Steven L. Rosenhaus, author created

Score

Written for Ms. Emily Casey and The United States Naval Academy Band.

O Danny Boy
(Londonderry Air)

Music: Traditional
Lyrics: Frederick Edward Weatherly (1913)
Arranged by Steven L. Rosenhaus

Lento ♩ = c. 52   **3**

Flute

Oboe 1 2

B♭ Clarinet 1 2

3 4

E♭ Alto Saxophone

B♭ Tenor Saxophone

Bassoon

B♭ Trumpet 1 2

3 4

Horn in F 1 2

Trombone 1 2

Euphonium

Tuba 1 2

Timpani

Bells

Percussion   Snare Drum   Bass Drum

Soprano

O, Dan-ny boy,   the pipes, the pipes are call - ing   from glen to glen   and down the moun-tain

Piano

© 2023 Steven L. Rosenhaus (ASCAP)

Figure 7-4   **"Danny Boy," © 2024 Steven L. Rosenhaus**, author created

Figure 7-5 **Ludwig v. Beethoven, *Trio, Op. 1, No. 1*,** screenshot of a work in the Public Domain.

S KYTICÍ V RUCE
Bagatela

Figure 7-6 **Joseph Suk, *Bagatela, opening*,** screenshot of a work in the Public Domain.

Note that in both examples the piano part is full-sized, but the other parts are shown smaller by about 25 percent. Traditionally pianists play from the score in works like these and not from a separate piano part. If the ensemble is larger but is still considered to be a chamber group, the piano will play from an independent part.

PDFS AND PAPER SCORES

We mentioned earlier that all of the major music notation programs offer preset layouts and preferences, but that those may need some adjustment to suit your needs. Here are some things to pay attention to in preparing your scores and parts:

   * *The page size.* In the United States, instrumental concert music is usually produced by established publishers on paper that is anywhere from 9" x 12" to 11" x 17" paper. These sizes, mostly hovering at the 9" x 12" to 10" x 13" sizes, are recommended by the Major Orchestra Librarians' Association (MOLA) for music reproduction for instrumental scores and parts. They make these recommendations based on the need for legibility. It's interesting that 9" x 12" paper, only slightly larger than standard 8.5" x 11" U.S. letter size paper, can make a big a difference in legibility. Choral music and other vocal music are mostly done on "octavo" pages sized 6.75" x 10.5". Self-publishing composers who sell physical sheet music, or distribute their works over the internet, tend to stick with the 8.5" x 11" format. This is mostly because home printers here can only handle that size or 8.5" x 14" "legal" paper. Self-published band and orchestra scores with many staves are often printed on "legal" paper, with the parts done on 8.5" x 11". Some folks go all out and buy printers that make oversized pages, printing on paper that's even larger, and then cutting it down to the desired size. Other self-publishers or small publishing houses simply get the work done to the required size by a local print shop.

   If you're satisfied with an 8.5" x 11" page layout you should have no issues printing or making PDF files of the score or parts. If you would rather use a 9" x 12" format, remember to set that size for the music notation file *and* the print parameters ("Page Setup" in most programs). On Mac computers the ability to "print" to PDF files without any additional software is built in; on PC computers, as of this writing, you need to use Adobe PDF as your "printer" and customize its settings under "Properties" or "Preferences." Once a PDF of your music is created you should be able to print it out on 8.5" x 11" automatically from a Mac, or by reducing the size of the page to 92 or 93 percent. You will have to experiment at first to get the proportions right. Why do it this way? If you're an optimist with a desire to have your music sold by an established publisher, you can provide them with files already set up with the proper page format. One major *caveat* is to make sure the music on the page, no matter what the page size, is large enough to be legible. Few things can make for a bad experience of reading music than having the music too small to read without squinting or worse.

   * *The page layout.* A layout is comprised of (1) the number of measures in a system; (2) the number of systems on a page; and (3) the number of pages.

Let's work backward. Examine any book and you will find that the number of pages will *always* be a multiple of four. If there isn't enough text to complete a set of four, you'll find blank pages at the end. (This happens less often with printed music for reasons we'll see.) Home printers can do the front and back of a sheet of paper at best, but professional printing presses do multiple pages at one go. The most efficient have always done so in multiples of four; two on the front, two on the back. When you work out the layout for your score keep that in mind, and be sure to include any front matter (instrumentation listing, program notes, etc.) in your page count. Also notice that odd-numbered pages are always on the right (referred to as "recto" pages) and even-numbered ones are on the left (called "verso" pages).

The process of determining the number of systems and the number of measures in each system is called "casting." The number of systems on a page should be as consistent as possible from one page to the next. This is easy with symphonic orchestra or concert band works, as they tend to have one system filling each page. Smaller ensembles and solo works will have more systems per page. Be sure to leave some white space between systems so performers don't get confused (and it gives them room to mark up the music). Score pages generally start on page 1 or another recto page after front matter. *Front matter* refers to non-music pages that give information, such as the title, writer and publisher credits, program notes, performance or conductor notes, and, perhaps, biographical information about the composer. Do your best to wind up with a *total* number of score pages that is divisible by four. Parts can start on either recto or verso pages, depending on where page turns wind up. If a part starts on page 1, there *must* be a page turn at the end of the last system. A good page turn consists of one or more measures of rest, depending on the music's tempo, that gives the performer enough time to turn the page and prepare to perform the next section of music.

The number of measures per system depends on the complexity of the music. The more complex the notation and the smaller the rhythmic units used, the fewer number of measures will fit in one system. Don't cram measures on one system only to have only a few on the next *unless* there are reasons of complexity or note values involved. Here are two examples from a work of mine, "Springs Eternal" for flute, two violins, and cello. Figure 7-7 shows a system consisting of only four measures. The music is replete with varying and some mildly complex rhythms and other factors requiring additional room in the system.

Figure 7-8 from later in the piece is far less complex rhythmically, and six measures fit the system easily.

One hint in setting up your music for printing the best way possible is to pay attention to both the number of systems on a page and the number of measures in each system and not just let your music notation program

Figure 7-7 **"Springs Eternal" expert, mm. 35–38. "Springs Eternal"** © 2021 Steven L. **Rosenhaus**, author created

Figure 7-8 **"Springs Eternal" expert, mm. 164–169. "Springs Eternal"** © 2021 Steven **L. Rosenhaus**, author created

to determine them automatically. Another hint is to find a balance between having too much "white space," that is the areas where there is no notation or text, and crowding. The goal is to make the music as comprehensible and easy to read as possible, but without having to constantly turn pages. If you're printing your music, you also don't want to waste money on using too much paper for a work, but you also don't want to squeeze everything in to too few pages to be cheaper.

** The type of printing paper.* Even if you're not going to self-publish your music, it makes sense to give it the best physical representation you can. PDF files present no problem beyond any issues with the layout itself, but various aspects can affect how a printed piece of music looks and feel. This is even true with the paper on which you print the music. When possible you want to have your music printed on paper that will stay upright on a music stand, that has good contrast (the "black" of the toner or printer's ink against the "white" or beige of the page), and is opaque enough to prevent "bleed through."[6]

Most laser or inkjet printers are designed to print on 8.5" x 11" (letter size) and on 8.5" x 14" (legal size) paper, often referred to as "bond" or "printer" paper. Paper is usually sold in packages of five hundred sheets, or one "ream," and is classified by size, weight, and "brightness." The brightness of a paper stock is not the same as its "whiteness." In the printing industry, brightness is measured on a scale of 0 to 100, referring to the paper's ability to reflect blue light. Whiteness is a paper's ability to reflect all colors. A paper's whiteness is subjective, it's described with adjectives instead of a numerical scale.

You can get the most common letter-size paper at many stores, even at some pharmacy chains; this paper is usually twenty pounds. in weight, and has a brightness rating of around 92. This is fine for any business documents, letters, *etc.*, but it's all too often inadequate for printing music. Twenty-pound paper tends to curl and fall off music stands quite easily, and its thinness results in a lot of bleed through. It's okay in a pinch, but nowhere near what we expect from a professionally produced piece of music.

Most publishers print their products on much heavier "text" paper, something in the seventy- to eighty-pound. range for parts (so they absolutely stay on the stand) and sixty- to seventy-pound. range for scores (which are usually laid flatter on a stand for conductors). Interestingly, and useful for us, sixty-pound *text* paper has the same density and thickness as twenty-four-pound *bond* paper. There is much less bleed through with either of these. Text paper doesn't work well on home printers though (it tends to jam the printer and there's no guarantee the toner or jet ink will stick to the page), so twenty-four-pound bond is the better option, especially if you find one with a higher brightness rating of 94 to 97. Note that the MOLA guidelines mentioned earlier call for paper that is "60 or 70 lb weight (100–120 gsm) offset paper in white or off-white should be used, and shiny or overly textured finishes should be avoided."[7]

* *Using a laser printer versus an inkjet printer.* If I were writing this book even five years ago I would have recommended using only a laser printer for your music, as inkjet prints still inclined to smudging and spotting on the page. Improvements in the technologies for home printing have improved such that those issues rarely arise, and either type of printer can give you better than adequate results. Nothing beats off-set printing or even the latest large-scale commercial laser printers, but any good home printer on good (that is, thick and bright) paper will represent you just fine. Still, each printer has its strengths and weaknesses.

Inkjet printers use small nozzles to deposit ink drops onto a page. This makes it possible to print bright color images, even high-resolution photographs. Most inkjet printers use four color cartridges: cyan (a shade of blue), magenta (not a pure red), yellow, and black. Some newer models add colors like a lighter cyan or magenta and gray. The inks are either water-based or solvent-based.

Inkjet printers boast the ability to print high-quality text, graphics, and images. If you want to print not only your music but also colorful covers for self-publishing, inkjet printers can be very useful. You should also know the downsides of inkjet printers though.

- The nozzles are focused through a print head, and the print head can be prone to damage and clogging from the various inks.
- Ink cartridges can be expensive and, with some printer models, if you run out of one color you must replace the entire cartridge unit of all four (or more) colors.
- Inkjet printers are great for small runs, but not for high volume printing; they tend to print more slowly than laser printers and print heads, as mentioned above, are disposed to damage and clogging.
- Some printers tend to bleed the ink sideways, blurring images.
- If an inkjet printer isn't used for a long time, the inks can dry out.

Laser printers are the alternative for home printing. Instead of ink these units use a combination of electrostatically charged toner—essentially a special ink powder—and a heated fuser to apply the toner to paper. The "laser" part is how the fuser works: the beam of light focuses the toner to the proper place on the paper and heats it sufficiently to fuse it on the paper's surface.

Laser printers work fast, much faster than most inkjet units, making them great for high volume print runs and more frequent or constant use. Like inkjet printers they can produce sharp prints. Laser printers usually offer a lower per-page cost than their inkjet counterparts. Lastly, laser printers usually require less maintenance than other types of printers and last longer. There are downsides to laser printers of course.

- Laser printers cost more at first compared with inkjet printers. (Inkjet printers themselves can be relatively cheap, but the ink cartridges and eventual need for repairs will make up for the up-front savings.) Color laser printers are *very* expensive.
- Toner cartridges are far more expensive than inkjet cartridges (but print more and last longer). Color toner cartridges are even more expensive.
- While the per-page cost for standard black toner printing is lower than for inkjets, the costs to print in color is higher. Printing in color using a laser printer also takes a bit longer per page than straight black.

Everything mentioned about printers assumes home equipment that prints on standard letter-size and legal-size paper. There are wide format inkjet and laser printers, but there seem to be more inkjet printers available. Some are designed to be used in home offices, others are for more ambitious commercial use. Home office units can handle up to 11" x 17" paper (the size of two 8.5" x 11" sheets combined). Prices can be very expensive for wide-format printers of any type. Finally, if you know you need to print five hundred or more copies of a work at a time, you can go fully professional and have the music printed using the offset method. Offset printing is done by creating a plate (some type of metal), inking the plate and transferring the ink from the plate to a sort of rubber blanket. The blanket is then pressed against paper to print. One form of offset printing uses the lithographic process, which relies on the repulsion of oil and water. Offset lithography is the norm for producing large volume, high-quality work. Newspapers, magazines, books, and more are all printed using offset lithography. Established music publishers traditionally use it too, although there has been a shift toward large-scale, high-volume laser printers over the past decade as well.

* *Binding.* If you're providing physical scores and parts, you will need to bind anything with multiple pages. There are different types of document binding, each with its strengths and weaknesses. Let's focus primarily on scores for this.

- *Loose sheets.* This is *only* for one- or two-page parts, the latter with the second page printed on the second side of the paper. Any part consisting of more than two pages will need to be bound in some way.
- *Comb, wire, and spiral binding.* These three methods are available at most print shops and stores like Staples. Each requires holes of some sort be punched on one side of the score, and then a plastic comb, metal wire, or plastic-coated metal wire shaped in a spiral are attached through the holes. Each method is fairly quick, although not when producing large quantities, fairly inexpensive (averaging under ten dollars per binding in 2024) and, mostly, holds up well. Of the three spiral binding seems best; it lets pages lie flat and, unless there are too many pages, everything stays intact for a long time. Pages don't fall out. Wire binding is second best for this. Try not to use comb binding, as pages tend to tear on the hard plastic combs edges and make noise when you turn from one page to the next. One trick to use when spiral binding: use a *bigger* spiral than you would normally use for any other document to ensure pages turn effortlessly and quietly.
- *Saddle stitching.* Probably the most professional-looking *and* effective way to inexpensively bind a smaller document like a score of four or more pages. The score or multipage part is printed on double-wide paper (17" x 11", for example), folded in half (8.5" and 8.5" across, respectively), and then stapled on the fold of the spine with the pointed edges on the inside. At least two staples along the spine should be used, more if you are printing 9" x

12" scores or parts. There are special staplers available with a long "reach" for binding large pieces of paper. The main advantage of saddle stitching is its small cost and relative ease of application; it's good for producing large quantities too. The disadvantages are that there is an upper limit to the number of sheets of paper that can be saddle stitched. Too many and the staples simply won't fit, but even if they do, scores or multipage parts with a lot of pages won't stay open or lie flat.

- *Perfect binding or PUR binding.* Sometimes also referred to as "paperback binding," perfect binding is fairly complex process. Folded groups of pages are clamped together, glued, and then ground down at the folds. This removes the folds themselves but keeps the pages together. The process continues, applying hot PUR glue (a synthetic adhesive) to the new spine, then applying "side glue." The binding ends with the cover being glued onto the spine. The cover is soft (like a paperback novel), but thicker and more durable than the pages inside. Professional PUR binding requires a lot of trimming as well as gluing and letting the various glues set, so it takes more time than saddle stitching. Perfect binding is good for scores with many pages of heavier paper stock, and pages can open flatter than with saddle stitching. On the downside the glues can dry out, allowing the book/score to lose pages. Still, professionally published scores intended for performance are usually either perfect bound or saddle stitched.

- *Hardcover or case binding.* Better for library editions than for performance, hardcover binding makes for a beautiful, sturdy, and long-lasting book of fewer than one thousand pages. Pages are bound in sections (groups of four, eight, twelve, or sixteen sheets, folded and glued) or as single sheets; the binding process itself is similar to perfect binding. The difference lies in the cover. As the name implies, a rigid hard cover is used, and it is attached to the interior with endpapers. An endpaper is glued to the spine of the book's interior; the ends on either side are then glued to the inside of the cover. Hard covers can be printed or imprinted (embossed) with titles and other information. The process takes more time than PUR binding and costs more. Scores that are case bound are best for study rather than performance, as pages will not lie flat without breaking the spine's binding.

- *Coptic stitch binding.* Stitch binding is an interesting method for creating books. Instead of gluing, interior sections are sewn. Those sections are then sewn together and, finally, sewn to a hard cover. The main advantage in using Coptic stitch binding is that pages lie flat. The downsides are that it's labor and time intensive, and the look is only as good as you can make it. It might be good for scores, especially oversized ones, but not at all for parts.

- *Wrappers.* When printing anything for two or more instruments that cannot play from the same score or book (like music for piano, four hands), you will need to keep everything—score and parts—together. The best way to do this is with a "wrapper," which is basically the sort of stiffer paper used for booklet covers folded, but not attached to, the contents. The wrapper is printed identifying the product's name, instrumentation, composer and/or arranger, publisher, catalog number and, sometimes, the price, grade level, and other additional information. Wrappers are printed separately from the contents due to the difference in paper weight and consistency and are made slightly wider than two adjacent sheets of paper aligned. (If two 9" x 12" sheets are adjacent to measure 18" x 12", for example, the wrapper might measure 18.5" x 12" and up, depending on how many pages of score and parts there are.) Wrappers should fit around the contents without overlapping in any direction.

* *The print size.* As said earlier, one way to turn off a prospective conductor or other performer immediately is to make your music difficult to read. If everything is too small you make the reader work harder, and that's on top of already trying to "hear" the music internally as your potential musical advocate reads the score for the first time. The *MOLA Guidelines for Music Preparation* issued by the Major Orchestra Librarians' Association strongly recommends a minimum staff size of 4 mm, measured from the bottom to the top of each staff for scores, with note heads large enough for a conductor to read easily enough at the podium. MOLA also suggests that parts use a staff size range of 7.0 mm to 8.5 mm. String parts have a "sweet spot" of 7.0 mm because the players share music stands; winds, brass, and other instruments who do not share should get parts with 7.5 mm staves.

If you're writing for a very large ensemble of twenty-five to thirty-five separate lines, and are printing at home, *don't* try to fit your score on letter-size paper. Go for a larger paper size; start at 8.5" x 14" (legal) size and go up from there if your home printer (or your local professional printer) can handle it, for more vertical room. Another way to keep things legible is to use your music notation program's sizing parameters (assuming they have that ability) to increase the whole page's content, certain staves, or even note heads. Don't just go with your music notation program's defaults when it comes to scores. Experiment.

Not every instrument needs its own staff, especially when there are multiple parts that play a lot of rhythmically similar things. You can have *two of the same instruments* on one line easily when they're playing the same rhythms; each part's stems can go in opposite directions when they're not performing the same rhythm. If two wind or brass instruments are playing in unison, just add "*a2*" above where it starts. If you look again at Figure 7-1, you'll see that Flutes 1 and 2 are sharing one staff; they start out "*a2*" but end their phrase splitting into two different notes. Unless noted otherwise, you should always assume the first instrument plays the higher note, and the second instrument plays the lower one. At the same time, Trombones

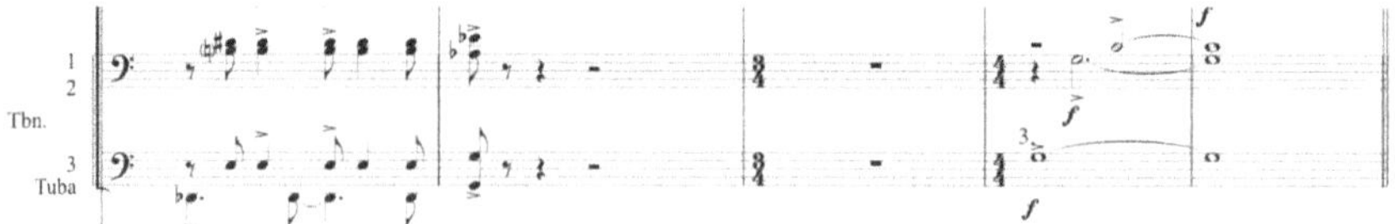

Figure 7-9 *Sussex Celebration,* excerpt. © 1998 Steven L. Rosenhaus, author created

2 and 3 also share a staff but here start out playing different pitches in the same rhythms. Starting at measure 6 they both play the same pitches with the same rhythm, so they get an "*a2*" there. If one player drops out but the other continues, indicate who is playing with their number and give the other part the appropriate rests if needed. In the Bassoons 1 and 2 part at measure 6 the line gets a "1" to show that only Bassoon 1 is playing. When the other part returns it helps the conductor (not to mention the player!) to state or restate the dynamic. Make sure any verbal or numerical indications are large enough in the score for the conductor to see, but not too large that they make it difficult to read the rest of the score.

In the short excerpt from my own *Sussex Celebration* for orchestra (Figure 7-9), Trombones 1 and 2 start out playing the same rhythm but become independent after two bars. Trombone 3 and Tuba—written on the same line to save vertical space in the score—are independent to start. The tuba then drops out but the trombone comes back in later. The score doesn't show rests for the tuba in the last two measures in the score for the sake of maintaining a clean look in the score, but the instrument's part does include them.

** Printing on covers and wrappers.* You already know the basic information that goes onto a front cover (for booklets) or wrapper (for large-scale works with many loose sheets of paper). Musicians expect to see that information in certain places, based on years of going to music stores and browsing through sheet music bins or racks. Aim to put the most important information on the front within the first three inches from the top; that would be the title, the composer, and the instrumentation ("Full Orchestra," "Band," "Flute, Clarinet, and Piano," and so on). If printing choral music, aim for the top two inches (and relatively smaller type sizes).

If you're printing covers and wrappers in color, make sure they are legible *as printed* and not just when you prepare them on a computer screen. Colors work very differently, as pixels from when they're made up of ink or toner dots. Contrasting colors work, as does "good old" black ink on a white background.

Lastly, if you're self-publishing and expect to produce large numbers of works, consider making a generic cover that you can "overprint" with the specific information. The generic cover should not have any text; all of that would be done in the over printing. That way you don't have to "reinvent the wheel" each time you put out a new work, and all of your publications will have a specific and consistent "look."

"LIVE" VERSUS COMPUTER-GENERATED RECORDINGS

There is no question that a well-produced score is always a composer's asset, but so is a recording for your potential performer to hear. Not every conductor, instrumentalist, or singer wants or needs a recording to determine whether to perform your work or not, but should they ask for one it can only help your cause. It's a time saver for them and gives them some idea of what you're after. You can, depending on a number of factors, offer a "live" recording or one that is computer-generated, that is a MIDI demo or what I call an "audio mockup." There are advantages and disadvantages to each.

A live recording is only as good as the performance itself *and* how well it's recorded. If the recording is of a work's premiere or a read-down by friends doing you a favor, a live recording could be beneficial if you're looking for a subsequent performance. Even if there are mistakes it will give the listener an idea of what to expect of the music. Nothing beats the sound of live musicians making music. Besides, most musicians won't be as critical of a live recording as you might think. They *know* what it's like to, say, come in a half-beat early or sing a wrong note, and they will likely feel sympathetic for the performers on the recording. They can also "listen past" the recording to the intent of your composition, especially if they have a well-produced printed score in front of them.

The only thing harder for a composer than getting a premiere of a work is getting a second performance. There's a mystique in presenting a premiere, but that mystique disappears once the premiere is over. But if you have a good recording of the premiere to present, it could help build interest in the work.

Making a live recording can be simple and cheap, like recording a performance on your phone with a bunch of musician friends in exchange for pizza. Or it can be done expensively, paying for musicians, a recording engineer, and for renting a recording studio or other space in which to make the recording. And there is an entire range in between of ways to make a live recording.

Live performance recordings aren't always possible to get. MIDI demos can work in lieu of them. Audio mockups have advantages too. They can provide precise, accurate "performances" that won't suffer from the almost inevitable mistakes that can happen when human beings make music. With the right equipment, programs, and sound libraries, you can make recordings that sound as almost as good as any made by musicians.

But even with "human playback" functions—essentially mini-programs within a larger music notation or sequencing program that mimic the quirks of live performance—computer-generated audio can sound *too* precise, *too* perfect. It's all subjective to be sure, but most musicians can guess correctly when a recording has been computer generated. Also, the sheer expense of good sound libraries, and the time and effort it takes to use them and your other music apps, can make creating good demos a challenging task.

Here's a tip when offering a recording whether it's "live" or a MIDI demo: never apologize for anything you think is wrong with it. Instead, make the listener aware of whatever the issues are, but just as a fact. Don't color that fact with a negative opinion. If you're giving someone a MIDI demo, say that it is one; do *not* try to pass it off as a recording made by real musicians. If it's a live read-through, say so and leave it at that. If it's a recording of a live performance and it's not a "perfect" one, just remind the listener that it is indeed a live performance. "Perfect" live performances rarely happen, and live demo recordings are perfect only after there are multiple takes and your engineer has "comped" the best bits together. Ultimately, recordings are to be used as a demonstration of the music, as well as continuing the good first impression you made. A recording, honestly presented, demonstrates your professionalism and the right amount of confidence.

NOTES

1. There are several useful books about music notation. *Behind Bars: The Definitive Guide to Music Notation* by Elaine Gould, Alfred Music, 2011, is considered by many to be *the* book on the subject. Another book that can be of assistance—if you can find a copy—is the long-out-of-print *The Art of Music Engraving & Processing* by Ted Ross, Hansen Books, 2nd Edition, 1970.

2. Hand-copying music for publication is practically a lost art. Much music was copied onto non-animal-skin vellum that had staff lines printed on the back. The vellum was translucent (you could see the staves on the "front" side), and the copyist would draw *everything* on the front side in opaque black ink using specific pens and nibs (pen points). The music would then be printed using cyanotype, a process similar to printing architectural blueprints. Printing blueprints this way is another process that has given way to computer generation of files and laser printing over the years.

3. The MOLA guidelines found at **https://mola-inc.s3.eu-west-1.amazonaws .com/files/mola3/MOLA-Guidelines-for-Music-Preparation.pdf** tell you exactly what professional orchestras—the New York Philharmonic–level ensembles of the concert world, expect to see when they receive scores and parts.

4. If there is a separate piccolo part it appears first in the score order *or* beneath the flute line(s). The reason for doing it the second way is that flute part *tessituras* tend to ride high with a generous use of leger lines, whereas many piccolo parts don't use

them quite as much. In other words, the order is based on the available vertical space on the score page.

5. The horn, *aka* French horn, is unique in its ability to blend well not only with other brass instruments but also wind instruments. It lends a certain warmth, not to mention covers a wide range, that is useful in the quintet setting. Some quintet scores reverse the order of the horn and bassoon based on the instruments' relative tessituras in the music.

6. "Bleed through" is pretty much what it sounds like: the appearance on one page of what is printed on the other side. The thicker the paper, the less likely you will see things coming through from the other side of a page.

7. "gsm" means "grams per square meter."

Chapter 8

CONTRACT (AGREEMENT) BASICS

A good negotiation is one where both parties walk away equally unhappy.

—Source unknown

What, exactly, is a contract? A *contract* is the formalization of a relationship between two parties, and of each participant's obligations to the other. In simplest terms, someone (or some entity) makes an offer and another person (or entity) accepts it within defined conditions. Contracts can get complex. Agreements you're asked to sign may not make sense to anyone but an attorney, that is someone trained in understanding how contracts work. I am not an attorney and can only speak from experience and my own research. *I cannot give you any legal advice.* As I've said elsewhere, don't take any legal action—including negotiating and signing contracts—without first consulting with an attorney. I'll remind you throughout this chapter with the phrase "consult your attorney" or "CYA."

You are a party to contracts throughout your life. Apartment rental leases are legally binding contracts. Services are secured through contracts. As musicians, and especially as composers, we frequently deal with contracts as well. Contracts generally consist of several things:

* *A contract is an agreement between parties.* A "party" is a participant in the agreement. Each can be a person, a group of people, a business, and the like. The most common sort of contracts or agreements is between just two parties, but there may be more.

* *Each party to a contract accepts certain obligations and responsibilities.* These may be financial, work-related, and more. Contracts not only lay out

who is responsible for what obligations but also any potential consequences if those obligations are not met.

** These obligations are enforceable by law.* Depending on the type of contract and where (in what state in the United States) it is made, different laws may apply, but the basics are the same: each party is required to fulfill its obligations under the agreement. The "potential consequences" mentioned above, in addition to the obligations and responsibilities, are enforceable by law.

** Each party must agree to the terms of the contract; there must be mutual assent.* "Mutual assent" is, in fact, the legal term for both parties having agreed to a contract's terms. A contract is not legally enforceable if signed "under duress," that is if one party is tricked, forced, pressured, or intimidated to sign. But if you, or your attorney, neglect to go through a contract presented to you, you cannot claim you signed it under duress later. So what constitutes duress?

- A threat of violence against you or others for whom you care.
- Economic pressure. This can take many forms.
- Bad-faith negotiations by the other party.
- Fraud or other misrepresentation.
- Intentional omission of important information connected to the contract.
- Unconscionability, that is having terms so clearly inequitable that it shouldn't be enforced.
- Terms that cannot be satisfied.
- Terms that would result in breaking the law.

Also watch out for situations in which another party uses "undue influence" to persuade you to sign an agreement. The people most susceptible to undue influence are the elderly, especially those living alone or who don't have trustworthy relatives nearby, but anyone can fall prey to someone intent on abusing you in this manner.

** A contract must include at least four of six elements to be considered legally enforceable: offer, acceptance, awareness, consideration, capacity, and legality.* Interestingly, "legality" and "capacity" are sometimes left off in discussions of contract elements, presumably because those aspects can be inferred from the rest of the document.

- The *offer* is the reason for the contract. It is a statement of what one party is willing to be obligated to do or provide within the terms of the agreement.
- *Acceptance* is when the person on the receiving end of the contract accepts the terms and conditions proposed by the offering person(s) or entity/ entities. Such acceptance must be definite, documented, and indisputable, and within the terms of the agreement. No terms may be changed

after the offer is accepted. Signing a contract is the clearest way to document acceptance.

- *Awareness* is a generally accepted expression in contract negotiations to mean that both parties are aware they are entering into an agreement, that they are doing so of their own free will, and that they are each actively participating in the process. This is to help protect both parties in case of duress, fraud, deception, or undue influence.
- *Consideration* is what each party "brings to the table," that is what they promise to do, provide, or pay in exchange for the other party's own contribution to the agreement. Any time you buy something, money is your consideration and the item you buy is the seller's.
- *Capacity* is the participant's legal capability to sign the agreement, that is to provide acceptance. It means that everyone involved needs to be aware of, and understand, the terms, obligations, and consequences before they sign a contract. The usual examples of those who may not have the capacity to sign an agreement are minor children, people who do not understand the language in which the agreement is written, or someone under the influence an illegal substance.
- The *legality* of a contract covers two aspects. The first is that a contract must comply with the laws within the jurisdictions where the contract is to be enforced. If you live in one state but you are asked to sign a contract with, say, a publisher in another state, it is very likely the contract will include language supporting its compliance and enforcement with the publisher's state. The second aspect of legality is not something we composers would normally encounter but is worth noting: contracts involving illegal activity in the form of products or services are considered unenforceable.[1]

Federal contract laws mostly deal with contractors, that is, businesses who provide goods and services to the government. The federal government, for example, has the right to cancel a contract if the need for the service or product provided is no longer needed. Every state and territory has laws regarding all other types of contracts, including those involving intellectual property such as works of art like music. This is the best reason of all to have an attorney conversant with intellectual property law. They can look over any contract you may be asked to sign or, conversely, have a contract drawn up on your behalf. You'll see examples later in this chapter to give you an idea of the sorts of things to expect, but keep in mind that every situation is different. Have an attorney working on your behalf if possible.

A good agreement incorporates the six elements discussed above, and those elements are expressed in generally accepted ways. The specific order of items may vary, but the first three presented here are fairly standard as presented.

* The date on which the contract is to be entered.

* The names (and addresses of record) of the parties involved.

* A brief description of the purpose of the agreement.

* What the first party is offering, and what its obligations are to be.

* What the second party is offering in accepting the first party's offering, and what obligations it will take on in doing so.

* Additional issues to be covered specific to the situation. (These may be included in the previous two items.)

* Any enforceable consequences of either party's failure to fulfill the terms of the agreement.

* Optional language covering any continuance of the agreement should one party or the other dies, become incapacitated or, if it is a business, should it be dissolved, sold to another entity, or close due to bankruptcy. (The language on this can vary widely.)

* Most contracts end stating that they are "the entire agreement between the parties" or something similar, and that its terms are binding unless changed and agreed to in writing by both parties, *and* that the agreement is to be governed by the state in which it is made.

COMMISSIONING CONTRACTS

Some composers define "commission" simply as a request from someone to write a piece of music in exchange for a performance, and in essence that's true. Among composers and performers who are friends this happens all the time; these informal situations are usually referred to as "handshake deals." But a more formal agreement is necessary once you add in things like commissioning fees for the composer, deadlines by which the composer has to deliver the music, any copyright and legal issues, and so on.

Commission agreements are for the sole purpose of having one party—called "Commissioner"—to commission you—the "Composer"—to write a work in exchange for certain financial and/or other obligations and responsibilities. In most cases the people or legal entities commissioning you won't have the experience of drawing up commissioning agreements. In those cases, it's up to you, or your attorney, to draft it. The odd thing about this is you will be drafting the contract as if it's *from* the commissioning party *to* you, because they're the ones legally proposing the agreement.

The first item in a typical contract is a short paragraph giving the date of the agreement, the names and addresses of the parties involved, and the reason for the contract. In the example below and elsewhere in this section anything in [brackets] is something you would need to fill in.[2]

AGREEMENT MADE THIS [Date] between [NAME OF PERSON(S) OR BUSINESS(ES)] (hereafter "Commissioner"), [full address of Commissioner], and [YOUR| NAME] (hereafter "Composer") of [your address], for the composition of a work for [FORCES such as orchestra, band, chorus, *etc.*], to be premiered by [NAME OF EXPECTED PERFORMERS].

What comes next varies in order and content from contract to contract depending as always on the specific circumstances. Things are broken down into numbered items, beginning with what the Commissioner wants and promises to do for it. Below is some of the language I've drafted, or have agreed to, for previous commissioning agreements as examples. Remember, there is much here that is negotiable.

1. COMMISSIONER hereby commissions COMPOSER to compose a work for [FORCES]. In making this commission, Commissioner agrees:
   A. To pay Composer a commissioning fee of [AMOUNT IN WORDS ($AMOUNT IN NUMERALS)] dollars for the composition of the musical work and the delivery of a fair copy of the score and one set of parts.
   B. Commissioner further agrees to pay Composer a non-refundable payment of [ONE HALF, OR OTHER AMOUNT] of the commissioning fee upon the signing of this agreement by both parties. Commissioner agrees to pay Composer the balance of the commissioning fee upon the delivery of the completed musical score.
   C. All aspects of the composition of the work are to be determined solely by Composer, including but not limited to: the title of the work, the number of movements, the musical language or style, the duration of the work, and instrumentation within the parameters set forth in this agreement.

Item 1 defines what the Commissioner wants, what the Commissioner agrees to pay for it, and what the Commissioner does and does not have control over. One negotiable point is **Item 1 B**'s half-on-signing payment. This is something I put into most of the commissioning agreements I negotiate, for three reasons. Being paid something up front is a sign of good faith on the part of the Commissioner; it's an impetus for me to work diligently to get the music written on time; and it puts some money into my pocket so I *can* write and not be concerned about financial matters as much. There's more on this up-front payment a little later in the agreement describing how it works. **Item 1 C** should be important to every composer reading this. This is an assertion of Composer's *moral* rights, the ability to have control over what is composed beyond anything Composer and Commissioner agrees to in the contract.

Item 2 outlines the responsibilities and obligations of the Composer in such an agreement and that the composer does indeed agree with the terms:

2. COMPOSER, in accepting this commission, hereby agrees:
   A. To compose a score of a duration of [number written out (number as numeral) to number written out (number as numeral)] minutes of music, but in no case shorter than [number written out (number as numeral)] minutes, or to exceed [number written out (number as numeral)] minutes of music. The music will be original in origin or may include arrangements of other music determined to be in the Public Domain. The work shall be composed for the instrumentation to be determined and mutually agreed upon by Commissioner and Composer; such instrumentation need not be finalized until the completion of the score.
   B. To provide a fair copy, hand-written, professionally copied, or computer generated, of the completed score and one set of parts for performance purposes. Composer will deliver the completed score no later than [DATE]; Composer will deliver the parts no later than [DATE]. Commissioner automatically grants an extension of either or both delivery dates in the event of any technical difficulty, personal illness, injury, infirmity, bereavement, or emergency, natural disaster, civil unrest, or Acts of God that might delay or otherwise hinder the fulfillment of the commission.
   C. Composer grants [NAME OF PERFORMER(S)] the exclusive right to premiere the commissioned work for a period of [AMOUNT OF TIME] from the delivery of the score. Right of exclusivity for the premiere performance may be extended by mutual agreement between Commissioner and Composer.
   D. Composer agrees to credit Commissioner in the program notes of the first public performance of the work and in any published edition of the work. Wording of the Commissioner's credit is to be mutually agreed upon by Commissioner and Composer.
   E. Commissioner shall be permitted to create archival audio and/or audiovisual recordings of one or more public performances of the commissioned work, provided such recordings are not distributed or offered for sale to the general public. Commissioner shall furnish Composer with one (1) complimentary copy of any such archival recording. In addition, Commissioner and Composer shall each be permitted to place such audio and/or audiovisual archival recordings on their respective websites or any other social or business

networking websites, such as Facebook, to which they belong, provided such recordings are not used for commercial purposes; any use of such archival recordings for commercial purposes are to be negotiated and mutually agreed upon separately from this agreement by Commissioner and Composer.

Item 2 A describes the Composer's obligation to compose the work, the durational range of the finished music (the timing not being precise due to the vagaries of performance as well as composition), certain aspects of the musical content, as well as any delimitations of instrumentation. **Item 2 B** specifies the composer's obligation to provide a "fair copy" of the score and parts, if any. The term "fair copy" means the delivered music needs to be legible, cleanly produced (nothing smeared or otherwise preventing reading the music), and usable. This item also sets delivery dates for the score and, separately, for any parts. In setting delivery dates refer back to the Chapter 5 discussion about schedules. Just remember to plan backward from the proposed premiere date whenever possible. Finally, section 2 B automatically grants the Composer an extension if needed due to anything preventing the completion of the work in a timely manner that is out of the Composer's control (sickness, death in the family, other emergency, or the ever-present Acts of God).

Item 2 C grants the performer(s) the exclusive right to give the premiere of the work within an agreed upon amount of time from the date of the score's delivery. This is an optional and negotiable item. Depending on the circumstances you can set any length of time for the duration of exclusivity, but I have found that one year from the score delivery date is often the most mutually beneficial. If the performers haven't given the premiere within the specified amount of time, they automatically give up their exclusive right to perform it. They can still perform it, but you're not locked into having them perform it first. You're free to get other performances.

Item 2 D is another optional element, giving the Commissioner and/or performer(s) written credit in the program notes and/or in the published version of the music if there is one. This is another successful negotiating point, especially if a commissioning party is told their name can appear above the title of the work in the score and parts if and when the music is published.

Over the past few years I have been incorporating **Item 2 E** into my commissioning agreements. This grants the Commissioner permission to create archival audio or audiovisual recordings of the premiere, and allows them and the Composer to put those recordings up on social media like YouTube, Facebook, and so on. Some people will do it anyway in flagrant violation of copyright laws, but giving them specific permission to do it makes you a hero of sorts in their eyes. That said, it *must* be clear that any recording they make cannot be done for commercial purposes. They can't make any money from the sale of such recordings unless they first negotiate and pay for the proper mechanical and other licenses separately from the commissioning agreement.

Item 3 describes items of mutual understanding between the parties. These include issues of copyright, certain permissions, and the results and remedies of possible scenarios.

3. COMMISSIONER and COMPOSER agree that:
   A. Composer shall retain all rights of ownership to the music, including that of copyright and commercial recording and release. As sole owner of the music, Composer and Composer's publisher, if any, are entitled to any performance royalties generated by the performance of the music, to be collected by the Composer's Performing Rights Organization.
   B. Composer agrees that Commissioner shall be permitted to keep a full set of score and parts to the commissioned work. Commissioner shall have the non-exclusive right to publicly perform the work after the premiere, without additional fees except for those performance royalties detailed in Section 3.A. above.
   C. In the event that the commission is cancelled by Commissioner before the completion of the work, Commissioner and Composer agree that Composer's signing fee of one half of the commissioning fee shall constitute payment in full.

Item 3 A should be in every commissioning agreement; it should *never* be a negotiating point. No commissioning party should ever take your copyright. The only exception is a situation where turning over the copyright is the norm, like when writing for visual media. When in doubt, though, hold on to your copyright as tightly as you can. **Item 3 B**, on the other hand, is one of those bits you offer because it's easy to do. The Commissioner gets to keep the set of score and any parts, and the right to give subsequent performances.

Item 3 C is a special clause regarding payment. There was a suggestion in Item 1 B to have a portion of the commissioning fee be paid on signing the contract, with the rest to be paid on delivery of the score. This is the reason why: in case the Commissioner cancels the project while you're working on the music but haven't finished it, you will at least have the portion paid up front. In book publishing, this used to be referred to as a "kill fee," when book publishers regularly gave the author an advance against royalties. Kill fees are there to compensate the writer, or in this case composer, for the work already put into the project before the undertaking was stopped.

The next two sections are what lawyers might consider "boilerplate," that is standardized text that can be used in similar documents with little or no changes:

4. This agreement shall be binding upon Commissioner, Commissioner's heirs, executors, administrators, successors or assigns. Composer's heirs, successors and assigns, including any conservator and guardian, and the executor of administrator of his estate, shall retain all of Composer's rights and remedies under this agreement.
5. This document constitutes the entire Agreement between the parties. No modification, amendment, waiver, termination, or discharge of this Agreement shall be binding unless executed in writing and signed by the party to be charged. This Agreement shall be governed by the laws of the State of [YOUR STATE] in which it is made.

Item 4 explains that the agreement remains in force, giving the Composer all of the "rights and remedies" spelled out in the agreement no matter who takes on the financial and legal activities on the Composer's behalf. **Item 5** is the statement of the contract being complete and in agreement between the parties. There can be no changes can be made and agreed to, unless those changes and the agreement to them are put into writing, and that the contract is to be in accordance with the laws of the state in which the contract was made. The very last part of the contract should be self-explanatory.

This Agreement is hereby executed as of the day and year first set forth above, as witnessed below by the parties involved.

[Your signature]   [Commissioner signature]
(Your name)/"Composer"   (Commissioner's name)/"Commissioner"

Date   Date

Most commissioning agreements are on a one-to-one basis, between one commissioner and one composer. When initiating a consortium commission, in which there are multiple commissioners, it's best to draw up separate agreements for each participant. If there is a lead commissioning party, they will pay a higher "buy in" fee to the composer in exchange for the right to give the world premiere of the work. All of the other commissioners would then each receive a similar contract granting them the exclusive right to premiere the work *in their area* (city or state), but always *after* the world premiere. When you do a consortium commission without a lead commissioner, each participant would pay the same commissioning fee and would not have any restrictions as to when they hold their performance; that would be provided it would be within the agreed upon duration from delivery of the score.

PUBLICATION AGREEMENTS

If you don't want to, or can't, self-publish your music but still want it to be available to consumers, you'll have to get it published through an established publisher. Assume you've done your research and have learned which publishers to approach and how. Then assume you've submitted your work and that a publisher has decided to take it on. The publisher then sends you a contract to sign. Publication agreements between a music publisher and a composer vary widely, ranging from one-page contracts in plain language to multiple-paged tomes filled with legal minutia and the most convoluted and impenetrable language even lawyers can have trouble comprehending. This is all the more reason to learn and understand what you'll typically find in a publishing contract, preferably with the assistance of an attorney. As I've said, I am not an attorney, let alone one versed in copyrights and contracts, and cannot give you legal advice. I've signed many a publication deal and can point out some of the more noticeable features that appear in many such agreements, but always, *always*, consult your attorney—CYA.

Publication agreements for concert music composers are similar to, but are not exactly like, those for pop songwriters. The two types of publishers differ in approach. Pop music publishers are more interested in getting the works in their catalogs used in film scores, "cover" recordings (that is, recordings of the same song made by different artists), and more. More importantly, they *actively* pursue those income-maximizing possibilities. This active pursuit rarely happens in the classical music world. Yes, classical music publishers will negotiate and issue mechanical, synchronization, and other licenses on the composer's behalf, but they don't often search out such transactions beyond basic advertising or catalog distribution. Put another way, pop publishers tend to be more *proactive*, while concert music publishers tend to be *reactive*. Also, publishers signing a songwriter will often require a certain number of songs be written within the durational terms of a contract, while classical music publishers usually don't impose such minimums. In fact, classical music publishers tend to focus more on making the music available to consumers. Educational music publishers do as well, so any discussion here applies to both.

* *The work.* Most concert music publishers will offer a contract for one work at a time. You can submit several works at the same time, but you never know if they'll publish all, some, or none. This goes back to the discussion in Chapter 6, "Publishing Your Music," about what publishers look for in

selecting repertoire: "You're not the only composer submitting works, and publishers have to determine if a work (1) is good, (2) will sell, (3) doesn't oversaturate their catalog with similar works, and (4) will sell." Besides these factors, classical music publishers are more interested in a work's performance record at the time of submission. This is unlike a pop publisher, whose focus is on songs they think or hope will become hits. Both types of publishers are interested in the composer's or songwriter's track record too.

* *PROs*. Many agreements include language acknowledging any composer's existing agreement with a Performing Rights Organization and its terms. The publishers themselves have to be members of the same PRO as the composer; this is why many publishers will have often have at least two companies under their business umbrella, one for each PRO. When performances generate royalties the PRO will split them evenly between the publisher and the composer.

* *Ownership*. Composers have to verify the music being contracted is solely theirs, original, that they have all rights to it, are legally allowed to make the contract, *and* that no one else has a legal claim on it. In other words, the publisher wants to make sure that you yourself wrote the music, that you own it (usually proved by the copyright notice and, better still, the copyright registration). By asserting that it's your composition and that no one else can claim it, you're absolving the publisher of any attempt to plagiarize or infringe on another work's copyright.

A publishing contract is where you allow the publisher to take over the copyright, that is to become the copyright claimant of record. They will now own the music legally. But you retain moral rights, and those are defined in other parts of the contract and the laws of the state in which the contract is executed. It can be emotionally nerve-racking to sign away the copyright on your creation the first time (or second, or third), but unless you self-publish you have to accept that this is the way the industry presently works.

* *Contract duration*. Publishing contracts are frequently immutable when it comes to their duration, which is almost always "forever." I have yet to come across a publisher who would take on a work for anything less, especially among the largest publishing houses. A very few agreements, however, allow for the possibility a work may fall through the cracks of the production process and just not get published in a timely manner, allowing for the rights to the work to revert back to the composer with no penalty to either party provided the composer actually asks for that reversion. Some might even allow the reversion of rights to occur if the work has not sold or otherwise generated significant income within a given time period, or if the publisher has allowed it to go "permanently out of print."[3]

* *Financial terms*. Income you receive based on sales will come to you *after* those sales are made *and* after the publisher has collected the monies

and adjusted the amounts for any returns of the product (your music). As mentioned earlier, the book publishing industry used to be known for giving advances against royalties, essentially betting the sales of a book will pay for that advance.[4] The music publishing industry, on the other hand, has seldom offered them.[5] An advance against royalties is money paid to you ahead of time—money that would otherwise be royalties paid to you after sales. This money must be recouped, earned back through the actual sales. Until then you do not receive any royalties. Say you get an advance against royalties of one hundred dollars ($100). The publisher would then have to sell enough music to generate that one hundred dollars in royalties to pay itself back. Starting with the cent over that $100 you would be back to earning money.

The Chapter 6 discussion on print royalties gives 10 percent of the retail selling price as the industry norm for sheet music. Some publishers might offer less, but not below 5 percent of retail. Some might offer a higher royalty rate, but *very* rarely, and even then it's usually not more than 12.5 percent of retail. Licensing generally pays higher royalties, most often 50 percent, be it for mechanical licenses, synch licenses, and such. Somewhat surprisingly any income earned internationally in any form also warrants a fifty-fifty split between the composer and the publisher. Some publishers may pay less though, so read (or have your attorney read) your contract carefully to make sure.

Legal terms. In addition to the legal information that appears in most contracts (the boilerplate) and the other items, there are some specific issues that come up in many publishing contracts. Some agreements will have language dealing with potential infringement by a third party of the composer's work. Here is an example:

> Any legal action brought by Publisher against any alleged infringer of any Work hereunder shall be initiated and prosecuted at its sole expense, and of any recovery made by it as a result thereof, after deduction of the expenses of the litigation, including reasonable counsel fees, the percentage set forth in [citation of a previous paragraph] shall be paid to Composer.

It means that if the publisher of your music learns of a likely infringement of one of your works with them, the publisher will take the alleged infringer to court on its own, and on your, behalf. Any restitution, that is money, resulting from the litigation would be paid to you after the publisher deducts the costs associated with the court case.[6]

Unfortunately, infringement cases can happen in either direction, and someone could bring one against you and the publisher. There's a clause for that too. Here's a sample:

Upon commencement of any legal proceeding or assertion of any apparently bona fide[7] claim against Publisher alleging any facts constituting a breach of any of Composer's warranties and representations hereunder, Publisher shall serve notice thereof upon Composer, and until such claim or proceeding has been finally adjudicated or settled by Publisher, any and all payments becoming due to Composer under any agreement between Composer and Publisher may be withheld by Publisher. Publisher shall have the right to settle or otherwise dispose of such claims or proceedings as in its sole discretion it may determine, in good faith with respect to Composer. Composer shall fully indemnify Publisher from any and all losses, damages, penalties and costs, including reasonable counsel fees incurred by Publisher in connection with defense of any such claim or proceeding.

Let's break down the "legalese." First: if the publisher is told of, or sued for, your work allegedly infringing on someone else's, the publisher is required to notify you of it *and* to withhold any payments due you earned by your work until the matter is resolved. If the case is then resolved in your favor, and infringement isn't proven, there is no problem. Traditionally in such civil cases, the loser of the suit could be required to pay the winner's court costs, and perhaps more. If you and the publisher *lose* the case, though, the last sentence of the clause kicks in. "Composer shall fully indemnify Publisher" is an elaborate way of saying *you* will pay the costs of the case. How you pay will vary; it could be a garnishment of current and/or future royalties or you could get a large bill to pay outright.

There's a clause I try to get into every publishing agreement I sign if it's not already there. It establishes the agreed-upon right of the composer to audit the publisher's financial records with respect to income generated by the work being published. Here's what I usually propose to the commissioning parties; for the record, I use "his" as my pronoun in my agreements.

Composer shall have the right, by representatives of [his/her/their] choice, to audit Publisher's books and records with respect to sales of the Work. Such audits shall be conducted during regular business hours upon reasonable notice in writing to Publisher, but in no event more than once during any twelve-month period. Such audit shall be conducted at Publisher's offices, at Composer's expense.

This clause could come in handy if you discover irregularities in your royalty statements, or if you have information leading you to believe there might be some financial malfeasance going on. The onus is on you the composer to have the books audited, though. You have had to get the audit done, with the least imposition on the publisher and at your own cost. Don't do it yourself, of course; have someone with an expertise in forensic accounting, like a CPA, do it. For the record, to date I have never had to make use of this clause, but I feel more comfortable having it in place. If it's not in a contract offered to you try to negotiate to have it put in.

This brings up a point about royalties. Income from sales and other sources can take a long time to make their way to the publisher. Once they're entered into the publisher's records, those records have to be updated and reconciled. Rather than go through the obvious hassles of paying royalties as soon as they're available, publishers send out statements and any associated monies on a regular but infrequent basis. Some send them once a year, others twice a year, and others still send statements and royalty checks four times a year. The average among publishers seems to be twice a year. As to when, exactly, you can expect to receive those statements and monies will depend on the publisher and their immediate circumstances. Many will do it on the schedule explained in the sample below that pays once a year for printed products and twice a year for all other income:

> Within ninety (90) days after the end of each calendar annual period with respect to printed product royalties, and semi-annual period with respect to all other royalties, Publisher will render statements together with payment or royalties then due, if any. Publisher may deduct from such royalties any or all of any outstanding indebtedness then owing by Composer to Publisher under this or any other agreement. Composer shall be deemed to have consented to all such statements and accounts and some shall be binding upon Composer and not subject to objection for any reason unless specific objection in writing stating the basis thereof is made to Publisher within one (1) year after such statements and accounts are rendered.

In this example, you would receive a print royalty statement once a year, within three months after the end of the previous calendar year. The year ends December 31, so you would expect to receive the statement (and any money noted in the statement) between January 1 and March 30 of the following year. No matter when most publishers say you'll receive statements you should note that they're ordinarily dealing with hundreds of composers or their estates, and that receiving them in the first sixty of the ninety-day period is unlikely. The same goes, in this example, for the twice-a-year statements for other income.[8]

OTHER KINDS OF CONTRACTS

The discussion of mechanical licenses in Chapter 2 on "Income Streams: Definitions and Explanations" describes what those licenses are, and how they're commonly used. If your music is published by a traditional publisher you don't have to be concerned about how mechanical licenses are negotiated, issued, and implemented, but if you are self-publishing, you should learn whatever you can.

There are two types of mechanical licenses. If a work has never been commercially recorded before, the person or entity wanting to make the first recording will need a "Mechanical License and Authorization for First-Time Recording." (Some call the last part "for First-Time Recording of Song.") Such licenses are contracts that must be signed by both the performers or their legal representative(s) or their record label and the music's copyright owner (you). Permission to record something first is *not* automatic, and you as the copyright owner must agree to it.

> [COPYRIGHT OWNER], the copyright owner of [NAME OF WORK], written by [COMPOSER'S NAME], authorizes [LICENSEE] to record and distribute [FORMAT OF RECORDING].

In this opening sentence, we learn who is involved, what music is involved, and what the licensee wants to do with the music.

* *Copyright owner.* That's you.
* *Name of work.* That's your composition.
* *Composer's name.* That's you again.
* *Name of person(s) asking for the license, or licensee.* That usually means the performers.

The licensing agreement will then go on to require the recording's catalog number(s), the name of the recording label(s), the names of the principal recording artist, and the anticipated date of the recording's initial release to the public. In Chapter 2's hypothetical scenario of the Second Tier String Quartet commissioning you to write your Third String Quartet, we conjectured that they would want to record the work. As they would be making the premiere recording this would be the license they would need. What comes next in the agreement are the specific terms.

> [LICENSEE] agrees to pay the mechanical royalty rate of [RATE] and issue statements and pay royalties on a quarterly basis. The work's owner[s] acknowledge that they are the sole owners and that they have the right to authorize this first recording. The work's owner[s] do not require a notice of intention to obtain a compulsory license be served or filed. We acknowledge receipt of this agreement and agree to its terms.

Mechanical royalty rates are determined by a number of considerations, including the country where the recording and reproduction takes place, whether there are statutory rates that are treated as a baseline for negotiations, the specific format of the mechanical reproduction (digital download, CD, streaming service, etc.), which may have its own rate. The size of your business may be a factor too. Established publishers tend to have more clout and can command higher royalty rates for the works they control; conversely, you as a self-publisher may not do as well. That said, you will usually not be able to get more than the standard compulsory rate. The Copyright Office of the Library of Congress has a group of Copyright Royalty Judges whose sole job is to determine and set those compulsory rates and the terms for the mechanical royalties for "Physical phonorecords; Permanent downloads; Ringtones; Limited downloads; and Interactive streaming."[9] The most current rates as of this writing were set as of December 31, 2023; they're shown in Figure 8-1. You can expect them to be updated by the time you read this.

The next portion of the license will have the performers' or record company's name(s), address, the signature of the appropriate representative, and the date on which the agreement is signed. You as the copyright owner then fill in similar information.

Once your work has been recorded the first time, anyone else wanting to record it *must* file a "Notice of Intention to Obtain Compulsory License." There is one exception, however: In 2018 the Music Modernization Act created a compulsory mechanical license for *streaming* copyrighted music, *even if it is the first recording of that music to be released.* The Notice should be filed through the Harry Fox Agency (HFA) or the Mechanical Licensing Collective (MLC) depending on the licensee's specific needs. As discussed in Chapter 2, HFA handles all mechanicals for physical products while MLC does similar work for the digital reproduction of music. See Figure 8-1 for rates set as of this writing.

It's important to know that potential licensees need to file their Notices *before distributing* their recordings of your music, and no later than thirty (30) days after the phonorecords (physical products) are manufactured and prepared for sale, or files (for downloading or streaming) are ready for distribution. For more information about the legal aspects of mechanical licenses, check out the Copyright Office's Circular 73, "Compulsory License for Making and Distributing Phonorecords."[10]

(Compulsory) mechanical license agreements are similar to those for first-time recordings, with some expected differences.[11] Expect to see these items:

* *"Agreement made and entered into* [DATE NUMBER] *day of* [MONTH], [YEAR] between [YOU] ("Licensor") and [RECORDING ARTIST or LABEL] ("Licensor"). This is pretty much the norm for contracts, that is

Mechanical License Royalty Rates

Copyright Royalty Judges issued rates and terms for the use of musical works in Physical phonorecords; Permanent downloads; Ringtones; Limited downloads; and Interactive streaming.

CATEGORY	RATE	EFFECTIVE DATE
Physical phonorecords	12.4 cents or 2.38 cents per minute of playing time or fraction thereof, whichever is larger, for physical phonorecord deliveries and permanent digital	December 12, 2023
Permanent downloads	12.4 cents or 2.38 cents per minute of playing time or fraction thereof, whichever is larger, for physical phonorecord deliveries and permanent digital	December 12, 2023
Ringtones	24 cents per ringtone	*
Limited downloads	The formulas for determining rates may be found in *37 C.F.R. §385.10 through §385.17*	*
Interactive streaming	The formulas for determining rates may be found in *37 C.F.R. §385.10 through §385.17*	*

* Effective date not determined by Copyright Royalty Judges (CRJs) . Final rule issued by CRJs, see *74 FR 4510*, indicates that effective date is governed by 17 U.S.C. 803(d)(2)(B).

LATE FEE

The Copyright Royalty Judges established that a licensee shall pay a late fee of 1.5 percent per month, or the highest lawful rate, whichever is lower. See *37 C.F.R. § 385.4*

Figure 8-1   U.S. Mechanical Royalty Rates as of 12/31/2023, partial screenshot of https://copyright.gov/licensing/m200a.pdf

stating when the agreement is being put into effect, and who are the participating parties.

** Ownership and compositions.* This is where you verify you own the composition (which is listed in this portion) and have the right to grant the license.

** License.* This is the granting of the mechanical license to make the phonorecords, etc. It is usually non-exclusive and allows for world-wide distribution. The rates are stated in this section, most often as a variation of "the statutory rate in effect at the time the recording is released, and any royalty stated in terms of a percentage of the statutory rate shall apply to the statutory rate at such time." The phrase "any royalty stated in terms of a percentage" of the statutory rate is referring to how the royalty income will be split. If your work is unpublished or self-published, you would get 100 percent. If the work is published as a work for hire the publisher would get 100 percent. If you have a publishing agreement with a traditional publisher the mechanical royalties would be split evenly between you and the publisher, 50 percent for you and 50 percent for the publisher.

For any number of reasons the licensee may want to pay a smaller royalty rate than the compulsory amounts. The requested reductions may not be drastic and in fact might not be much more than a reduction to 75 percent of the amount set by the Compulsory Royalty Judges. Whether you accept any such reductions or not is up to you, but be sure of what you're being asked to give up and what should you expect in return instead.

** Accounting.* This section defines how frequently the licensee will provide royalty statements and any associated monies, how and when the licensor can audit the licensee's book if there are any significant discrepancies or potential malfeasance, and how and when the licensor can terminate the agreement if the licensee hasn't provided those statements and monies with the amount of time stated in the contract.

• Credit. This section is to obligate the licensee to give you credit as the composer of the work on any label copy or other permanent packaging used for the recording. Similarly, credit must be provided for any digital recordings, assuming they are formatted to handle and display the information. The next few sections are, essentially, boilerplate. This is followed by signatures and countersignatures to complete the agreement.

• Warranty and Indemnity. This section holds the licensee harmless in case of any legal against the composer or publisher.

** Assignment.* This is the "we agree to this contract" portion of the agreement.

** Term.* This is the duration of the contract. With mechanical licenses it's not unusual to have them in effect "for the life of the copyright on the composition" (of the original music).

* *Effective Law.* This is another way of saying where, that is in which state, the agreement is being made.

* *Licensing Information.* This is the basic information about the licensee, including:

- Artist
- Song Timing
- Album Titles
- Release Date
- Label Name (if any)

Synchronization licenses were also discussed in Chapter 2 and, as with mechanical licenses, the following information is of more use if you're self-publishing. Synchronization licenses are needed by anyone wanting to use your music in some audiovisual medium, whether it's for movies ("motion pictures"), television (broadcast, cable, streaming), videograms (physical products like DVDs), trailers, or other audiovisual advertising for the previously listed media using the music. The term "synchronization" is used in the literal sense, in that the music is synchronized to the action on screen in some way. The format for a contract synchronization (or simply "synch") license is much the same as for the other licenses and agreements we've seen so far; only the details are different. Here are some items and terminology you'll see:

* *The basics.* As with the other contracts, synch license agreements start off with who is involved, what work is being requested and, very generally, in what way the music is to be used. The licensee in this case is the producer of the audiovisual project.

* *Grant of audiovisual license.* This is where you or your publisher grants a non-exclusive right to record your work in synchronization with any audiovisual medium (most agreements include something like "now known or created later"), and to give public performances of the work as long it is in synchronization with the audiovisual. In other words, they can't just play the music; it has to be in the context of their film, television episode, etc. This portion of the agreement also gives the producer public performance rights including via television, providing the broadcasters have performance licenses with your PRO. If a televised performance is not licensed by a PRO it must be cleared directly through you or your publisher. This license is strictly for works to be exhibited within "the Territory," that is the geographic or political area defined elsewhere in the agreement. See the section on "Territory" below.

Lots of movies and television shows license not only pop songs as you would expect, but classical works as well. The 1973 movie *The Exorcist* used a wealth of concert music for much of the soundtrack, including excerpts from five works by Krzysztof Penderecki (*Kanon for Orchestra and Tape*, the Cello Concerto, the 1960 String Quartet, *Polymorphia*, and *The Devils of Loudon*); the *Fantasia for Strings* by Hans Werner Henze; and George Crumb's *Threnody I: Night of the Electric Insects*. For the movie *The Elephant Man* (1977), John Morris wrote most of the score, but for the final scene the producers decided that nothing worked better than what they had been using as a temporary ("temp") track, Samuel Barber's *Adagio for Strings*. The *Adagio* was also used in the movie *Platoon*. Classical music even makes its way into comic book–based movies like those in the Marvel universe. Arvo Pärt's *Berliner Messe* was used in the 2015 film *Avengers: Age of Ultron*.

** Grant of videogram license.* This is similar to the audiovisual license, but it's geared to physical products including but not limited to DVDs. When this is part of the agreement it is usually for distribution of the videograms intended for home use in the territory covered.

** Trailers.* Here you or your publisher grants the producer the right use your work in connection with the exploitation of the project. Trailers are the advertisements made to "sell" the upcoming release of a new movie or television show.

** Reservations of rights.* Here you're reserving and maintaining all rights not granted in the agreement.

** Modifications to composition.* Changing one's music is a major sore spot for almost all composers, so this clause is important. As one sample agreement puts it, "Producer shall not make any change in the fundamental character of the music or use the title or any portion of the lyrics, if any, as the title or subtitle of the film without written prior authorization from Publisher." Movie producers normally use the music they license "as is" for the most part, although they may commission a new arrangement for title credits and so on. As for using music titles for movie and television show titles, well, it happens a lot more often than you might think. For example:

- *American Pie* (movie title based on a song by Don McLean)
- *Boogie Nights* (movie taking its title from the 1977 disco-funk song by Heatwave)
- *Life on Mars* (the title of a song by David Bowie used for *two* versions of the same show, one British, one American)
- *My Girl* (movie using a song by The Temptations as its title)
- *Stand by Me* (movie using Ben E. King's song as its title)
- *What I Like About You* (television series using the title of a song by The Romantics)

Interestingly, there aren't many—if any—classical works whose titles have been used as the name for a film or television show. Forbidding the use of a song's title without permission as a clause in a mechanical license agreement makes moral sense, but as you read in Chapter 1 on "Copyright," titles can't be copyrighted. Whether such a clause is enforceable is a topic of discussion for contract and copyright lawyers to hash out.

* *Territory.* This is essentially where the license occurs.

* *Audiovisual license payments.* Synch licenses can be paid as a onetime fee, as royalties with an advance, or as straight royalties, all depending on the project and, likely, the size of the project's budget. (Indie films may make a onetime payment because the likelihood of earning royalties down the road is lower than for major blockbuster movies, for example.) Such onetime fees are paid once the movie or television show is exhibited (shown), or within a specified amount of time (usually less than a year) from the signing of the agreement.

Royalties are based on the negotiated percentage of net profits from public performances of the movie or show. Any advance given on those royalties are always considered nonrefundable but recoupable (they can be earned back before royalty payments resume).

* *Videogram license payments.* These work the same way as payments for the audiovisual license portion above, with one exception. With videograms there is also a *pro rata* option. The term *pro rata* describes a calculated proportion of something, usually in equal portions. In this case the producer agrees to pay you or your publisher a percentage of a specified percentage of the net revenue for all videogram income, including all sales, licenses, and any other income sources.

This "percentage of a percentage" works as follows: unless your music is the *only* music used and licensed in the film or show, you will have to share the net income royalty with other copyright holders. A hypothetical scenario would have ten works used in a movie that goes straight to Blu-ray DVD, and you've written and self-published one of those works. If the sales are such that one hundred dollars in royalties is generated, then that would be divided evenly among the licensors, including you. Each would receive a *pro rata* share, in this case ten dollars, in royalties.

* *Payments and statements* is the section dealing with royalty earnings. In these contracts it is customary for the royalty period to be quarterly (every three months), with the statements and associated monies to be sent to you or your publisher within at least a month after the end of a given quarter. The producer is allowed to withhold amounts to account for anticipated returns, refunds, etc., of physical products (videograms), but they must pay out the withheld money no later than a specified time—usually a year—after it is reported on a quarterly statement.

* *Favorable rates.* This applies to videograms, where income can be generated pretty much indefinitely from the sale of physical products. If the law changes and mechanical royalty rates are increased, producers are required to either pay the increased royalty rate or delete the composition from the movie or show.

* *Audit.* This is similar to the suggested audit clause mentioned in the earlier discussion on commissioning contracts. It's the limited ability to examine the payor's books with regard to the payee's royalties, *etc.*

* *Warranty.* You or your publisher confirms the ability to enter into the agreement.

* *Credit.* Here you or your publisher define how you want to be credited and under what circumstances. If there is other music being used, you can ask for credit similar to the others; as a single "card" in the main titles in all forms of the film, show, or videogram; and in all paid advertising similar to all the other compositions used.[12]

* *Samples.* You or your publisher should, contractually, receive an agreed-upon number of copies of the movie or show, in *each* format in which it is released.

* *Term.* This is usually for the length of the copyright on the music.

* *Termination and breach.* This spells out under what conditions the music's copyright holder may terminate the agreement. The conditions that come up most frequently are a producer's failure to make timely royalty payments or to provide credit as originally agreed.

The agreement wraps up with the expected clauses: "This agreement can only be changed or amended in writing and signed by both parties" is one; "this agreement shall follow the laws and regulations of the State of [YOUR STATE]" is another. The contract is then signed by both parties.

No matter what kind of contract you deal with, knowing more about how they work can only help you negotiate properly. Even so, don't do it alone unless you're an attorney versed in copyright law or contracts as well as a musician, and even then, consider getting an attorney. CYA. Even if you use the lawyer for only the first few contracts, you'll be better informed and better protected.

LAWYERS

A lawyer's services can be expensive, but *not* having an attorney to look after your interests can be even more expensive. Music is considered intellectual property. As a composer you create it, but when you do it becomes *your intellectual property*, something you can own, allow others to access in some way, or to sell outright. Lawyers specializing in intellectual property, especially music, deal with copyright (and patents, and trademarks) and contracts. Finding attorneys who are good at what they do, have the experience and knowledge to deal with your specific circumstances, and, something intangible, is a "good fit," can be time- and effort-consuming, but there are ways to do it to make it a bit easier.

Start with recommendations from your colleagues in the music business or from friends and relatives. You're looking for someone with a focus on the music business, copyright, contracts, or intellectual property law in general. But *don't* hire an attorney suggested by someone with whom you're already doing business. There could be a conflict of interest; the same lawyer could wind up representing both sides of a negotiation and might be biased in favor of the first party to hire them.

You can also find an appropriate attorney through your local or state bar association. Bar associations, made up of attorneys themselves, are self-regulating and policing in order to maintain high standards. Most operate referral services, and can give you a selection of attorneys appropriate to your needs. Another source for finding lawyers is through music business directories if you have access to them.

If money is tight, consider finding an attorney who would work for free or *pro bono publico,* which is usually shortened to just *pro bono.*[13] In New York City, for example, there is an organization called the Volunteer Lawyers for the Arts. If a pro bono attorney can't help you, they should be able to help you find someone who can.

The next step is to "vet" your potential lawyer, that is investigate and evaluate the person you're considering handling your legal affairs. Look at their website. How big is the firm? What services do they provide? Can they provide more individual attention? Is the website itself done professionally or haphazardly? What experience do they have in the music business? How much of their practice is devoted to the music business? Have they gotten reviews on sites like the lawyer review site Avvo?[14] Have they been disciplined or punished by their state bar? Don't hire an attorney with a record of discipline if you can help it.

Try to narrow down your list of possible attorneys to just three or four, and then arrange for a consultation with each. Find out ahead of time what the consultation costs. Don't schedule a meeting with an attorney who will charge more than you can afford. Find out how long the consultation will be. Consultations can be as short as fifteen minutes or go longer, depending on the questions you need to ask and the answers you get. Ask ahead of time what the attorney wants you to bring to the consultation, like a contract you need to have looked at.

Go into the consultation with a list of questions, including how long they've been practicing music law or intellectual property law, and what aspects of music law do they *not* handle. How do they communicate with clients (e-mail, text, telephone, *etc.*)? Who will do the actual work, the lawyer you're hiring, or others on staff like associate lawyers, paralegals, *etc.*? Then you can ask what they charge and how that rate is calculated. If you don't need an attorney on a regular basis, which is kept on retainers, ask what typical charges would be for the specific jobs you expect to have for them.[15] Show up on time, take notes, thank each candidate for their time, and then decide which attorney you want representing your interests.

NEGOTIATING ISSUES AND COMPOSER-SPECIFIC ISSUES

* *What should never be negotiable?* Contracts may include some things that seem reasonable at first glance but would not be in your best interests. These are the most common and the most potentially damaging items that should be excluded or at least modified to be in your favor.

* *Your moral rights.* Moral rights are your ability to control the eventual fate of your works, which make them the most important part of any contract you'll sign as a composer. You are entitled to receive credit for the work you create, and for that work to represent you in the form in which you created it. Put another way, moral rights are your right to attribution and the right of integrity. Your basic moral rights also allow you to ensure no modifications are made without your consent, to withhold publication or distribution of your work before you are satisfied with it in its entirety and to control that publication or distribution, and to allow you to retract or withdraw a work from sale or distribution. These rights prevent the distortion, modification, or revision of your work *no matter who owns it* (that is, who is the copyright holder), not to mention to help deter infringement and plagiarism. U.S. laws protect moral rights through several copyright, trademark, privacy, and defamation statutes. Also note that *moral* rights are not *financial* rights.

It should be said that moral rights are hardly ever asserted in the United States, either in agreements or in courts of law. Most contracts never actually use the term "moral rights," in fact. Most contracts that deal with copyright licenses will include a *waiver* of moral rights instead of transferring or licensing them. A waiver is a voluntary surrender of a particular right or privilege.

Any time you are asked to sign an agreement with a publisher or other business, or if you're self-publishing and have to negotiate contracts and licenses, be aware of any items dealing with moral rights. Any decently written agreement will cover most of what you need to your benefit, but not always and not always in satisfactorily ways.

- *Your right to limit, in particular ways, how your music is used.* Most likely this won't come up for concert music composers, but it happens a lot to songwriters. Music is used for advertising or political use with which the composer disagrees or feels would tarnish the composer's reputation or dilute the effectiveness of the music in some way.

For example, a politician with whom a songwriter disagrees vehemently decides to use one of the songwriter's songs at a rally. The songwriter has a clause in the song's contract that it cannot be used for any political use, either at all or without specific permission. If the politician asks for permission to use it—and, unfortunately, many politicians or their teams don't bother—the songwriter or the publisher of the music could say "no." Other examples would be the use of your music in advertising or other promotional works for products or services with which you disagree on moral or other grounds. There are some composers and songwriters who completely prohibit the use of their music for *any* promotional work, be it for products, services, or political causes.

Do you absolutely need to have this sort of item in a publishing contract? That will depend on what the music is, how you think it could be used, and how strongly you feel about that potential use.[16]

* *What can be negotiable?* We've covered a number of negotiable items in this chapter, and they vary with the type of contract involved. Let's sum them up.

- *Money.* Clearly this is the *most* negotiable item in any agreement with certain exceptions. Publishing contracts, for example, tend to stick to the publisher's own norm for royalties (like "10% of the retail selling price"). Commissioning contracts, mechanical licenses (within limits), and other licenses, are negotiable. Knowing the budget of the commissioner or licensee should make it easier to negotiate. If you know what they can afford, and know what you really need and want in compensation to do the work or supply the license, you can come to an agreement. Try not to "lowball" your asking price for your music—asking for less than what others charge or what you feel your work is actually worth—unless you know the party you're dealing with has an extremely low budget *and* you really want to work with them. In some cases, the budget for what is being requested is low, but there's additional money available for something else you can provide. For example a commissioning fee budget may be "X" but you really should be charging "Z." If the work is to be conducted and you are also a conductor as well as a composer, you could offer to conduct the premiere for the difference, "Y." Or you can offer to do a "greet the composer" session before or after the concert if you're local for a small honorarium.

- *Payment.* There are no legally defined payment schedules or methods of payment for commissioning agreements, or for most licensing agreements, within certain limits. *How* you are paid is up to you and the other party; some people are fine with PayPal or other mobile payment services, while others prefer checks. It's negotiable.
- *Commissioning credit.* Clearly this only applies to commissions. One of the biggest selling points of commissions is the commissioner's bragging rights—"I/We commissioned this work"—and nothing strokes the ego of a commissioning party, be it person, business, school, or even religious institution, like knowing the music will give them credit for commissioning the work right there on the score and parts right there above the title, or at least in the official program notes. (It's bragging rights for the composer too, but let's keep that among ourselves, shall we?)
- *Permission to record.* This, too, is a negotiable item for commissioning agreements. Granting commissioning parties the right to make *archival* audio or audiovisual recordings of the premiere performance and to post them on social media like YouTube or Facebook is a clear "win-win." For one thing, you're tacitly acknowledging that they would probably make a recording anyway but that you're making it acceptable and legal for them to do it, as long as it's *not* for commercial use—as long as they're not going to sell or offer streaming or downloads of the work for money. The other "win" is that you will automatically have a demo recording of the work that you can use to shop the music elsewhere.
- *Duration of exclusivity of the premiere.* This is another commissioning contract item. The exclusive right to premiere the commissioned work is considered an inherent right for the commissioning party, but offering it within a defined period of time always seems better. Perhaps it's because the length of time allows for the vagaries of life; something may delay a premiere by months or even longer. Some terms, including the duration of exclusivity, can be amended and agreed to in writing by both parties.
- *Subsequent performances.* This commissioning agreement item is completely optional and negotiable. Any such contract can include language giving the commissioner express permission to give subsequent performance once the premiere has been given and provided the composer's PRO is notified of each performance.

There's not much "wiggle room" when it comes to publishing contracts. These are the most likely items that can be negotiated in a publishing contract:

- *Money.* In this case the publication royalties are fairly standard, 10 percent of the retail selling price. You could, if you has major name recognition, negotiate a slightly higher royalty, as much as 12.5 percent, but otherwise 10 percent should be fine. Caution though: If offered 10 percent of *wholesale*, please remember that works out to 5 percent of the retail selling price, and you should push for 10 percent or higher of retail.
- *The right to audit the books.* This is explained in detail earlier in this chapter. Most publishers will not balk at including this clause into their contract with you, especially if they are one of the larger publishing firms that keeps records well.
- *Right of approval.* This is extremely rare but not unheard of. In these unusual cases a composer will have the right to approve any arrangement, edition, advertising, cover design, and more before anything goes into print. The only exception that happens frequently is the writer receiving "first proofs" of the music when they come from the engraver. You proofread the music, mark up the music or make a list of corrections, and return it to the editor to have it fixed by the engraver.

ABOUT GETTING PAID

Commissioning fees should be paid in full by the time the completed score is delivered to the commissioning party according to the terms laid out in your commissioning agreement. This can be done (1) paying the fees up front at the signing of the commissioning agreement, (2) paying it in installments (e.g., half at signing, other half on score delivery), or (3) paying it in full on delivery of the score.

Commissioning fees can be paid to you in the form of traditional paper checks, or as direct deposits into your bank account, or via one of the digital payment services like PayPal, Apple Pay, Venmo, and others. Which is used depends on who, or what entity, is commissioning you, and which method of payment is most convenient for both parties.

Royalty statements and payments of *any* sort—print, performance, mechanical, and so on—must be sent to the copyright owner or the authorized agent of the owner on a regular, mutually agreed upon basis. The frequency of receiving statements and royalties depends on the type of agreement signed. Royalty payments can be made, as with commissioning fees, by check, direct deposit, or digital payment service. Statements can be provided on a business' website, sent as digital files (usually PDFs), or as printed paper statements. PROs in the United States, for example, all now have the ability to direct deposit performance royalties into members' bank accounts.

The bigger the business the better it is at record keeping and providing statements and royalties. Smaller organizations may not be as efficient, but they also might be quicker to pay because they're dealing with smaller numbers. Each situation is different. One of the bigger questions that frequently comes up for composers—not to mention for musicians in general, unfortunately—is *what happens if I don't get paid?*[17]

The first step is to prevent getting cheated out of the money due you in the first place. A contract or agreement needs to establish clear expectations and obligations, including those for payment, before you begin composing. This helps avoid problems later on.

The payment of a portion of a fee when signing an agreement, or partial installment payments throughout the process of a project helps too, particularly for commissioning contracts. If you do work that has you writing invoices, send them—dated—and include your full contact information along with the name of the project (commission, *etc.*), the name of the payee (the person or business who owes you money), and instructions for paying (such as "Make check payable to: [YOUR NAME]"). If you feel it necessary, include a statement of late fees (like "There will be a late fee of [AMOUNT OR PERCENTAGE OF BILL] added if payment is not received in [NUMBER OF DAYS].")[18] Have a follow-up system: set up a calendar with the date the money is due, the date when late fees will begin to accrue, and when the next step—whatever you determine that to be—will occur. Is this all necessary? Probably not, but it is the way "big business" operates and it can only help you.

Say that, after sending multiple letters requesting payment and even imposing late fees, you still haven't been able to collect monies due to you. The next step could be to send a letter saying you may be forced to pursue legal action if the payment isn't received with a specified amount of time. Two to four weeks is the normal range for such things. No one likes having to go to court to get paid or having to pay money owed. Certainly, no one likes the legal expenses and time lost. Such letters could convince the payee to close the matter by paying. These letters should be written by your attorney if possible. Nothing frightens a reluctant payor than seeing a letter on an attorney's letterhead. If that doesn't work, and the amount is significant enough to warrant it, you can call in "the big guns," that is your attorney, to take legal action by way of a civil lawsuit. For amounts varying from $2,500 to $25,000, states have special "small claims" courts.

Hopefully, though, you will be paid in full and on time and never have to resort to these drastic alternatives. Still, it's helpful and somewhat comforting to have these options available.

NOTES

1. For some of us any discussion of contracts may seem overly complex, perhaps something like this: **https://youtu.be/G_Sy6oiJbEk?si=xXHgkbGYSt9BEo5W.**

2. The examples provided are just that, examples. Have your attorney help draft your own commissioning contract template.

3. "POP" means "permanently out of print," which in turn means what you think it means: the publisher is no longer making it available in any form. Interestingly, that does not mean they are relinquishing ownership, or control, over the work's copyright. If the work is recorded or performed the publisher will happily take any fees or royalties generated. The abbreviation "TOP" means "temporarily out of print," which means just that. The publisher has plans to print more copies of the music.

4. With rare exception book publishers have eliminated the practice of giving authors advances.

5. One exception was when Excelcia Music first started. Those of us composers who had works published with the company in that first year of business received small—but very meaningful—advances on the sales of their work. This was a way for the publisher to say "thank you for publishing with us, for trusting us with your music, and for believing in us in our work to sell your music." It only happened the one time, but it made a *huge* positive impression on me and, no doubt, on the other composers whose works were published with Excelcia that year.

6. Such cases are held in the civil courts of the state in which the publisher brings the case, which is always the state in which the publisher officially does business.

7. The term *bona fide* is Latin for "in good faith."

8. There are more reasons for publishers to limit the number of times per year to distribute royalty statements and their accompanying monies. In holding on to the royalties for a while, the publisher gets a chance to have it earn interest from their own bank accounts and other investments.

9. **https://www.copyright.gov/licensing/m200a.pdf.**

10. **https://www.copyright.gov/circs/circ73.pdf.**

11. Here's one sample mechanical license agreement; there are others available online: **http://www.newmandecoster.com/pdf/mechanical.pdf.**

12. A "card" or intertitle or title card, is a piece of filmed printed text edited into the movie or show. Cards are used to give the title and appropriate credits ("Directed by," "Produced by," "Music by," *etc.*).

13. *Pro bono publico* is Latin for "for the public good."

14. **https://www.avvo.com.**

15. A *retainer* is a fee paid to secure the services as required. Retainers require service contracts and payments can be done in full up front, as partial payments, or as periodic payments. A lawyer on retainer is expected to take care of any legal matters that arise for the client. The bigger your business, the more likely you would need an attorney on retainer; one-or-two person operations like self-publishers probably won't need it, but a larger, corporate structured business probably would. The largest businesses will often have "in-house counsel," that is lawyers on staff.

16. In October 2004, the songwriter John Hall of the band Orleans commented that George W. Bush's presidential campaign had not asked permission to use his song "Still the One" at campaign events. His publisher sent a "cease and desist" letter to Bush's campaign, and the campaign dropped the song from their playlist. Later, in 2008, John McCain's presidential campaign *also* tried using the same song without permission and once again Hall and his publisher stopped it. (He did allow the 2008 Democratic National Convention to use it after Senator Ted Kennedy's speech, however.) More recently in 2024, the singer Celine Dion's management team and Dion's record label Sony Music Entertainment Canada, Inc. learned that a campaign rally in Montana for Donald Trump and J.D. Vance had used "the video, recording, musical performance, and likeness of Celine Dion singing 'My Heart Will Go On.'" This was unauthorized, Dion's team said; Dion did not and "does not endorse this or any similar use."

17. A great resource on this and other topics is the website for the Freelancers Union. Here is the link to some recommendations they make about getting paid: **https://freelancersunion.org/the-freelancers-guide-to-getting-paid-on-time/.**

18. Late fees are usually set as being incurred if payment has not been received by multiples of thirty days: thirty days, sixty days, or ninety days.

Chapter 9

FOLLOW UP

People don't care how much you know until they know how much you care.

—Theodore Roosevelt, 26th president of the United States

Your work has been commissioned, written, performed, and received enthusiastically by the audience and performers. You're done now, you can go home and get to work right away on the next project, right? No. You have to follow up. In fact, you have to follow up each step of the way. But "following up" can mean different things. It could mean to follow one thing with something similar or in addition. Film sequels and numbered musical works ("Symphony No. 2") are examples. It could involve taking further action, like sending a thank-you note to someone after they've done something nice for you. And it can mean continuing contact with someone or a business to learn of any effects, good or bad, caused by earlier actions. Here are some examples in the composing world.

* You've written a work for a band that has become *very* popular with, say, middle school students. Although most composers bristle at the idea of repeating themselves you might consider following up with a new work in a similar style just this once.

* You've written a work for string trio and the performers have been rehearsing it. You follow up some time after they've had a chance to get to know the work, to learn if anything needs adjustment or correction, and to take further action by making those adjustments or corrections.

* For this last example, reread the first sentence of this chapter. It's at this point, after the performance, that you follow up. You do this by contacting the people who commissioned and/or performed your music and learn of any

153

comments, compliments, and complaints about it, especially the things that worked well and those that didn't.

With certain written agreements, following up is a contractural matter, but the onus isn't always on you. If you or your publisher issues a mechanical license it is is up to the licensee to follow through by sending statements and any associated monies on a regular, predetermined basis. If your music is published through a traditional publisher, that publisher is also required to send statements and any monies on a routine basis.

Following up or following through is, when you think about it, really paying attention to detail. It's not *just* about paying attention to the details of your commissioning agreement or the method of payment. Sometimes it's about the social interactions that come along with them.

And following up isn't only for commissioning situations either. When applying for grants the grantors will customarily let you know if or when they've received your application and when you should expect the results. Submitting works for possible publication takes considerably more patience, but also some follow up throughout the process. If a publisher doesn't acknowledge receipt of your work within a reasonable amount of time, it's okay to ask if they have received it. If they say it will take "x months" to let you know if they want to publish it and you haven't heard from them for a few weeks beyond that "x," it *might* be okay to inquire about it—but consider that on a case-by-case basis. There are also situations in which you're working in some way with musicians on a performance of your music; that's a topic for a more detailed discussion later in this chapter.

Chapter 4, "Presenting and Promoting Yourself As a Composer (Preparing to Get Lucky)," suggested sending an e-mail, text, or even a physical note to someone you've met, to keep the lines of communication open. Let them know you *enjoyed* meeting them at whatever the occasion was. You can even add you hope to be in touch with them, or work with them again if that is applicable. If they've requested a link to your music or for scores or recordings, your message can include those. If you get to send those materials or links, you'll need to wait. Let them find time in their schedule to look over your score and/or listen to your recording. *Be patient; don't harass people.* People are busy, and you should assume that someone of any importance is even busier. If you haven't heard back in a week, or even two, then you can drop a short note making sure they received what you provided. Don't ask what they thought of your work, because if they haven't checked it out yet *they* will feel embarrassed and that will not serve you well. Just asking, "Did you receive the files I sent?" is a nice, unpressured way of reminding them that you did provide the materials, that they are expected to check it out, and that they should give you a response (no matter when or what that response may be).

You will need to find a balance between applying too little psychological pressure and too much. Too little and it comes off as if you don't care or, worse, that you're unprofessional. If you apply too much pressure it will imply that you care *too* much, that you're desperate. Balancing both following up and having patience are considered signs of professionalism.

PRE-PERFORMANCE PUBLICITY

Some composers are uncomfortable self-promoting; they might feel it beneath them as artists to "hype" themselves, or they could simply be uncomfortable or shy in self-promoting situations, or they don't think they're good at it. These are all legitimate feelings and are not to be dismissed or denigrated. But while you don't have to go to "hype" extremes, a bit of honest self-promotion can only help draw interest to your music. It's your music itself, after all, that deserves the attention. Even if the performers presenting you work do their own promotional work, there can always be a bit more which *you* can do help draw an audience or gain more exposure. Here are some things I've done at one time or another.

* Offer to do a pre-concert lecture on the piece—a "meet the composer" session—with a question-and-answer period. This might draw some audience on its own. Your willingness to speak with the audience makes you more approachable and, therefore, helps your music seem more approachable as well.

* Offer to meet the audience after the concert. Guaranteed, you will get all kinds of comments and questions.[1]

* Offer to be interviewed on a local radio or television station, or on satellite radio or a podcast. Newspaper interviews, particularly in local communities, are quite nice to do.[2]

* Promote the concert on behalf of the performers. Mention it on social media, send out e-mails or even physical flyers, and so on to the people most likely to go to the performance. Don't bother folks who live on the West Coast to come to a concert on the East Coast, for example. Limit your outreach to people within easy commute of the concert. Except for the flyers, all of this only requires your time and computer skills and no money. You can make basic flyers (or use the performers' own for copies) at home, and you can mail them cheaply enough using the USPS.

In Chapter 5, "The Gig," there's mention of self-promotion opportunities that can arise during a project of any kind. Whether it's to announce your signing a significant agreement—an exclusive publishing deal for example or, say, a commission from A-list musicians—you have the chance to promote those events using a *press release*. Admittedly, press releases are considered old-fashioned, yet they work. As defined earlier, a press release is a statement provided to news media giving information about an upcoming event or significant matter. If a newspaper, magazine, news program, or other reporter of news finds it interesting, or even they just need "filler" for an empty spot on a page or in a program, you've gotten free publicity.

Before discussing the content, you need to know that a press release always starts with three things:

1. *The date to be released.* This is when the information should be disseminated. Because of time lags between when releases are received and when they can be published or aired, most say "FOR IMMEDIATE RELEASE." You can of course adjust things accordingly.
2. *The date of release.* This is the date you are sending the release. This will help the recipient keep track of things.
3. *The name(s) of the contact person(s) and contact information.* This can be you, your publisher, or whomever is sending out the release on your behalf. That's the "point person," the one the recipient will text or call or e-mail (or send a physical letter) to get further information or, hopefully, to arrange an interview.

The basic format for the text in press releases can be described as an inverted triangle of information, with the widest part of the triangle at the top providing the most important information, and the pointed end at the bottom giving the least important. Figure 9-1 is a visualization of the concept.

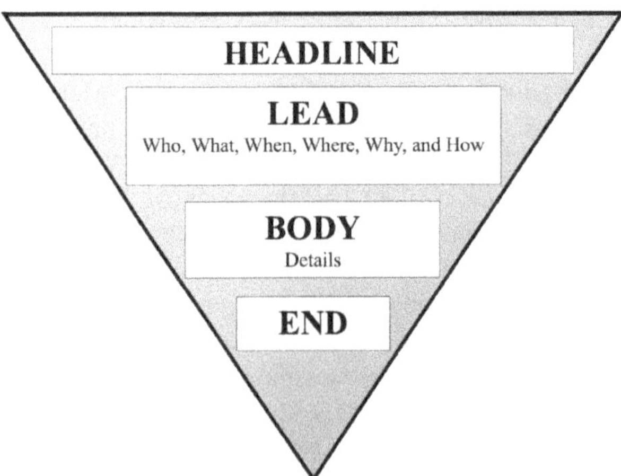

Figure 9-1   Press Release Inverted Triangle, author created

The first thing the recipient of a press release will see is the *headline*. This consists of one concise sentence saying what the release is about, and it needs to grab the reader's attention. For example, say you're J.P. Composer and you want to promote an upcoming premiere. The headline of your press release might read something like this:

**Hypothetical Ensemble To Premiere New Work By
J.P. Composer At Schmarnegie Hall On June 3rd**

You'll notice the headline anticipates the next section of the press release (the "lead") by succinctly giving the "who" (the Hypothetical Ensemble *and* the composer), "what" (the premiere), "when" (June 3rd), and "where" (Schmarnegie Hall). It does not include the "why" and "how" information, as that can be provided in the lead and/or body sections of the release.

The *lead* ("LEED") is the most important part of a press release. It expands on the headline, providing the same information in more complete sentences, and adds pertinent information not already covered. The "why" portion could mention the work was commissioned and why. The "how" could be anything, even how the composer came to the ensemble's attention. Everything after this section will be interesting and even necessary, but it won't be as essential.

The *body* of a press release is where you fill in necessary details. Those can entail information about the composer, the performers, the music, the reason for the work, and so on. Some publicists say this is the perfect place for a quote or two from someone connected with the event. This is also where you can put the cost of admission and location information.

The *end*, of course, wraps things up. If you haven't put things like ticket prices or driving directions in the body portion, you can put it here. You can also mention things in this last section like "there will be a wine and cheese reception in the lobby after the concert where you can meet the composer and performers." Lastly, this is where you put any "For more information" contact information or website URL.

After the last paragraph of your release skip a line, then put "###" centered, like this:

###

This indicates the end of the release. If your press release runs more than one page, put "MORE" in a similar spot on the first page and "###" at the end of the last one. You can also put the number of words used in the body of the release centered on the next line ("360 words" for example). This comes in handy for newspaper and magazine editors when they're determining if your press release will fit a particular page.

###

360 words

Here are some time-tested tips for writing good press releases:

* Write the text of the release in complete, grammatically correct sentences in "standard" English. A press release is not a text or a social media posting. Don't use texting abbreviations[3] ("lol," "thanq," etc.) or slang unless it's part of a title or name of something or someone significant to the release. If someone has to look it up on the Urban Dictionary website, you're better off not using it.[4] And please, *please*, make sure everything is spelled correctly, and that the words you use are the right ones in the first place. Don't just by run your text through a spell checker. I've seen countless releases, not to mention newspaper articles, and even the occasional whole book replete with incorrect words spelled correctly. Get someone else to proofread the text, preferably someone whose command of language better than your own.[5]

* Use action verbs whenever possible. "The Hypothetical Ensemble will perform . . ." is better than "There will be a performance by the Hypothetical Ensemble of. . . ." The words "will perform" make the sentence active, while "will be a performance of" is passive and makes the sentence more cumbersome.

* Stick to the most-important-to-least-important concept when writing the text. Make sure the sentences are in the right order.

* It's usually better to write a release without thinking about its length, and then edit it down to what is essential. For most writers it seems easier to pare down something lengthy than to add something later. Try to be thorough but succinct. Aim for one page. You can have a two-page release, if necessary, but if you haven't gotten your point across with the headline and first two paragraphs your release clearly needs more editing.

* Think of press releases as "bait" for enticing the media into being interested in your work, in the performance, and so on. It could lead to someone else following up and featuring you and/or your work in more depth. In keeping with the previous suggestion, think of giving the reader a "taste" of something good, and leave them wanting (to know) more.

* Don't send out press releases haphazardly; be selective. Know your market, that is, know whose positive response would benefit you the most. Don't, for example, send a release to the *Source* magazine unless your work actually has some connection to rap and hip-hop.

* Also, be selective in how many releases you send out and why. If you send out a release at every stage of a project—referred to as "papering" your contacts—it will dilute the impact of your more important releases.

* It's not a bad idea to include a photo or two with your press release, along with the identification of anyone in the photo listed left to right. If sending releases digitally attach the photos as thumbnails and allow the recipient to select which, if any, they'd like in better resolution. Thumbnail photos have smaller files and are easier to send. If you have a website where you can post

high resolution photos for downloading, all the better; just include a link in your release.

A circumscribed but useful tool is the Public Service Announcement or PSA. A PSA is a short message, written as a script or recorded for playback and distributed by the audio and audiovisual broadcast media—without charge—to raise awareness about an issue (health and safety for example), event, or to help change behavior ("Don't smoke!"). PSAs can be found on television or radio during commercial breaks and on social media and various websites like YouTube. Keep in mind the PSA's purpose; you're limited in how you are allowed to use it. PSAs should only be used for events and other things that are for the public at large, free or asks for donations, and benefits the community or society in general. Here are some examples.

* Announcing a *free, open-to-the-public* performance that includes your music.

* Publicizing a *free and public* lecture or discussion about your music and how it relates to the community in which the event takes place.

* Announcing a new *community-focused* project that includes your work, and that if any money is involved it is to go to a nonprofit organization that will serve the community.

Note that the examples are all free and/or beneficial to the community. PSAs should *not* be used for things like:

* "Regular" concerts for which admission is charged, unless the performers are under a nonprofit umbrella and donations are solicited instead of ticket charges. (CYA for that!)

* Announcing your latest commission, album release, or publication.

Assuming your reason for writing and distributing a PSA is appropriate, it should check off these criteria:

* *It needs to be authentic.* To be a true PSA it needs to be linked to a 501(c)(3) nonprofit, tax-exempt organization, preferably with local or national recognition. Generally you have to submit a PSA to the public affairs director of a television or radio station with certain information:

• The official name of the 501(c)(3).
• A description of the event (or initiative, or cause).
• The name of the event, as well as its date, time, and location.
• The associated website URL, if any.
• A description of who the organization benefits, and what portions of the proceeds go to the beneficiaries.
• Your name, title, and contact number (I would also provide an e-mail address).

* *The PSA needs to be simple and quick.* PSAs should be offered in two versions, one for thirty seconds (65–90 words) and one for sixty seconds (150–180 words). Provide both versions so stations can choose as they need to fill airtime. Also provide the scripts for each, because some stations would rather enlist one of their own hosts read the PSA live. You could also provide a fifteen-second script for live reading purposes.[6]

* *Follow up.* Stations may say something like "due to the volume of PSAs we receive, we are unable to acknowledge receiving your submission." You will need to follow up with phone calls and e-mails a bit after you've submitted your PSA. In any case it's an opportunity to "sell" the virtues of the reason for the PSA to get the station to air it. Short of that you can include a "yes/no" form along with the submission or give them a way to answer online.

Formatting a PSA is relatively easy. It should have a title, the script length, an optional heading of the PSA (in all uppercase letters), followed by the text. Figure 9-2 shows a typical PSA.

REVIEWS

Let's get this out of the way: *reviews of new compositions are rare and damn challenging to get, and a good review is twice as difficult as that.* Fewer newspapers exist to begin with and those that do rarely have *a* music reviewer—let alone a staff of reviewers—to come to a concert featuring your music and give it the critical attention you think it deserves. Television stations, not even the smallest local ones, don't seem to review concerts or recitals at all, although they might do a short bit on an upcoming one. That's likely to be the timing for any interviews as well. Satellite and internet radio stations barely acknowledge classical music's existence, and only a very select number of magazines or journals review new works in print or online. Sheet music gets reviewed in journals and newsletters aimed at performers or educators dealing with the specific genre (flute works, band pieces, etc.), but never enough to cover everyone's music. Disheartening, right? So what *is* a review and how do you get one?

A *review* is a formal critical appraisal of the composer's work in performance (or print). A *good* review offers some background information about the work, the composer, and things like placing the work in historical context. All reviews, good or bad, also rely on the reviewer's informed but ultimately highly personal reaction to what is performed and how. A good reviewer should aim for positivity and sympathy for the composer's musical goals. Some college and university music programs offer study tracks and even degrees in music criticism, blending a knowledge of music with that of

THIRD TIER STRING QUARTET PSA

YOUR OPTION: 30 SECOND SCRIPT

THE THIRD TIER STRING QUARTET WILL GIVE A FREE PERFORMANCE FOR THE SCHMARNEGIE MEWS COMMUNITY ON SUNDAY JUNE 3RD.

The Third Tier String Quartet, advocates for the Schmarnegie Mews renovation initiative, will perform to celebrate the project's receiving funding on Sunday, June 3rd at the SM community room, 3 Jones Boulevard.

The performance will feature the premiere of John Q. Composer's work "Rosins."

Admission is free, tax-deductible donations to the Schmarnegie Mews Renovation Initiative are welcome.

Contact the Schmarnegie Mews Renovation Initiative at www.smri.org for more information, or call 555-111-1111.

Figure 9-2   Sample Public Service Announcement (PSA), author created

journalism. There is also a long tradition of composers working as reviewers themselves. Claude Debussy wrote criticism under the pen name "Monsieur Croche,"[7] and Virgil Thomson served as a highly respected music critic for the *New York Herald-Tribune* from 1940 to 1954. Whether reviewers are a composer or a trained music journalist, they each come with their own biases, preferences and, on occasion, their own agendas.

Reviews come in three basic varieties: "loved it," "hated it," and "mentioned" or "meh." We composers naturally want reviews of the first type, the more enthusiastic the better. We *love* to quote reviews like these. Severely negative reviews, on the other hand, can be taken as a reflection on the reviewer's disposition at the time (remembering that reviews are, after all, highly subjective), as something to be ignored entirely, or a statement that might have some credence. Maybe the reviewer heard something in the music you missed in the composing. You may not want to quote that review, but perhaps there's a point or two you can learn from it. It might not seem so, but the worst type of review is the one that is non-committal, the "mention" or "meh" review. It's said that the opposite of love is not hate but apathy, and that applies to new music reviews too. A "mention" or "meh" review is more of a statement that the performance happened, and that the reviewer showed up, listened, but didn't find anything in the music worth discussing. An old adage comes to mind: "If you can't say something nice, don't say anything."

Composers want reviews to have someone *not* themselves say "this music is good, this composer is good." We don't want to seem self-serving even when, to be honest, we have to be. Reviews can lend composers and the music they write respectability, help interest potential audience in the music itself, and even bolster a composer's sense of self-worth. Reviews often provide composers with feedback not possible from significant others, general non-musician audiences, and even other musicians. In practical terms, nothing beats quoting a good review to make composers seem a bit more important to the music world and even to themselves.

Actually getting a concert reviewed is extremely difficult and not always possible. But on the "you never know" basis, here are some things you can do to give yourself the best chance of getting your work reviewed.

* *Send a press release.* If you're sending it to a local paper, it's okay to play up any local connections. If your work is tied to an external event such as a historical celebration or honoring or celebrating someone in the community, definitely emphasize that aspect. Remember that the intention of a press release is to grab someone's attention so that *they* follow up. (If the circumstances warrant it, you can also send out a PSA as discussed earlier.)

* *Use your networking skills.* Talk to people you know, learn about whom they might know who would be amenable to reviewing your work. All it takes is one person to say, "Hey, I know the reviewer for the [insert name of newspaper or television station]. Would you like me to contact them?"

* *Do your homework to find media that reviews concert music performances.* Some magazines (mostly online at this point) review classical music performances, such as *Musical America Worldwide*, the *Classical Review*, and the online-only *Bachtrack*.[8] Other magazines and journals, like the *National Review*, don't specialize in music, but will sometimes have articles and essays on musical subjects. Things change frequently and unpredictably, so even the sources I just mentioned may or may not exist, or they may

change their review policies by the time you read this. You'll need to do some digging to learn what publications and shows currently do reviews.

Formal reviews aren't the only way to get feedback you can use publicly. Getting positive comments from performers, notable non-musicians, or any audience members can put an interesting "spin" on your bio that could grab extra attention. Any positive comments about a specific work can be helpful, and it puts a personal touch to your work and how people relate to you.[9]

POST-PERFORMANCE PUBLICITY

Aside from reviews, not a lot of publicity can be done after a premiere. That said, what is possible can be effective in expanding the audience for your music.

** Start promoting your next performance.* In fact this should happen during the current performance and continue afterward. If there are program notes at your premiere, include a mention of the next performance of your work. (You don't have to give all the details; give just enough information to intrigue the reader.) You can also do this during a "meet the composer" session before or after the current performance.

** Post about the concert on social media.* If you have photos post those too. They can be of the performance itself or "behind the scenes" and "after the concert" photos. If you have videos, even (or especially?) short ones, *definitely* post those. Get followers to wish they hadn't missed that performance and to start thinking about going to the next one.

** Get audience feedback.* This is something more for your performers to do than you, or maybe you could do it together. Perhaps provide a QR code in the concert program to a survey about what the audience members heard. You're likely not to get a large response (anything over, say, 3 percent of possible respondents is considered awesome) but it could be instructive. And by listening to what people have to say, you're demonstrating appreciation for the audience's support.

FOLLOWING UP WITH THE PERFORMERS

Whether you're dealing with professional, amateur, or student musicians, it's always a good idea to stay in touch with them after your work is premiered or given a subsequent performance. It's a sign of courtesy and professionalism; caring enough to continue communication *after* you've gotten what you wanted—a performance—proves your consideration for others. Your relationship could become a long-term, mutually beneficial one as a result and, better still, even develop into outright friendships. Perhaps the only thing better than having repeat customers (that is commissioners and/or performers of you music) is having *friends* who support you and your work professionally too.

Following up before a performance is important as well. During the composing process you can give periodic progress reports—not too frequently, just once in a while—to show you haven't been idle and that you've been thinking about *their* piece a lot. The composing process is a mystery even to us composers, so an occasional update to the music's recipient tends to have a reassuring influence. During the rehearsal schedule staying in touch *as needed*, assuming you're not directly involved in the performance, allows the musicians to let you know of any possible issues with the music. It gives you enough time to fix, add, or delete things as necessary. That too is reassuring, for you as well as the performers. And whether you've written for pros, amateurs, or students, a meeting either in person or via the internet can be of interest and assistance in the performance.

It's a good idea to contact the musicians to say "thank you" a short time after a performance. You can do it at any point from the next day to about a week later, but don't do it as an obligation. Offer your thanks from the heart. People who have given your music their all deserve a true, warm response from you.

At this point, "once the dust has settled," you can also ask for feedback about the piece itself if you're willing to hear it. We composers don't think about feedback often enough, but it's an essential component of our growth and refinement of our craft. Learning what the musicians think works, or what doesn't, can help the compositional process. For large ensemble works, it's better to get those reactions from the conductor. If you were the conductor though, get it from the players. Asking them for feedback and listening, really listening to them shows you value their opinions. Whether or not you ultimately agree with the comments and suggestions you receive, they may lead to some revisions of the work or get you thinking about a new work.

NOTES

1. Hopefully you'll only get compliments from audience members after a performance of your music, but you can't please everyone all the time. When someone *doesn't* like what they heard, it's rare to say so to your face. Instead you might get something like: "That was an *interesting* work. Where do you get your ideas?" Or there's: "I don't like modern music, but I like your work." (This is usually said with an actual sneer at the word "modern.") My all-time favorite after-concert comment, though, is "I've never met a *living* composer before." Aside from the obvious snarky

question—"How many dead composers have you met?"—you need to appreciate the truth in the statement. That person has never met anyone who creates music before, so you're helping them have a brand-new experience.

2. No matter where and for whom you're being interviewed, whether it's on national television or a small-town newspaper, *always* be respectful of the interviewer and the place you're in. Don't put on "airs"; don't come across as if you're more important than anyone else around you. It comes off as pretentious, obnoxious, and self-aggrandizing—and that's not the way to win people over. The best way to handle interviews is to relax as much as you can, be yourself, and stick to the basics: why you're there (to participate in the premiere of your new piece), what the audience should expect of the piece (in non-patronizing but non-technical terms), and some good words about the musicians you're lucky to have performing it. Stay positive. And if you can't find anything nice to say, save it for your memoirs.

3. Here's a good resource for texting abbreviations, just for fun: **https://www .internetmatters.org/resources/text-dictionary/#navigation.**

4. Urban Dictionary's URL: **https://www.urbandictionary.com.**

5. Not only has this book been given a good going-over by editor Michael Tan, but it was also "beta tested" by a few friends whose command of the written word I trust.

6. Fifteen, thirty, and sixty seconds all seem too short to get a lot of information to a listener or viewer, but with good, concise scripts PSAs at these lengths can be very effective.

7. Literally, "Mr. Eighthnote."

8. New York Classical Review: **https://classicalreview.com.**

Bachtrack: **https://bachtrack.com.**

Musical America Worldwide: **https://www.musicalamerica.com/pages/ ?pagename=meet-the-journalists.**

Classical Review actually has local branches, such as the New York Classical Review, and similar local *Reviews* for Boston, Chicago, Washington (DC), as well broader areas like South Florida, Texas, and Utah.

9. Sometimes the responses one gets can go beyond your expectations. I once had the opportunity to communicate with Oliver Sacks, M.D., who was revising and expanding his book on music-related disorders, *Musicophilia.* One thing led to another and I wound up sending him some of my music. His note back to me included this: "I have been listening with enormous pleasure and admiration of your music—an astonishing range of pieces, I never knew what to expect next. . . ." To be honest, I wish more reviews of my work would be that enthusiastic. It was also, frankly, an ego boost to see me later described as an "eminent composer" in Sacks's revised book.

Chapter 10

FINANCES

Nothing is certain except death and taxes.

—Benjamin Franklin

Like it or not, we composers are in the music *business*, and a big part of that is dealing with our personal and business finances. Unless you've grown up around CPAs or tax attorneys, or you have as much interest in your finances as you have in your music, you'll at least need the basic information presented here.[1] Some of it might be obvious, but it won't be obvious to everyone. As a reminder, I can't advise you on anything financial, tax-related, or legal; *only your own accountant or attorney can give you financial or legal advice.* When it comes to your finances, consult your financial advisor. And since that phrase will come up very frequently in this chapter, let's abbreviate it to "CYFA."[2]

SOME FINANCIAL DEFINITIONS AND EXPLANATIONS

* *Income* is the money you earn either through wages, fees, royalties, or investments. Wages are earned through work done for one boss or entity, on a regular basis during specific hours. Fees are paid on a onetime or limited number of times bases, such as commissioning fees. For composers, royalties are monies earned from performances, sales of sheet music, or sales of audio or audiovisual products. Investments can range from a simple bank account to day trading on the New York Stock Exchange. See Chapter 2, "Income Streams: Definitions and Examples," for a discussion on possible composer

income sources. Non-monetary goods or services might also be considered income, such as property like real estate, or work done in exchange for other things.

* *Expenses* are the monies you spend. Expenses can be personal (rent or mortgage payments, utilities for your home, and so on) or for business (certain pieces of equipment, services, supplies, and pretty much anything you pay for to conduct your business as a composer).

* *Taxes* are compulsory contributions to federal, state, and/or local governments. There are different types of taxes levied at all levels of government, but the three basic ones imposed at the federal level are the income tax, Medicare, and Social Security. Depending on the state there can be income tax and disability insurance. The ones that concern us here the most are the income taxes. In the U.S. federal income, tax rates vary depending on the level of income; the lower the income the lower the rate; the higher the income the higher the tax rate. These rates change yearly, ordinarily to adjust to current inflation rate. At this time forty-three states and the District of Columbia levy taxes on individual income. Consult your financial advisor (CYFA) to be sure about state income taxes, but know that you *must* pay federal income tax on income earned. Taxes are not considered expenses, although they do affect what's left in your bank account at the end of the year.

* *Employment status* is how you define what you do for tax purposes. If you're like me and have the figurative "seventeen jobs at any given time," you could consider yourself an employee, self-employed, or both.[3] You are an *employee* if you work on a continued basis for an employer (*aka* boss) under supervision at a specified pay rate, and paid on a regular basis (say, every two weeks). Employees have a written or implied contract for the work they do. You're *self-employed* if you hire out your services on a one-time or short-term basis, are not regularly supervised, and are paid once the work is completed (or through other arrangements as with commissions).

As indicated earlier, you can be both an employee—working at your "day job"—and self-employed at the same time. Composers have juggled both for hundreds of years. Beethoven, for one, had some patronage early in his career from Prince Lichnowsky, which effectively made him an employee, but his primary income later was through performing, teaching, commissions, and print royalties from sales of the sheet music of his works. An employee receives Form W-2 at the end of the calendar year (or as late as February of the next year), showing the gross income earned during the year, the amounts of taxes and other deductions made, and the net income after those deductions. The self-employed are supposed to receive Forms 1099 around the same time from those who pay individually for their services or goods; any income over $600 requires you and the IRS receive a 1099. There are different 1099s to cover different kinds of non-wage income, the most common for composers being the 1099-MISC. None of the Forms 1099 withhold money for taxes; they only show gross monies paid or earned. Be aware though that not every person or entity who pays you for your work will issue a 1099, even if they've paid you over six hundred dollars. The safest move is to *report all of your earnings* come tax time.

One of the more challenging aspects of dealing with our finances is keeping track of it all. For composers just keeping track of income alone is more difficult because of the different possible income streams:

* Commissioning fees.
* Performance royalties from your PRO.
* Print royalties, especially if you have works with different publishers.
* Mechanical royalties (and remember there are two types of those!).
* Synchronization fees.
* Bartering. This would be trading your art in exchange for some non-monetary compensation (living rent-free, for example).

That list can be longer if you record your own music, perform it in concert, and if you belong to the musicians' union, and longer still if you also invest your money in various ways. When recording our finances we need to use one of two accounting methods, consistently: accrual or cash. The *accrual* method is reporting income as you *earn* it. The *cash* method is reporting the income when you *receive* it. Whichever you use, be sure to record all of your income and expenses, and keep those records up to date. For keeping income records, keep these ideas in mind:

   * *Keep a record of* all *of your income.* Assume anyone paying you is notifying the IRS of that payment even if they pay you cash. The IRS tends to look at musicians as "low hanging fruit," that is, easy pickings for audits because a longtime stereotype of us being notoriously bad at bookkeeping. The more complete and accurate your record keeping, the less likely you'll incur an audit. You can create an income record as part of an Excel or other spreadsheet app or as some sort of physical chart. Your accountant can advise you on how to set it up. No matter how you receive money, keeping a straightforward record of your income will make it a lot easier to file your taxes and to prevent those dreaded audit letters from the IRS from being mailed to you.

   * *Keep your accounts up to date.* Whether or not you use physical checks, you get monthly checking account statements from your bank. Online banks also provide statements. It's all too easy to ignore them and just loosely keep track of what's in or out of the account, but don't. It's worth the time and effort to reconcile your account each month, and it's an opportunity to keep track of money coming in and from where. Some people check their

accounts on their phones very frequently, sometimes obsessively. Please be aware that every time you check your account, especially in public, you're opening yourself to having your phone hacked. Your information, and likely your money, can be stolen. Unless you're in a situation where every penny counts and you absolutely need to keep tabs on your finances, try to limit the frequency with which you check them and then try to make sure your connection is secure. Using mobile data on your phone is usually more secure than using WIFI, for example.

Mobile payment services like PayPal and Venmo are used with increasing frequency because they're seen as fast, convenient, and relatively secure. They're accessed through dedicated phone apps and are designed to be easy to use. Payments are made, essentially, from one person's phone to another. Proof of transactions are transfer receipts that show up on your phone as a screenshot or scan. The transfer receipt includes the payer's account number either in full or just the last five digits; the account holder's full name as shown in their account; the amount; and the date of the transaction. It may include a transaction number assigned by the service as well. Mobile payment services are not banks, however. They don't provide any of the other services banks provide, including (currently) interest on money in your account. They are also not FDIC-insured.

Notice the phrase "considered relatively secure" in the preceding paragraph. Information stored on your phone can be subject to hacking, or your phone could be lost or stolen and your information then accessed—especially if you don't lock your phone with a password. Also, if your phone stops working it will be problematic, to say the least, to get the information off that phone and onto another securely. If you're using mobile payment apps be sure to follow the installation instructions carefully and with extra attention to any security steps. Lastly, if you use a mobile payment service, find out if they provide monthly statements of activity. If they do, keep and go over those records at least until you file your end-of-year tax returns. If they don't, be sure to keep the transfer receipts.

As of 2024, if you receive $600 or more in payments within a calendar year through a mobile payment service, the service may be required to withhold 24 percent of those funds for tax purposes. PayPal, for example, says "Once you receive $600 in payments for goods and services within a calendar year, tax laws require us to withhold 24 percent of such payments when you have not confirmed your taxpayer status by either providing your US tax ID or completing a Certificate of Foreign Status. This 24 percent is sent to the IRS as backup withholding for any potential income tax due on those payments." This is a definite CYFA situation. Mobile payment services will also issue a Form 1099-K at the end of the calendar year with the amounts you earned through them, with one copy of the form going to the IRS and another going to you.

** Issue invoices when possible.* An invoice is a bill listing the goods or services you are providing, the amount of money due for those goods or services, and other information. Invoices are especially useful when working with individuals, small groups, or schools, and mostly when dealing with commissions. The best reasons to issue invoices are for both you and your client to maintain good recordkeeping for tax purposes, and to have a "paper trail," that is a way to "follow the money," in case of a dispute by either party. A good invoice will include:

- *The date of the invoice.* This date not only notifies the recipient of when you have sent the invoice but it effectively starts a count-down clock on when payment is due.
- *An invoice number.* I recommend setting up an invoice numbering system to help you keep your records straight. You can use any system that works consistently; some folks just start with "001" and go up from there, or you can include the year, like "2024037" with the "2024" being the year. Whatever invoicing system you use, just make sure it's consistent and accurate.
- *The payor's name and physical address.* This is a clear statement of who needs to pay you, and the address is there to ensure the correct person is receiving it.
- *"Please remit payment to" followed by* your *name and address.* This is most useful if you are to be paid by a physical check. Allowing payment by any other means should be described in the body of the invoice, but keep your name and address as the payee.
- *Your telephone number.* This is optional, but it can come in handy should any questions regarding payment come up and the payor needs to contact you quickly.
- *The body of the invoice.* Here is where you describe briefly, but with some details, what services and/or goods you have provided. This is also where you spell out the fees and other charges.
- *Total amount due.* Having spelled out the fees and other charges in the body of the invoice, you now total them all up and give that total here.

Here's a typical invoice in Figure 10-1. Create your own and include other information such as your e-mail address, payment due dates, or statements about any late payment fees.

There is a discussion on keeping accurate contemporaneous records of your income and your expenses later in this chapter. For now, the important thing to know is that some expenses are considered *tax deductible* and others aren't. The term "tax deductible" is used to define expenses (items, services,

<table>
<tr><td colspan="2">Invoice Number: <u>**2028001**</u>   Date: ________</td></tr>
<tr><td>For:</td><td>[PAYOR'S NAME]
[PAYOR'S ADDRESS 1st Line]
[PAYOR'S ADDRESS 2nd Line]
[PAYOR'S ADDRESS 3rd Line, if needed]</td></tr>
<tr><td>Please remit payment to:</td><td>[YOUR NAME]
[YOUR ADDRESS 1st Line]
[YOUR ADDRESS 2nd Line]</td></tr>
<tr><td>Telephone number:
E-mail Address:</td><td>[YOUR TELEPHONE NUMBER]
[YOUR E-MAIL ADDRESS]</td></tr>
</table>

FOR SERVICES RENDERED:
COMPOSITION COMMISSIONING FEE (< for example)

Describe here what you've done (composing, arranging, *etc.*) in what way (instrumentation here), for whom (who will perform the work, in this case, and when). You can include information regarding additional aspects of the services provided (a dedication in the score, and so on).

Fee (for the composing here, including anything you're providing, like a set of score and parts):
[$ AMOUNT]

Additional charges (if any, like shipping and handling):   [$ AMOUNT]

TOTAL AMOUNT DUE: [$ TOTAL AMOUNT]

(Optional, and open to alteration)
Payment is due no later than ninety (90) days from receipt of this invoice.

Figure 10-1 Sample Invoice, author created

etc.) that may reduce the taxes you have to pay in a given year. Here are some things the IRS lists as possibly deductible expenses, which could apply to anyone depending on their circumstances. They could also apply whether you take the standard deduction or you itemize your expenses.[4]

- Alimony payments.
- Business use of your car. (That is, the use of your car only when it is used for business.)
- Business use of your home. (This is a tricky item. CYFA!)
- IRA contributions.

- Health savings account contributions.
- Penalties on early withdrawals from savings.
- Student loan interest.
- Teacher expenses.
- *Some* work-related education expenses *if* you serve in the military or government, or if you're self-employed, or you have a disability.
- Moving expenses for those in the military.

Not everyone takes the standard deduction, and not everyone needs to itemize. According to the IRS, taxpayers who normally have a standard deduction of zero *should* itemize expenses. The people who fall into that category are: (1) married and filing a separate return, with their spouse is itemizing; (2) those filing a return for a short tax year due to a change in the annual accounting period (ask you financial person about this); or (3) those people who are considered nonresident aliens or who are considered dual status aliens during the year, but are either not married to a U.S. citizen or who is a resident at the end of the tax year.

When you *itemize* your expenses, you're cataloging everything you've spent during the year for business purposes. You're essentially telling the IRS, "This is what I spent on 'x' for my business" (whatever "x" is). Itemized expenses, according to the IRS, can include:

- Medical and dental expenses.
- Certain taxes paid. In this case these can be *either* state and local income taxes or sales taxes, but not both, as well as real estate taxes. What taxes are not deductible are things like federal income taxes, license fees (although the IRS doesn't define what sort of licenses they mean), and employment taxes. (CYFA!)
- Home mortgage interest.
- Gifts to charity. This refers to organizations, as per section 501(c)(3) of the Internal Revenue Code, which are "charitable, religious, educational, scientific, literary, testing for public safety, fostering national or international amateur sports competition, and preventing cruelty to children or animals. The term *charitable* is used in its generally accepted legal sense and includes relief of the poor, the distressed, or the underprivileged. . . ." and so on.[5]
- Casualty and theft losses (but only if those losses are derived from federally declared disaster areas).
- Certain miscellaneous deductions.

Once you've been paid and you've entered the transaction into your records, what do you do with the money? Where do you keep it? There are many options but the best one to safeguard your funds and keep them accessible is still having accounts in a bank. Banks can have a physical presence with branches across the United States or even just within your state, or they can be online, or both. There are several reasons to keep you money in bank accounts.

* Most banks are insured by the Federal Deposit Insurance Corporation (FDIC), which guarantees your money will be there and accessible no matter what up to a certain amount. The is an independent agency created by the federal government to help maintain financial stability and public confidence in the U.S. financial system.

* Most types of accounts offered by banks allow your money to earn interest. Banks use your money to make more money—that's for another book entirely—so you gain something for their use of it. The interest rates are miniscule, but that's still more than you would earn stuffing your cash under a mattress for safekeeping. As of this writing, online banks are paying slightly more in interest, but all banks' interest rates are subject to the whims of the economy.

* Banks, unlike some mobile payment services, are required to give you monthly statements showing all of the transactions with a certain cycle. The cycle is usually calculated by the month. This makes your record keeping easier, especially if you keep your accounts up to date.

* Banks where you have an account allow you to cash physical checks. This is done in person only, but you can also deposit the check via an Automated Teller Machine—an ATM. You can then withdraw an amount equal to what you deposited, provided your account has enough money in it beforehand to cover the withdrawal.

* You can have money direct deposited into your bank account. This is useful when payments to you are made on a regular basis. PROs offer direct deposit of performance royalties, for example.

* All U.S. banks now offer access to their own ATMs with the use of bank-issued card at no charge. You can also use almost any bank ATM to access your own account—usually for a fee imposed by the other bank. This makes getting cash when you need it a "no brainer," and makes depositing cash and checks a lot easier as well.

* Just as you can have money direct deposited into your account, you can arrange to have regular payments made from your account through electronic transfers as well. Sometimes this requires filling out forms and providing a voided check to the payee like a power company or another utility. How easy or difficult it is to set up depends on whom you're paying and in what bank you have an account.

* Many banks now have mobile banking available, either through their website or, more frequently, through a proprietary phone app. At the very

least this enables you to "bank anywhere" and not have to wait on a line in bank branch. Of course you can only do electronic funds transferring; there is no way to conduct any cash-based transactions.

* Banks offer a lot of services that are good to know about even if you don't think you'd ever use them. You can have a cashier's check drawn, in which you give them the money and they write the check under their name. A bank can also issue a certified check with funds taken from your account, but the bank certifies that you can cover the amount. Either is good for dealing with large amounts of money or money used in business transactions. Banks also offer money orders for less formal transactions and smaller amounts. A money order is similar to a cashier's check in that you provide the money and the bank writes the order.[6]

* Seeing the metaphorical writing on the wall, some banks have gone beyond just online banking to offering their own mobile payment services like Zelle. The only real difference between these and the standalone services is that these are tied directly to your bank account.

* Yet another service banks offer is loans, all kinds of loans. Any loan is an agreement between you and the bank in which you borrow a certain amount of money and promise to pay it back with interest. Mortgages are loans, as are car loans and boat loans, as well as what is generally referred to as business loans used to expand a business or purchase equipment, *etc*. But banks *never* give you a loan just on your good word that you'll pay it back. There is a *lot* of paperwork involved and you have to prove you have something of significant enough value, called *collateral*, to back up your promise to pay off the loan. If you need a loan, first talk with your financial advisor before applying for one.

But wait, there's more:

* Banks offer investment opportunities such as CDs (Certificates of Deposit); money markets (which function in much the same way as checking accounts); and, if you have a large amount of money with the bank, there are additional investments like access to the bank's brokerage branch available. CDs and money markets are covered by the FDIC, but not brokerage investments, so again, consult your financial advisor before diving into them.

* Banks can also provide financial advice usually depending on the amount of money you have in your accounts with them, but consider this with caution. A bank's advice will often be based on the bank's own investments and other services and "products" they provide. Your financial advisor should be someone with *fiduciary responsibility*, that is someone is who legally and/ or ethically responsible to advise and perform fiscal work for you, with only *your* best interests at heart. That is a topic for a completely different book by someone more conversant with that level of finances.

If you decide to deal with a bank you have choices as to what types of accounts you should have. Most banks offer a variety of products and services: checking accounts, savings accounts, and debit/ATM cards, and more. Many also offer their own credit cards.

* A *checking account* or "demand deposit account" is for conducting transactions on a day-to-day basis. Money you deposit into the account (by a bank or other financial institution) is held there on your behalf and available "on demand" immediately and as frequently as you need or want. The funds are considered "liquid" and considered, in accounting terms, as cash. Funds can be accessed by writing physical checks or through electronic transfers like using a bank card or debit card (see below). You can use your card to withdraw or deposit money at a bank branch or an ATM (Automated Teller Machine). People these days don't use physical checks nearly as much as previous generations did. More are using their debit cards or their cell phone app equivalents. Some businesses, too, are moving to payment services like Venmo, Apple Pay, and the like, or doing direct deposits. Still, physical checks are a viable option for now. Checking accounts earn interest on the money held there, but that interest is almost always small and almost always taxable.

* A *savings account* is similar in that you deposit money into it and earn interest on that money. Deposits and withdrawals are done at the bank branch or via an ATM with a debit/ATM card tied to the account, or through other electronic transfers. No physical checks are involved unless you are depositing them. Savings accounts are protected by the FDIC in almost all cases. The main difference between a checking account and a savings account is the purpose for each. You use a checking account to have money readily accessible for transactions. Checking accounts are for paying bills, depositing income, and so on. Savings accounts, by contrast, are for saving money. Savings accounts generally earn a slightly higher interest rate than checking accounts. But earning interest, even at a low rate, can be helpful.

* A *credit card* is a sort of loan. With a credit card you make purchases not with money you have at hand as with a checking account, but as loans which you have to pay back to the financial institution who issued the card. Credit cards are ubiquitous and most are accepted everywhere in the United States, the European Union, and elsewhere. Purchases can be made with credit cards in person, online, or via physical mail (within limitations).

Credit cards come with an individualized credit limit, a set amount over which you cannot spend at any given time, and they are subject to monthly interest charges that are added if you do not pay the charged amount in full when you receive the bill. You can pay off a bill in full or, if you want to or have no choice, pay smaller amounts to keep a balance that adds interest with each billing cycle. Most credit companies suggest a minimum monthly installment in those cases. That can add a lot of money to what you owe though, as it keeps adding interest charges to the total and those interest rates can be high. Credit card debt has become a major problem in the United States. Ultimately, it's better to pay off any credit card bills in full or as quickly as possible.

  * *Debit (or ATM or bank) cards* are tied directly to your bank account, and you're limited to what you can spend by what is in that account. They are usually tied to your checking account. The primary purpose of debit cards is to allow you transfer money electronically to another bank account. There has been a significant increase over the past decade in the number of people paying for purchases with debit cards instead of physical cash or checks. The differences between a debit card and a credit card are:

- Debit cards function as "digital cash," allowing you to make purchases easily. They do this by directly accessing your bank account.
- Most debit cards function as ATM or bank cards too, allowing you to perform transactions at ATMs and bank teller windows. That includes deposits as well as withdrawals. With a debit card you can withdraw cash immediately, with no waiting period. You are only limited by the amount of money in your account or if there is a "hold" on an amount that was recently deposited and is still being processed.
- Debit cards do not charge interest *per se*. Theoretically, you are limited to what you can spend by what is in your account. If, however, you have an account with certain privileges, you can spend a bit over your funds on hand and be charged *overdraft fees*. If you use a debit card, do your very best to avoid overdrafts.
- A credit card, on the other hand, is a loan based on what the card issuer determines to be your line of credit. It allows you to make purchases on money borrowed from the credit card company. Credit cards run on regular monthly cycles; you receive a statement listing all purchases and payments made during the billing cycle, plus any interest that may have accrued.

Finally, you should be aware of some major differences between traditional banks and online banks. The good points are pretty clear. Online banks are currently paying slightly higher interest rates, and they boast charging lower or even no fees for certain things like overdrafts or "insufficient funds" fees. Online banks also offer better ATM access than brick-and-mortar banks, in that more ATMs accept them. Using the ATMs may still incur use fees though. Overall, online banking can be easier, more portable, and possibly more profitable than traditional banking.

On the other hand, most online banks are comparatively unknown to the general public, while just about everyone in the United States has heard of banks like Chase, Citibank, and Bank of America, to name a few. Many online banks don't provide the various service "products" that traditional banks offer, like car loans, mortgages, and so on. Perhaps the biggest issue with online banking is when you are withdrawing or depositing cash. Withdrawals can be especially difficult if you need to withdraw a large amount of money at one time. Most ATMs impose a limit on the amount of money you can withdraw in one day, and those limits can range anywhere from four hundred to one thousand dollars. This could present major issues when dealing with emergencies, paying bills promptly, and more. Another concern is the possibility of having your account hacked, since most people who use online banking do it on their cell phones. If your phone is stolen, for example, you're not only losing your phone and the contacts in it, *but you're also losing your bank account information and access.*

Online banks can be subject to service interruptions when they're overwhelmed by too many account holders trying to use them simultaneously, or when they're doing data backups, or if there is a major power outage or system crash at the bank's headquarters. Lastly, most online banks provide chat bots on their websites and A.I.-run "operators" on their phone lines, and very little in the way of actual people with whom you can discuss issues. Despite the list of negative aspects, online banking is improving daily and can be considered as a viable alternative to using a traditional bank. It's your choice but be sure to do your "homework" to determine which is better for your situation.

COMPOSERS AND THE IRS

The Internal Revenue Service (IRS) is a division of the U.S. Treasury Department. It has three important functions: (1) to enforce the Internal Revenue Code (or IRC), (2) administer the federal tax laws, and (3) collect federal taxes from U.S. individual and corporate taxpayers. Their stated goal is "to provide America's taxpayers top quality service by helping them understand and meet their tax responsibilities and to enforce the law with integrity and fairness to all."[7]

The IRS tries to be fair, but like most government agencies at the federal level they're perennially and woefully understaffed and under-supported. It takes lots of people power and computer work to handle the millions of tax returns filed each year. In 2023 alone, for example, the IRS processed over *163 million* federal tax returns and supplemental documents.[8] Tax laws and the Internal Revenue Code itself changes yearly. The result is that things can, and often do, slip past the return examiners. There are just too many returns to go over in detail all at once. That said your return may be looked at more thoroughly later, several years later in fact. This is why the IRS says you should keep your records for anywhere from three years to seven years depending on the circumstances. See the IRS website for what those circumstances may be. Your accountant, on the other hand, is more likely to err on the side of caution and tell you to keep those records for the full seven years no matter what. It certainly can't hurt.

No one earning a living likes the idea of being audited, no matter how honest and thorough they are in filing their taxes. A financial audit is an official inspection of accounts or, in this case, tax returns. Probably since the IRS first opened its doors there has speculation that IRS agents "like" to audit the returns of high-profile people or, based on long-standing stereotypes, those in careers who are perceived as not paying attention to the business end of what they do or just don't understand it. Fairly or unfairly, musicians are perceived to be in that second group. According to these suppositions, all of those groups might be considered the "low hanging fruit" mentioned earlier. There is no hard evidence proving any of these conjectures though. In fact, the IRS gives certain reasons for determining who gets audited.

- First of all, the IRS says they will usually not look back more than six years to question a return. If they find something amiss in one year, though, they might decide to look back further. But hold on to those records, folks!
- Being selected for an audit doesn't always mean there is a question or problem. Sometimes, the IRS says, returns are selected randomly based on a statistical formula. When that happens, they compare your return to others to see if they fit the "norm" for that group.[9]
- But sometimes your return is selected because of some issues or transactions, not with your return but with other taxpayers whose returns were selected for audit but have some financial connection to you.
- If there is an actual problem with your return—if, for example, you didn't declare a large amount of income from one source but your payor reported it as they should—your return will probably warrant an audit.

If the IRS finds something amiss, they won't start with an audit right away. First, they will send you a letter saying you owe additional money and that you should pay it or give a reasonable explanation why you don't owe it. If things don't go well, the next step is the dreaded audit. It can be a "paper audit" in which you or your CPA has to provide specific meticulous documentation to back up the information you've provided on your tax return. This can be done by physical mail with actual documentation, or it can be accomplished electronically. Your CPA is better equipped for this and has the authority to deal with the IRS on your behalf.

Audits can also occur in person, although you don't have to go down to the local IRS office. For in-person audits an IRS agent visits you, or your accountant, to look over your records in minute detail. I can't stress this enough: if ever there was a reason to have a CPA, it's that they can represent you, much better than you can, in dealing with the IRS. See "Accountants versus Doing Your Own Taxes" below for a more in-depth discussion.

If you keep good documentation—not just a shoebox filled with receipts and scraps—and file your returns accurately and truthfully, it's less likely you'll get audited. There are other ways to keep the IRS at bay, but keeping your records properly is the first and probably most important first step.

DOCUMENTATION AND ACCURATE "CONTEMPORANEOUS RECORDS"

If you only earn a salary and have no other sources of income such as bank interest, investments, gig work, etc., filing your taxes should be fairly straightforward. But if you are a freelancer, hold multiple jobs, have investments (even one Certificate of Deposit), or in any other way have more than one source of income, your need for keeping accurate documentation is essential. That is regardless of whether you or your accountant ultimately files your tax returns. When you file a tax return the IRS (and your state if they have an income tax) first requires certain personal information.

- *Your* Social Security Number (SSN) *or* Individual Tax I.D. Number (ITIN). If anyone else is included on the return their SSN or ITIN will be needed too.
- *Bank account and routing numbers for refunds or to pay by direct deposit.*
- *Your adjust gross income* and *the exact refund amount you received from your last tax return (if any).*
- *Your name as it is on record with the Social Security Administration (SSA).* You must notify the SSA if you've changed your name.
- *Your current address, and if that is a change of address since the previous tax return was filed.*
- *If you e-filed the previous year, your* self-select PIN.[10]
- *If you were a victim of identity theft, your* IP PIN.[11]

In addition to the information above you'll need to supply certain documentation. If you're working with a CPA, you'd normally bring these documents to the accountant for entering into your return.

- *Paycheck stubs or Forms W-2 or corrected W-2.* If you're providing paycheck stubs, you may only need the last one provided for the year showing the accumulated gross earnings, total deductions for the year, and the year's net income. Consult your financial advisor (CYFA) in any case.
- *Statements from banks, payment apps or online marketplaces.* As for paycheck stubs, some of these you may only need the last statement of the year showing the amounts to date, including any interest accrued. Again, CYFA.
- *Checks paid to you.* This would be to account for single instances of payment. You might not have to provide the checks themselves but rather a contemporaneous record of having received them. Once more, CYFA.
- *Records of digital asset transactions which, for tax purposes, is any digital representation of a value recorded on a cryptographically secured, distributed ledger or similar technology.* Digital assets, for the IRS's purposes, are considered property, not money. They include cryptocurrencies like Bitcoin, non-fungible tokens (NFTs), and other similar digital objects.
- *Unemployment compensation records.*
- *Contemporaneous records.* These are records kept in one place where you record transactions of monies paid to you and monies you've paid out, when those transactions occurred, and why. Keeping and providing accurate records and documentation to the IRS is where the whole "contemporaneous records" concept comes in. Put plainly, it means to have things recorded as they occur. Daily planners, spreadsheets, anything you can reliably use to log in the date of a transaction, the amount spent or earned, the person or organization with whom you've had the transaction, and the business-related reason for it, are all useful. To prove your records are in fact useful they must:
  - *Be accurate* in the information: who, what, where, when, why, how (much).
  - *Be accessible.* You should be able to produce your records easily and in a format that can be examined easily.
  - *Be complete and comprehensive.*

Rather than file your tax returns with a "shoebox of receipts," consider creating a spreadsheet to list your expenses. You can do this in programs like Excel, Numbers, QuickBooks, and so on. A spreadsheet program will help organize data into rows and columns and can calculate the numbers as necessary. You may do one sheet per month, listing days in one direction and categories of expenditures in the other. Expense categories for composers will vary (CYFA!) and must be *only* for business, but they *may* include:

- *Legal and professional services*, including your CPA's fee.
- *Insurance premiums*, for musical instruments, computer equipment, *etc.*

- *Union dues* if you belong to the musicians' other related union.
- *Subscriptions and memberships* that are clearly business related.
- *Office expenses.*
- *Depreciation*, for property purchased for business use expected to last at least one year. Such items can't be deducted in full as a business expense in the year in which it was purchased; instead the cost is spread out over a number of years and partially deducted each year on a Schedule C.
- *Supplies.*
- *Repairs and maintenance* like piano tunings and repairs, *etc.*
- *Postage and shipping.*
- *Printing and stationery.*
- *Travel and lodging* for those out-of-town gigs, performances, and so on. These can include vehicle expenses *only if they pertain to business*, as well as the costs of dry cleaning and laundry while you're on a business trip.
- *Meals and entertainment.* Be careful with this category. *Be sure* these expenses are for business only. According to the most recent IRS rules, these expenses are only 50 percent deductible.
- *Tips.*
- *Advertising and promotion costs.* This is handy if you're self-publishing or beating the metaphorical bushes to get commissions or performances of your work.
- *Business use of your home.* Be wary with this, as IRS is a stickler for the rules. Your use of the business part of your home must be *exclusive, regular*, and *only for your business*. It must be the *principal place of business*, a place where you meet or deal with clients, customers, et al., in the normal course of your business, *and* it must be a separate structure and not attached to your home and, again, used solely in connection with your business.

If you live in an apartment and you use a second bedroom as an office and *only* as an office, you might be allowed to claim it as an expense. To do that you would have to figure out the *pro rata* share of your home's costs, that is, the portion of your mortgage or rent, etc., for the room. It's not easy to prove to the IRS's satisfaction though. If you're not sure whether you can claim the expense of having a home office—you guessed it—CYFA.

- *Taxes.* This is a complicated topic and the details change yearly, but know that certain taxes will be considered deductible.
- *Other.* This could include things like the costs of creating and maintaining a dedicated website for your compositional work, or research expenses incurred in writing a new work, advertising, bank fees, licenses, and even certain educational expenses. (And yes, please, CYFA.)

After you've entered your expenses, do *not* get rid of your receipts and other documentation. Keep them for up to seven years. You never know if or when the IRS will question an expense, so having those physical items on hand "just in case" will be helpful. Keep the year's receipts, *etc.*, together in one place, organized in some way (chronologically, for example). Once you've entered your expenses into each month's spreadsheet, create another sheet with the same categories but only with each month's totals. (For example: January Supplies, $100; February Supplies, $300; and so on.) Then have the spreadsheet calculate each category's total for the year. These totals are what the IRS expects to see.

Whatever you do, *don't exaggerate your expenses.* You must have documentation to back them up. If you don't have that documentation, the amounts must seem reasonable, that is within the norms of other people declaring similar expenses, and supported in some way (the dates of the transactions, and so on). Drastic differences in expenses from one year to the next, increased or decreased, can also trigger a "red flag" to auditors.

In Chapter 8, "Contract (Agreement) Basics," you're encouraged to incorporate clear expectations and obligations in your agreements, so both parties are fully aware of them and are legally compelled to abide by them. Those include the other party's obligation to pay you. The discussion includes suggestions as to what to do when the other party hasn't paid within the terms of your agreement. But if after you've tried everything you can think of to legally encourage payment but there has been no effect, or if the person or business entity has gone out of business and liquidated before you could lay claim to the money due you, there may be tax implications in your favor. The money you haven't received may be considered a "business bad debt," which is defined by the IRS as "a loss from the worthlessness of a debt that was either of the following: (1) created or acquired in your business, or (2) closely related to your business when it became partly or totally worthless." It's important to know that you can only take a bad debt deduction if the amount you were owed was included in your gross income "either for the year the deduction is claimed or for a prior year." It seems this is more for those using the accrual method for accounting rather than the cash method.

You can also use a spreadsheet format to organize your income. Typical categories for income can be: Wages Reported on Forms W-2; Self-Employment Income Reported on Forms 1099-NEC; Self-Employment Income Not Reported on Forms 1099-NEC; Royalties Reported on Forms 1099-MISC; Royalties Not Reported on Forms 1099-MISC; and Other Income Not Reported on Forms 1099 or W-2.[12]

ACCOUNTANTS VERSUS DOING YOUR OWN TAXES

If you want to do your own tax preparation and aren't intimidated by the prospect, and if your income streams are few and straightforward, by all means do so. There are plenty of computer programs and online apps for the purpose and many are quite good, including (but not limited to): Intuit TurboTax, H&R Block Online, and TaxSlayer. Even the IRS itself now has an online setup, IRS Free File, that lets you file directly.[13] If you decide to do your own taxes, make sure whatever program or method you're using is consistent, accurate, up to date, and secure.

That said, the repeated suggestions for having an accountant or other financial advisor (CYFA) goes double here. The more sources of income you have, no matter what the total income from those sources may be, the more likely you'll need assistance filing your taxes. CPAs are required to stay abreast of the latest tax laws and changes to the Internal Revenue Code, and they can help you file your taxes with your best interests at heart legally and ethically. They can't do that without your input, though; they need your contemporaneous records and documentation to fill things out correctly.

You read in Chapter 8 that a lawyer's services "can be expensive, but *not* having an attorney to look after your interests can be even more expensive." Double or triple those sentiments and you get close to knowing how much you need a financial person. The question, though, is "what sort of financial person do I actually need?" Your basic choices are bookkeeper, accountant, and certified public accountant. Let's look at each.

* A *bookkeeper* works on the day-to-day aspects of your finances—literally, they keep your books. They maintain your records of transactions and post credits (income) and debits (expenses). Bookkeepers can also run payroll (assuming you're not the only one involved in your business), create invoices, and more. A good bookkeeper is trained in QuickBooks and other accounting software.

Bookkeepers don't need a specific degree or credentials. They can be licensed by the American Institute of Professional Bookkeepers (AIPB) or the National Association of Certified Public Bookkeepers (NACPB). While a bookkeeper can help prepare your data for filing tax returns, they don't have the training or education in tax codes; they cannot give you tax advice, help you with tax planning, and *cannot file annual tax returns on your behalf or represent you at an IRS audit.*[14] Bookkeepers generally charge less for their services than accountants and CPAs.

* *Accountants* do everything bookkeepers do, but they can also run financial reports, prepare statements and tax returns, and even spot trends in your business you (and a bookkeeper) would otherwise miss. An accountant will have a bachelor's degree from an approved university or college and will

charge more than a bookkeeper. Accountants, like bookkeepers, cannot file a return on your behalf or represent you at IRS audits, unless they are also licensed Enrolled Agents.

* A *Certified Public Accountant (CPA)* is someone who has passed a rigorous exam and continue their education throughout their career to maintain accreditation. They *can* file returns on your behalf and *can* represent you at an IRS audit. If you suspect financial malfeasance in your accounts (or, say, in royalty statements you've received) CPAs can conduct forensic accounting to determine if that is the case and, if so, to what extent. Certified Public Accountants' training and continued education gives them an edge a bookkeeper or "regular" accountant just don't have: an intimate knowledge not only of the Internal Revenue Code and state tax laws, but also how the IRS does things. CPAs are scrupulous, meticulous, and honest—they have fiduciary responsibilities to you as a client both by law and character. As you would expect, CPAs charge more than bookkeepers or accountants.

A word should be said about tax lawyers, even though there is little likelihood of your ever needing their services. Literally, these are attorneys who specialize in tax law. They practice in all sizes of law firms, as well as in accounting businesses, corporations, and even within the IRS itself or state tax departments. The role of a tax attorney is not to deal with the actual numbers—they don't maintain your books or file your returns—but they do advise clients on how to achieve favorable tax results in different financial transactions and stay on top of the latest developments in the tax laws. They might also monitor transactions to ensure they occur as they should. Like CPAs, tax lawyers can interact with the IRS on your behalf at audits or return reviews, and when dealing with things like mergers and other transactions. Some, when necessary, defend clients in court who are being prosecuted for tax evasion and other similar crimes.

ESTATE PLANNING

No one *likes* to discuss this topic, perhaps even less so than talking about taxes, politics, or dental work, but we need to at least acknowledge it. It'll be kept simple here, but please, CYFA to learn more about how to provide for significant others, offspring, and others, not to mention how to deal financially for your own care when you get past retirement age. It is literally never too early to begin working on this. You can start by:

* *Listing your assets.* These include:

• Cash-based assets like bank accounts, brokerage accounts, IRAs, etc.
• "Hard assets" like musical instruments, art works, even some furniture.

- Property in the form of real estate, vehicles (cars, trucks, *etc.*), and boats.
  * *Listing your liabilities.* These can include:

- Secured debts, that is debt incurred through loans secured with collateral, like mortgages, car loans, and more.
- There are unsecured debts too, including personal loans and credit card debt.

* *Designating your beneficiaries.* These are the people (or institutions or organizations) whom you wish to receive your assets. You can designate beneficiaries for bank accounts and certain other cash-based assets directly, or you can do it through a will you have drawn up. Speaking of which:

* *Drawing up a will and other paperwork.* The more you have in assets the more you will need a will and the more you need an attorney to help you draw it up. There's far too much to cover here about wills but know this: a will designates an executor to handle your estate according to your instructions, designates who gets what and how, and provides for things like providing for your children if you have them and even for your pets. A will might also deal with your wishes for your funeral. (Do you want a burial or cremation? Do you want a traditional service according to your beliefs or something else? All of this and more can be included in your will.) You also need to consider things like life insurance, health directives and proxies, and much more.

Last but not least, you should determine what happens to your music once you're no longer around to control or benefit from it. One possible course of action is to secure a separate representative, a music executor if you will, on behalf of your heirs. Like an author's literary executor, yours would only administer your musical estate and be paid out of your general estate. The duties of such an executor would include managing your musical assets, overseeing its commercial exploitation (publication, licenses, etc.). The duties would need to be spelled out in your will. A musical executor can be anyone. I recommend, however, someone younger than you by at least ten years, preferably with a background in music, intellectual property law, accounting, or any combination of those. You want someone who has an idea of your work's worth, and how to handle it to your heirs' benefit. But you'll need to have a detailed meeting about this with your attorney and, possibly, your accountant as well. Bottom line? CYA/CYFA.

NOTES

1. There are many good books about personal finances available, but few are focused on musicians. I recommend *Personal Finance for Musicians* by Bobby Borg and Britt Hastey (2023, Rowman & Littlefield) as a resource. It covers some of the

same topics discussed here, but also goes into things like retirement planning, insurance, investing, and even estate issues in greater detail.

2. The IRS Publication 334 "Tax Guide for Small Business" goes into detail about what is considered income, what is considered business expenses, and more. You can download it here: **https://www.irs.gov/pub/irs-pdf/p334.pdf.**

3. The "seventeen jobs" remark is obviously an exaggeration, but on the other hand I can honestly describe myself as a composer, arranger, conductor, educator, clinician, author, performer, and a few other things. For tax purposes though, I'm simply a "musician."

4. The IRS defines "standard deduction" as "a specific dollar amount that reduces the amount of income on which you're taxed. Your standard deduction consists of the sum of the basic standard deduction and any additional standard deduction amounts for age and/or blindness." The standard deduction is adjusted each year for inflation and varies "according to your filing status, whether you're sixty-five or older and/or blind, and whether another taxpayer can claim you as a dependent." Not all taxpayers are eligible. For a better idea of how this all works see the IRS website or, better still, CYFA.

5. Your favorite symphony orchestra is most likely a 501(c)(3) charitable organization.

6. A little-known alternative to getting a money order at a bank is to get one at the U.S. Post Office.

7. **https://www.irs.gov/about-irs#:~:text=The%20IRS%20mission%20is%20to,integrity%20and%20fairness%20to%20all.**

8. **https://www.forbes.com/advisor/taxes/taxes-statistics/#:~:text=How%20many%20tax%20returns%20are,tax%20returns%20and%20supplemental%20documents.**

9. You can learn more here about audit selection and how to prepare for an audit: **https://www.irs.gov/businesses/small-businesses-self-employed/irs-audits**. Your accountant, assuming you have one, would be of better assistance.

10. The self-select PIN (SSP) requires a five-digit PIN that can be any five numbers except all zeros that you choose to serve as your electronic signature. If using the SSP you must also enter your date of birth and either your prior year's SSP or your "original prior year adjusted gross income." Joint returns require each person to enter their own SSP to sign.

11. An Identity Protection PIN (IP PIN) is a six-digit number used to prevent others from filing tax returns using your Social Security Number or Individual Taxpayer Identification Number. The IP PIN is known only to you and the IRS Once you're confirmed as a victim of tax-related identity theft and your tax account issues have been resolved, you'll receive a notice with your new IP PIN each year. (You don't have to wait to have your identity stolen to apply for an IP PIN; anyone with a SSN or ITIN can get one, even if you're living abroad.) You can apply online or your CPA can do so on your behalf (with you filling out the paperwork). Also, you might be issued an IP PIN without having applied for one if the IRS has discovered you were the victim of someone else's tax fraud.

12. Form W-2 is the IRS form employers send to you *and* the IRS each year, reporting an employee's annual wages and the taxes withheld. Form 1099-NEC is used for "non-employee compensation," that is money earned as an independent contractor or freelancer *if* you have earned $600 or more from one person or business during the calendar year. Form 1099-MISC covers income to nonemployees in the forms of rent, prizes, healthcare payments, royalties, and more. PROs, for example, send members and the IRS Forms 1099-MISC showing how much in performance royalties they have sent. See the IRS website for more information, or just—you guessed it—CYFA.

13. **https://www.irs.gov/filing/free-file-do-your-federal-taxes-for-free.**

14. The only way for a bookkeeper to file a return on your behalf is to become an IRS-licensed Enrolled Agent. "Enrolled agents are subject to a suitability check and must pass a three-part Special Enrollment Examination, which is a comprehensive exam that requires them to demonstrate proficiency in federal tax planning, individual and business tax return preparation, and representation. They must complete 72 hours of continuing education every 3 years."

Chapter 11

USEFUL WEBSITES

COMPOSER ORGANIZATIONS

American Composers Forum, The   https://composersforum.org
Dramatists Guild, The   https://www.dramatistsguild.com
   For composers, lyricists, and librettists of musical dramatic works.
League of Composers/International Society for   http://leagueofcomposers.org
   Contemporary Music
New Music USA   https://newmusicusa.org
Society of Composers, Inc.   http://www.societyofcomposers.org
International Center for American Music, The   http://www.icamus.org/en/

COPYRIGHT INFORMATION

Copyright Alliance   https://copyrightalliance.org
Copyright Clearance Center   https://www.copyright.com
History of Copyright   http://www.historyofcopyright.org/pb/wp_fe548a29/
                          wp_fe548a29.html
   This provides a good general introduction to the history of copyrights and copyright law.
ISBN.org   https://www.isbn.org
   "ISBN" is the International Standard Book Number for published books.
U.S. Copyright Office   https://www.copyright.gov
   Where you can find all of the information and forms you need to protect your music. Some specific links are given in the footnotes of Chapter 1, "Copyright."

U.S. Copyright Royalty Board   https://www.crb.gov
    For information about mechanical royalties.
U.S. ISMN Agency   https://www.loc.gov/ismn/
"ISMN" is the International Standard Music Number for published music,
similar to the ISBN (International Standard Book Number) assigned to published books.

INTERNAL REVENUE SERVICE (IRS), TAX INFORMATION, AND OTHER FINANCIAL INFORMATION

Association of International Certified   https://www.aicpa-cima.com/about/
    Professional Accountants (AICPA)   landing/about
Federal Deposit Insurance Corporation (FDIC)   https://www.fdic.
                                                              gov/index.php/
MacArthur Foundation   https://www.macfound.org
Royalty Exchange   https://www.royaltyexchange.com/?_ga=1.159633983
                                                  .361740511.1489153659
    An interesting but mostly little-known service that, to quote their home
page, asks you to join "30,000 registered investors and make offers directly
on hundreds of royalty assets – from music catalogs to trademark royalties."
This might be of interest to those overseeing the estate of a deceased composer or songwriter.
U.S. Internal Revenue Service (IRS)   https://www.irs.gov
    For all information and forms relating to federal income tax and other
related topics.
U.S. Social Security Administration   https://www.ssa.gov
    For all information and forms relating to Social Security and related topics.

LEGAL INFORMATION

American Bar Association/Legal   https://www.americanbar.org/groups/
Services Division   legal_services/flh-home/
    The American Bar Association (ABA) is a national membership organiza-
tion comprised of attorneys whose intention is to promote legal and ethical
foundations in the practice of law. This specific page is open to nonmembers
searching for legal help. Sources are provided for those who qualify as low-
income, active-duty servicemembers and veterans, and people who need
"unbiased referrals to affordable lawyers." (Partial quote from the website.)

Avvo   https://www.avvo.com
   An online clearinghouse of sorts for those in search of attorneys in their location and/or expertise in specific areas of law. Avvo is part of Martindale-Avvo as part of Internet Brands.
National Directory of Volunteer   https://vlany.org/national-directory
   Lawyers for the Arts Organizations   -of-volunteer-lawyers-for-the-arts/
Freelancers Union   https://freelancersunion.org
   A nonprofit organization serving freelancers across the U.S., providing "education, advocacy . . . tools and benefits regardless of industry or income level." (Quoted from the website.)
Lawyer Legion/Attorney Directories   https://www.lawyerlegion.com/
   by State Bar Associations   promote-your-law-practice/
                                                   directories-by-state-bar
   A listing of directories of attorneys belonging to state bar associations. From there you can search your own state's listing of attorneys to find a suitable law-yer in your area and with the necessary skill set to work on your behalf.
Volunteer Lawyers for the Arts (New York City)   https://vlany.org

MISCELLANEOUS USEFUL INFORMATION

Bandworld   https://www.bandworld.org
   The site states that it is "dedicated to helping band students and directors worldwide," and it is the source of the grading chart mentioned in Chapter 6, "Publishing Your Music."
Cleveland Clinic   https://my.clevelandclinic.org
   This is the general URL for the Cleveland Clinic, whose report on multi-tasking is mentioned in Chapter 5, "The Gig."
Game Developer   https://www.gamedeveloper.com
Symphonic Blog   https://blog.symphonic.com
University of Oregon Libraries   https://opentext.uoregon.edu/
                                                   payforplay/front-matter/cover/
   Starting on this page you can access the book *Pay for Play: How the Music Industry Works, Where the Money Goes, and Why* for free as of this writing.

MUSIC NOTATION AND RELATED COMPUTER
APPLICATIONS

Note: Music notation and audio programs come and go with surprising frequency. The links listed here are current as of this writing.

Audacity (free audio editor/recorder)   https://sourceforge.net/projects/
                                                        audacity/
Dorico (music notation program)   https://www.steinberg.net/dorico/
Faber Music   https://www.fabermusic.com

In addition to being a music publisher (based in the United Kingdom), Faber Music is the publisher of some of the most useful books on music notation currently available, such as "Behind Bars, the Definitive Guide to Music Notation" (which is not hyperbole), and "Behind Bars: General Conventions (Theory)" (drawn from the full "Behind Bars" book for students). Both books are available in the United States.

Finale (music notation program)   https://www.finalemusic.com

Support for Finale was discontinued as of August 2024. This site may not exist by the time this book is published, but there may be redirects to other useful sites at that time for those who still use the program.

MuseScore (music notation program)   https://musescore.org/en
Noteflight (music notation program)   https://www.noteflight.com
Notion (music notation program)   https://legacy.presonus.com/products/
Notion/downloads
Sibelius (music notation program)   https://www.avid.com/sibelius

MUSIC PUBLISHING INFORMATION

Harry Fox Agency, The (HFA)   https://www.harryfox.com
For information about and use of mechanical licenses for physical reproduction of music. HFA is owned by SESAC.

Major Orchestra Librarians' Association (MOLA)   https://mola-inc.org/
                                                        resources/11631
The link is to the "MOLA Guidelines for Music Preparation." It is available in Chinese (2 forms), English, French, Japanese, Korean, and Spanish.

Mechanical Licensing Collective, The (The MLC) https://www.themlc.com
For information about and use of mechanical licenses for digital reproduction of music.

Music Publishers Association   https://www.mpa.org
Public Domain Information Project   https://www.pdinfo.com

PERFORMING RIGHTS ORGANIZATIONS (PROS)

ASCAP (Association of Composers,   https://www.ascap.com
Authors, and Publishers)

BMI (Broadcast Music, Inc.)   https://www.bmi.com
SESAC (Society of European Stage   https://www.sesac.com
Authors and Composers)

PRINTING

A note for self-publishers: There are many ways to print music; hundreds of businesses advertise that capability. Printing can be done at home with a laser or inkjet printer, with binding done as simply or intricately as you wish depending on your needs, budget, and skills. Your local print shop, Staples, FedEx Office, and so on can do the job at least as well as you can and a bit more cost effective if producing more than a few copies of your music at one time. Fully professional printers, a couple of which are listed below, are even more useful and cheaper (per unit) than your local shop for producing large quantities of sheet music or complex jobs like sets of scores and parts for symphonic orchestra or band compositions. One little-known fact is that some traditional publishers and even sheet music dealers print their own music or materials, and can make those services available to outside businesses. Knowing which companies are doing this and getting the right information will take some initiative and persistence in research.

Britannica   https://www.britannica.com

The general URL for the online version of what was once the most extensive encyclopedia in print, *The Encyclopedia Britannica*. See https://www.britannica.com/topic/printing-publishing for an interesting article on the history of printing and more modern printing techniques. See also https://www.britannica.com/technology/paper for information about paper.

American Forest & Paper Association   https://www.afandpa.org

For more detailed information about paper, how it's produced, and more.

Doxzoo   https://doxzoo.com/en-us/documents/music-score-printing

Although based in the United Kingdom, Doxzoo maintains a U.S. presence. They claim to do everything but the printing itself online, offering a wide range of standard paper sizes, weights, and textures, as well as different paper finishes and binding styles.

Engraver's Mark Music   https://www.engraversmarkmusic.com/
                                                                print-shop.html

The link takes you directly to Engraver's Mark's Music Print Services page. The company is based in Nashville, Tennessee, offers a wide selection of paper sizes, weights, and textures, and various methods of binding and finishing. The overall site (https://www.engraversmarkmusic.com) offers "full service music preparation for print and digital publication" (according to the website).

SELECTED BIBLIOGRAPHY

This bibliography is by no means a complete record of the sources and works I have consulted in writing *The Concert Composer's Business Handbook*. The books cited are the editions I have used; there may be subsequent editions available. Also note that several books listed for one chapter should be considered in others as well. The Kohn and Kohn book on music licensing, for example, is listed under the chapter on income streams but is also useful in researching contract basics. Finally, comments are occasionally given in a listing to explain the book's inclusion.

1. COPYRIGHT

Association of American Publishers, Inc. *Questions & Answers on Copyright for the Campus Community*, 7th Edition. Washington, DC, 2006.

Rae, Casey. *Music Copyright: An Essential Guide for the Digital Age*. Rowman & Littlefield Publishing Group, Inc. Lanham, MA, 2021.

United States Copyright Office. *Circular 1: Copyright Basics*. Washington, DC, 2024.

— *Circular 3: Copyright Notice*. Washington, DC, 2024.

— *Circular 15A: Duration of Copyright*. Washington, DC, 2024.

— *Circular 38A: International Copyright Relations of the United States*. Washington, DC, 2024.

2. INCOME STREAMS: DEFINITIONS AND EXPLANATIONS

Not all of the sources mentioned here apply directly to concert music composers but may be useful nevertheless.

Brabec, Todd and Jeff Brabec. *Music, Money, Success and the Movies: The Basics of "Music in Film" Deals.* ASCAP. New York, NY, 2002. The information was "obtained from the revised paperback edition of the book *MUSIC, MONEY AND SUCCESS: THE INSIDER'S GUIDE TO MAKING MONEY IN THE MUSIC INDUSTRY* by Todd Brabec and Jeff Brabec (Schirmer Trade Books/MusicSales. New York, NY, 2002). This focuses mostly on synchronization licensing.

Chertkow, Randy and Jason Feehan. *Making Money with Music: Generate Over 100 Revenue Streams, Grow Your Fan Base, and Thrive in Today's Music Environment.* St. Martin's Griffin. New York, NY, 2018. Mostly for pop musicians but much of the information is useful for concert composers as well.

Davis, Richard. *Complete Guide to Film Scoring: The Art and Business of Writing Music for Movies and TV, 2ⁿᵈ Edition.* Berklee Press/Hal Leonard. Boston, MA, 2010.

Hawkins, Kris. *The Working Musician's Handbook for Professional Success.* Rowman & Littlefield Publishing Group, Inc. Lanham, MA, 2022.

Horowitz, Steve and Scott R. Looney. *The Theory and Practice of Writing Music for Games.* CRC Press/Taylor and Francis Group. Boca Raton, FL, 2024.

Kohn, Al and Bob Kohn. *Kohn on Music Licensing, 4ᵗʰ Edition (with CD-ROM).* Aspen Publishers. Waltham, MA, 2009.

Radbill, Catherine Fitterman. *Introduction to the Music Industry: An Entrepreneurial Approach.* Routledge. New York, NY, and Abingdon, Oxon, UK, 2013

Singer, Dana. *Stage Writers Handbook.* Theatre Communications Group, Inc. New York, NY, 1997. Useful information for creators of musical theater works.

3. PERFORMING RIGHTS ORGANIZATIONS (PROS)

While there seem to be no books dealing specifically with PROs, the books by Chertkow and Feehan, Kohn and Kohn, Stim, and Williams are all good sources of information. The best and most up to date information you can get is from the Performing Rights Organizations themselves: ASCAP, BMI, and SESAC. See Chapter 11, "Useful Websites," for their respective URLs.

4. PRESENTING AND PROMOTING YOURSELF AS A COMPOSER (PREPARING TO GET LUCKY)

Papolos, Janice. *The Performing Artist's Handbook.* Writer's Digest Books, an imprint of F&W Publications. Cincinnati, OH. 1984. Note: Long out of print but some libraries still have copies and used copies may be found on online book sites for sale.

5. THE GIG

This chapter was mostly based on personal experience, with references to the books and other sources already mentioned. I list one useful book on scheduling here, but others are available and equally good.

Various authors, Jocelyn K. Glei, ed. *Manage Your Day-to-Day: Build Your Routine, Find Your Focus, and Sharpen Your Creative Mind.* Amazon Publishing. New York, NY, 2013.

6. PUBLISHING YOUR MUSIC

Carl Fischer, Inc. *Carl Fischer, Inc.: 1872–1972, 100 Years of Progress.* New York, NY, 1972.

Krummel, D.W. and Stanley Sadie, eds. *The Norton/Grove Handbooks in Music: Music Printing and Publishing.* The Macmillan Press, Ltd. Hampshire, England, and New York, NY, 1990.

Poe, Randy. *A Songwriter's Guide to Music Publishing.* Writer's Digest Books. Cincinnati, OH, 1990.

Winogradsky, Steve. *Music Publishing: The Complete Guide.* Alfred Music. Van Nuys, CA, 2013.

7. PRESENTING YOUR MUSIC

There are far too many books on music notation, both general and specifically for new concert music, to list here. But for presenting your music visually in the best possible way, you cannot go wrong with the books by Gould and by Ross.

Gould, Elaine. *Behind Bars: The Definitive Guide to Music Notation.* Faber Music. London, UK, 2011.

Ross, Ted. *The Art of Music Engraving & Processing, 2nd Edition*. Hansen Books. Miami Beach, FL, 1970. Note: Long out of print but some libraries may have copies and used copies may be found on online book sites for sale.

International Paper Company, Frank Romano and Michael Riordan, eds. *Pocket Pal, 21st Edition: The Handy Book of Graphic Arts Production*. International Paper Company. Memphis, TN, 2019. This is a truly handy compendium of information about paper, printing, binding, and more. This edition is out of print and there doesn't seem to be a later one issued. It is worth owning if you're self-publishing (or just interested) if you can find a copy through the usual online sources.

8. CONTRACT (AGREEMENT) BASICS

Gordon, Steve. *The 11 Contracts That Every Artist, Songwriter, and Producer Should Know*. Hal Leonard Books, an imprint of Hal Leonard LLC. Milwaukee, WI, 2017.

Stim, Rich. *Music Law: How to Run Your Band's Business, 10th Edition*. Nolo Publishing. Pleasanton, CA, 2021.

Williams, David R. *The Enterprising Musician's Legal Toolkit*. Rowman & Littlefield Publishing Group, Inc. Lanham, MA, 2020.

9. FOLLOW UP

Beeching, Angela Myles. *Beyond Talent: Creating a Successful Career in Music, 3rd Edition*. Oxford University Press. New York, NY, and Oxford, UK, 2020.

Pettigrew, Jr., Jim. *The Billboard Guide to Music Publicity*. Billboard Books, an imprint of Watson-Guptill Publications. New York, NY, 1989. Note: Long out of print but some libraries still have copies and used copies may be found on online book sites for sale.

10. FINANCES

Borg, Bobby and Britt Hastey. *Personal Finance for Musicians*. Rowman & Littlefield Publishing Group, Inc. Lanham, MA, 2022.

Tyson, Eric. *Personal Finance for Dummies, 10th edition*. For Dummies. New York, NY, 2023.

GLOSSARY

Acceptance, in contracts

The act of the person on the receiving end of a contract, in which the recipient consents to the terms and conditions of the agreement.

Accountant

An accountant keeps and maintains financial records, as well as run financial reports, prepare statements and tax returns and, depending on the circumstances, spot income or expenditure trends in a client's business. Accountants cannot file returns on your behalf or represent you at an IRS audit unless they are an Enrolled Agent.

Agent, composer's

An agent or representative who works on your behalf to help you get work. Composer agents are rare in the classical music world but are more common in the movie, television, and video game industries.

Arrangement, arranger

An existing work that is rescored, reharmonized, or otherwise adapted from its original form into something still recognizable but different. The person who creates it is called an arranger.

ASCAP

ASCAP is a Performing Rights Organization (PRO). The name refers to the "American Society of Composers, Authors, and Publishers," with "authors" meaning lyricists. It is owned by its membership and is not-for-profit.

Audit

The systematic examination, inspection, and assessment of an organization's or individual's accounts, most often to ensure those accounts are properly maintained, and are in compliance with the Internal Revenue Code (IRS), as well as any state or city laws. The IRS can conduct audits of federal income tax returns.

Automated Teller Machine (ATM)

A machine allowing a banking customer to perform basic transactions such as making deposits, withdrawing cash, and checking balances without having to go to a physical bank branch. ATMs are accessed using the customer's personalized bank card (also called a "debit card"). A bank's ATM will generally not impose a usage fee on the bank's own customers to access the machine. ATMs owned by a bank or other financial institution may impose a fee to conduct a transaction for someone who is not that bank's or institution's customer.

Awareness, in contracts

The act of both parties to a contract, in which they acknowledge they are entering into the agreement, that they are each doing so of their own free will, and that they are each actively participating in the process.

Bank, online

A financial institution with no "brick-and-mortar" physical presence in which most customer-facing transactions occur. Online banks rely on web sites, ATMs, and phone and other apps to interact with customers and have those customers conduct business.

Bank, traditional

A financial institution with a physical presence in the form of a "brick-and-mortar" building in which most customer-facing transactions occur. If a bank has more than one such building, each is called a "branch." Traditional banks may also have ATMs on and off premises, and may have online banking available.

Binding

The method by which collections of more than one sheet of paper are kept together intact. Binding methods include saddle-stitching, perfect or PUR binding, hardcover or case binding, and Coptic stitch binding.

Blanket license

A license negotiated and issued by a Performing Rights Organization (PRO) to a performance venue, restaurant or bar, television or radio station, or in other similar situations, to cover all performances of music covered by the PRO. Blanket license fees are based on the type and size of the venue or medium.

BMI

Literally "Broadcast Music, Inc.," BMI is a Performing Rights Organization (PRO). It is privately owned and considered "for profit."

Bookkeeper

A bookkeeper keeps and maintains financial records, usually for businesses. Bookkeepers do not require specific degrees or credentials, but they can be licensed by the American Institute of Professional Bookkeepers. A bookkeeper can help prepare tax returns for filing but does not have training or education in tax codes, and cannot give tax advice. Bookkeepers also cannot file tax returns on your behalf, give tax advice, or represent you at an IRS audit.

Call for scores

A request, usually from performers, for musical works that are appropriate to the performers' needs. Call for scores may require a small fee from the composer.

Capacity, in contracts

The participant's legal capacity to sign an agreement including the ability to be aware of and understand the terms, obligations, and consequences of the contract.

Certificate of Deposit (CD)

A financial product that has a fixed term with an average range of one month to five years, unlike savings accounts which have no fixed terms. In many cases CDs yield a higher rate of interest than savings accounts.

Certified Public Accountant (CPA)

A Certified Public Accountant is someone who has passed a rigorous exam and maintains accreditation through ongoing education throughout their career. CPAs can file returns on your behalf and represent you at an IRS tax audit. CPAs generally have intimate knowledge of tax codes at the federal, state, and local levels. Certified Public Accountants have, by law, fiduciary responsibility and must do what is legally and ethically in the best interests of their clients.

Commission

A composition commission is a request by one party (the "commissioner") for the second party (the "composer") to create a new work, usually in exchange for a performance, a commissioning fee, or both. Commissions can be informal ("handshake deals") or formalized in a commissioning contract.

Commissioning fee

The money paid to a composer to create a new composition.

Consideration, in contracts

What each party to a contract "brings to the table," what each promises to the other.

Consortium commission

A request by a group of commissioners (the consortium) for a composer to create a single new work. Each member of the consortium pays the composer the same predetermined amount except the lead commissioner, if any, who pays more in exchange for the right to give the world premiere. In most cases consortiums make commissioning affordable for the commissioners while providing the composer with proper compensation for the work to be done.

Contemporaneous records
Records—kept in one place—of transactions of monies paid to you and monies you've paid out, when those transactions occurred, and why.

Contract, also agreement
The formalization of a relationship between two parties, and of each participant's obligations to the other.

Copyright
Copyright is a type of intellectual property that gives its owner the exclusive right to copy, distribute, adapt, print, publish, perform, or record an original work, or to authorize others to do the same. Copyrights are applied to created original works, including literary works, visual art works (whether two-dimensional, three-dimensional, or in a digital format) and, of course, musical works. Copyright is automatically granted to works put into "fixed form," but registering a copyright with the Copyright Office of the Library of Congress helps ensure the full protection of U.S. copyright laws.

Copyright notice
A copyright notice is a literal notice on the fixed form of a created work, that it is protected by U.S. copyright law. Copyright notices consist of the symbol "©" followed by the year of the work's creation or copyright claim and the name of the copyright claimant (usually the composer). Copyright notices have not been required on musical works since 1989, but their use is recommended.

Copyright Royalty Board (CRB)
A panel of three copyright royalty judges that sets mechanical royalty rates for five-year periods.

Credit card
A card used to make purchases on a loan basis, limited by the card issuer's determination of your line of credit. Purchases are made by borrowing money from the card's issuing financial institution. Interest accrues on purchases not paid back in a timely manner.

CYA
Consult your attorney.

CYFA
Consult your financial advisor.

Debit card, also bank card, ATM card
A card that is used to make purchases by drawing funds directly from the card holder's account at the issuing financial institution. Debit cards also function as bank or ATM cards, allowing the card holder to conduct other transactions at ATMs.

Deduction, itemized
A reduction in the amount of income on which you are taxed at the federal level, based on a full listing of tax-deductible expenses incurred for business purposes in a given year.

Deduction, standard

The IRS defines "standard deduction" as "a specific dollar amount that reduces the amount of income on which you're taxed [at the federal level in a given year]." Eligibility to claim a standard deduction changes yearly and not all taxpayers qualify.

Digital Streaming Provider (DSP)

A service which offers music and other audio in streaming format.

Documentation, financial

Financial documentation consists of all receipts, contemporaneous records, and other documents which track what income you've earned and what expenses you've incurred for business purposes in a given year. Such documentation is used to complete income tax forms.

Download, downloading

The delivery of audio or audiovisual files over the internet, to be retained on a computer, phone, or other device for playback.

Employment status

Employment status is a definition of what you do to earn income for tax purposes. Work done as an employee is done on a continued basis for an employer under supervision at a specified rate of pay; the income earned is paid on a regular basis. Self-employment is work done by hiring out your services on a one-time or short-term basis, and you are not regularly supervised; income is paid once the work is completed or through other arrangements agreed upon in advance. A person can be both an employee and self-employed depending on the circumstances.

Enrolled Agent

Someone granted permission by the IRS to represent taxpayers at audits after having passed a three-part comprehensive test or by being a former employee of the IRS.

Estate planning

Estate planning is the organization of a person's financial assets and liabilities with specific preparations for their use and distribution once the person is retired or deceased.

Expenses

Expenses are monies spent for business or personal reasons.

Fair use

Probably the least understood concept in copyright law and most poorly defined. The term *fair use* is used to describe the allowance for small portions of a copyrighted creative work to be used for certain reasons under particular circumstances. These usually involve educational purposes but are not limited to them.

Federal Deposit Insurance Corporation (FDIC)

A federal agency that insures bank account holders their money will be available no matter what occurs, up to a certain limit. As of 2024 the standard insurance amount is $250,000 per depositor, per insured bank, and for each account ownership category. For example, if you have three accounts at three different FDIC-insured banks, each with $25,000, the FDIC would cover your money up to $75,000 if, say, all three banks were to fold or be robbed simultaneously.

Fixed form

A physical or digital form of a musical work that can be accessed directly (looking at sheet music) or via mechanical means (reading a file on a computer screen), but cannot be easily changed. Music handwritten in pencil can be changed easily with an eraser and a good pencil, but a score printed by a laser printer cannot be changed anywhere near as easily.

Gig

A musician's term for a job. Most recently the connotations have been broadened beyond the music business to mean any sort of temporary or freelance work, often with informal implications.

Grade level, for educational works

The amount of technique needed to perform certain musical works, ranked into five or six levels corresponding to the number of years an instrumentalist or vocalist has studied.

Grand rights

The right to perform a dramatic work with music that is intended for the stage, including operas, operettas, musicals, oratorios, ballets and other dance performances, and other theatrical works. Grand rights are secured by a production to have any of these types of works performed.

Grant

Money given based on an applicant's track record and/or potential for success in their work

Harmonice Musices Odhecaton

Literally *One Hundred Songs of Harmonic Music* (1501), this was the first collection of polyphonic music published using movable type. The collection was published by Ottaviano Petrucci in Venice, Italy.

Harry Fox Agency (HFA), the

The Harry Fox Agency, established in 1927, negotiates and issues licenses on behalf of music publishers and composers for the use of their music for mechanical reproduction via physical products such as records, CDs, audiotapes, and more.

Income

Money earned through wages, fees, royalties, or investments.

Infringement

Infringement is the use of a copyright-protected work without permission.

Intellectual property

Any object or intangible creation that is the result of human intelligence. The main types of intellectual property are trademarks (recognizable signs, designs, or expressions used to identify products or services), patents (for protecting the exclusivity of inventions), and copyrights (for creative works of art, whether literary, artistic, musical, and so on).

Internal Revenue Service (IRS)

The IRS, a division of the U.S. Treasury Department, is charged with enforcing the Internal Revenue Code, administering the federal tax laws, and collecting federal taxes from U.S. individual and corporate taxpayers.

Invoice

An invoice is a bill for goods or services, listing those goods or services, the amount of money due for them, and other information.

Legality, in contracts

The legality of a contract consists of two factors. The first is a contract must comply with the laws within the jurisdiction where it is to be enforced, usually in the state where the agreement is drawn up. The second factor is the acknowledgment that agreements involving illegal activity in the form of products or services are considered unenforceable.

License

In general terms, a license is an agreement in which one party is given formal or official permission to do something specific. A driver license, for example, gives the licensee permission to operate a motor vehicle. Licenses are granted in exchange for monies, goods, services, or (as in the case of a driver license) having proven qualified for them.

Mechanical license

A license giving permission to use a piece of music in the making of a sound recording, in exchange for an agreed upon rate known as a mechanical royalty. There are two types of mechanical licenses, one for physical products such as Compact Discs or vinyl (analog) records, and the other for digital recordings distributed as downloads or through streaming.

Mechanical Licensing Collective (The MLC), The

The Mechanical Licensing Collective (The MLC), established in 2018, negotiates and issues licenses on behalf of music publishers and composers for the use of their music for mechanical reproduction via digital products such as streaming and downloads.

MIDI demo, also audio mockup

A sound recording of a musical work, demonstrating its musical potential to potential buyers of the work's sheet music. MIDI demos are created using computer programs rather than live musicians.

Moral rights

The composers' right or ability to control the fate of the works they create, no matter who claims the copyright.

Network, networking

To network is to connect and interact with others, specifically to develop social or business contacts, or to exchange or acquire information.

Offer, in contracts

A statement of what one party to the agreement is willing to be obligated to do or provide within the terms of the agreement.

Party, in contracts

A named participant in a business transaction formalized in writing as an agreement or contract. Any contract requires a minimum of two parties.

Payee

The person or business being paid in a transaction.

Payor

The person or business paying in a transaction.

Performance

The act of presenting a musical work to be heard. Performances can be "live," presented by musicians for listeners to hear as the music is performed, or recorded and heard later.

Performing Rights Organization (PRO)

An organization or business that collects performance fees from various sources (live venues, television stations, etc.) and distributes them to their composer, lyricist, and publisher members as performance royalties. Performing Rights Organizations (PROs) work to protect their members and help ensure they are compensated for performances of the works they create. There are three PROs in the United States:ASCAP, BMI, and SESAC.

Permission

The consent or authorization given by one party to another to accomplish something. A license is a formal form of permission that usually requires a payment by the licensee, but not all permissions granted require payment or other considerations.

Plagiarism

Plagiarism is the false claim of a work's creation and/or ownership.

POP

Literally "permanently out of print." This is the situation in which a music publisher's stock of a work has run out but there is no intention to print more copies for sale.

Press release

An official statement issued to print, audio, and audiovisual news media to provide information on specific matters or to make an important announcement. In journalism, press releases are considered a "primary source" of information.

Print on demand

Music that is printed only when it is ordered for purchase. This is possible due to the digitalization of sheet music; the music is kept in the form of high-quality PDFs and printed as needed. No additional copies need be kept, keeping warehousing needs to a minimum.

Public Domain (PD)

The term *Public Domain* (or PD) describes works not protected, or no longer protected, by U.S. copyright laws. Works are considered PD when their original copyright has expired, in most cases when the work is produced by the U.S. federal government, when a work is not in a tangible "fixed form," works with no original author (such as certain folk songs) or, if the work was created prior to March 1, 1989, if the work was not given a proper copyright notice.

Public Service Announcement (PSA)

A short message written as a script or recorded for playback, distributed without charge to audio and audiovisual media to raise awareness about an issue, an event, or to help change behavior.

Publish, publication (music)

To prepare a musical work for dissemination and availability via printing and distribution of sheet music or by other means. This can be done by a company specializing in the production and sales or rental of sheet music—publishers—or by the creators of the works themselves. (See "Self-publish" below.)

Retail price

The price a consumer pays for a particular product, such as sheet music. The publisher of such a product sets the retail price (either as a "suggested retail price" or a hardline one) at the product's release. If the publisher doesn't sell directly to the consumer but through a store or other party, that additional party pays the publisher a reduced "wholesale price."

Review

A formal assessment and critical appraisal of a creative work.

Royalty

Money paid to a composer and/or publisher of a musical work for the sale of sheet music, or earnings from performance of the work, recordings ("mechanical royalties"), or other uses.

Sampling, sample

Sampling is the use of a fragment of one work for use in another, different work. Unlike plagiarism in which a whole work is claimed to be by another party than the one who actually created it, sampling uses specific ideas or recordings within a larger new composition. Unless the sample is Public Domain, a license must be obtained to be used legally.

Schedule

The organization of a list of tasks to be done according to a timeline.

Scholarship

Money given to a student who is currently enrolled or just entering a specific program in a college, university, or conservatory. The money is solely to support the student's education and is considered based on the student's academic record or other achievements.

Score order

The order in which a work for more than instrument or voice is presented in visual form. The general order is shown from top down as winds, brass, percussion, "other," and strings. The "other" consists of any unusual instruments followed by any solo or choral voices. Score order breaks down further, again generally, from highest ranged instrument/voice to lowest within each category.

Self-publish (music)

The preparation and distribution of music done by the creator of the work.

SESAC

Now known only by the acronym "SESAC," this Performing Rights Organization (PRO) began as the Society of European Stage Authors and Composers. It is privately owned and considered "for profit."

Sheet music

The visual representation of a musical work in fixed form and distributed either as physical paper products or as downloads for use on tablets and other digital equipment. Musicians, especially those who perform classical music, rely heavily on sheet music.

Small rights

"Small rights" is a sort of back-formation term, used in opposition to "grand rights" and is not used legally or in everyday business within the music industry. Nevertheless, it refers to any musical work that is not considered "dramatic," and it entails the rights to perform and otherwise use the music.

Streaming

The delivery of audio or audiovisual media over the internet instantly but not permanently. Files are delivered as small packets of data to be read and played by a consumer's streaming application, but the files are not retained or saved.

Synchronization ("Synch") license

A license to use copyrighted music in an audiovisual work. Two licenses are usually needed, one for the music itself and one for the recording of the music if using the original recorded performance.

Tax

A compulsory contribution to federal, state, and/or local governments. Federal taxes include income tax, Medicare, and Social Security.

Title

The name of a musical work (or other creative work). Titles cannot be copyrighted.

TOP

Literally, "temporarily out of print." This is the situation in which a music publisher's stock of a work has run out but there is an intention to print more copies for sale.

Use

"Use" is the term that describes the exploitation of music for financial or other benefit in all ways except performance. Mechanical licenses, publication, and synchronization licenses are all examples of "use."

Wholesale price

The price paid to a publisher by a music dealership or other business operating between the publisher and the consumer. Wholesale prices are considerably smaller than the retail price the consumer pays, most often by half.

Work for hire

A work created for which you have turned over all rights, including but not limited to copyright, to a third party.

Wrapper

A stiff paper front-and-back cover for a sheet music product consisting of a score and separate multiple parts. The wrapper is printed with the name of the work, the composer and other writer credits as needed, the publisher's name and any catalog information.

Appendix A
SUGGESTED COMMISSION TIMELINE

Commission Negotiations:

The determination, and mutual agreement, of the details of a commission, worked out by the composer and commissioning party. The negotiations should be completed in a timely manner to ensure that there is enough time for the composer to complete the commissioned work and for the performers to receive, rehearse, and premiere it once it is composed. The premiere date must be set at this point in the timeline to work out the optimum timing for the intervening stages between the formal agreement and the premiere.

Signing of the Commissioning Agreement:

This should happen as soon as both parties have agreed on all major points of the commission and the formal contract has been drawn up. Depending on the situation, the signing of a commissioning agreement may also signal the payment of the first portion of a commissioning fee, if any, to the composer.

Delivery of the Score:

Depending on the complexity and length of the score, the delivery of the score can be a few weeks to a few months prior to the delivery of the parts, and it may also initiate payment of the final portion of a commissioning fee, if any, to the composer.

Delivery of Parts:

Contingent on the musicians involved, the delivery of the parts could be from a few weeks to several months prior to the premiere. The musicians

must have sufficient time to rehearse the music prior to the premiere performance; this timing must be determined during the negotiation process.
Works for educational ensembles may require a longer lead time between
receiving the parts and the performance to accommodate academic calendars
and schedules.

Premiere:

The date of the first public performance of the work.

Appendix B
SAMPLE COMMISSIONING AGREEMENT

The sample agreement below is typical of commissioning agreements I use, but not everything is presented "as is" or is included every time. What is important is defining who is involved (presented in the first paragraph), what is to be done and for what compensation (shown in Item #1), and what the obligations and expectations are for each participating party (indicated in the rest of the agreement).

AGREEMENT MADE THIS (date) of (month), (year), between the [Commissioning Party Name], (hereafter "Commissioner"), [full address of Commissioning Party], and [Your Name], (hereafter "Composer") of [your full address], for the composition of a work for [forces: orchestra, band, etc.], to be premiered by [performer names].

1. COMMISSIONER hereby commissions COMPOSER to compose a work for [forces]. In making this commission, Commissioner agrees:
   A. To pay Composer a commissioning fee of (amount in words) ($ amount in numerals) dollars for the composition of the musical work and the delivery of a fair copy of the score and one set of parts.
   B. Commissioner further agrees to pay Composer an advance of one half of the agreed-upon commissioning fee upon the signing of this agreement by both parties. Commissioner agrees to pay Composer the balance of the commissioning fee upon the delivery of the completed musical score.
   C. All aspects of composition of the work are to be determined solely by Composer, including but not limited to: the title of the work, the number of movements, the musical language or style, the duration of the work, and instrumentation within the parameters set forth in this agreement.

2. COMPOSER, in accepting this commission, hereby agrees:
   A. To compose a score of a duration of [number in words] ([number in numerals]) to [number in words] ([number in numerals]) minutes of music, but in no case to be shorter than [number in words] ([number in numerals]) minutes, or to exceed [number in words] ([number in numerals]) minutes of music. The music will be original in origin or may include arrangements of other music determined to be in the Public Domain. The work shall be composed for the instrumentation to be determined and mutually agreed upon by Commissioner and Composer; such instrumentation need not be finalized until the completion of the score.
   B. To provide a fair copy, hand-written, professionally copied, or computer generated, of the completed score and one set of parts for performance purposes. Composer will deliver the completed score no later than [date]; Composer will deliver the parts no later than [date]. Commissioner automatically grants an extension of either or both delivery dates in the event of any technical difficulty, personal illness, injury, infirmity, bereavement, or emergency, natural disaster, civil unrest, or Acts of God that might delay or otherwise hinder the fulfillment of the commission.
   C. Composer grants [performer names] the exclusive right to premiere the commissioned work for a period of one (1) year from the delivery of the score. Right of exclusivity for the premiere performance may be extended by mutual agreement between Commissioner and Composer.
   D. Composer agrees to credit Commissioner in the program notes of the first public performance of the work and in any published edition of the work. Wording of the Commissioner's credit is to be mutually agreed upon by Commissioner and Composer.
   E. Composer agrees that Commissioner shall be permitted to keep a full set of scores and parts to the commissioned work and shall have a perpetual, royalty-free license to publicly perform the commissioned work.
   F. Commissioner shall be permitted to create archival recordings of one or more public performances of the commissioned work, provided such recordings are not distributed or offered for sale to the general public. Commissioner shall furnish Composer with one (1) complimentary copy of any such archival recording. Commissioner shall be permitted to place such recordings on social media including, but not limited to, YouTube, SoundCloud, and Facebook, as long as it is for streaming only, and not for downloading or any commercial purposes.

3. COMMISSIONER and COMPOSER agree that:
   A. Composer shall retain all rights of ownership to the music, including that of copyright and commercial recording and release. As sole owner of the music, Composer and Composer's publisher, if any, are entitled to any performance royalties generated by the performance of the music.
   B. In the event that the commission is cancelled by Commissioner before the completion of the work, Commissioner and Composer agree that Composer's signing fee of one half of the commissioning fee shall constitute payment in full.

4. This agreement shall be binding upon Commissioner, Commissioner's heirs, executors, administrators, successors or assign. Composer's heirs, successors and assigns, including any conservator and guardian, and the executor or administrator of his estate, shall retain all of Composer's rights and remedies under this agreement.

5. This document constitutes the entire Agreement between the parties. No modification, amendment, waiver, termination, or discharge of this Agreement shall be binding unless executed in writing and signed by the party to be charged. This Agreement shall be governed by the laws of [your state] in which it is made.

This Agreement is hereby executed as of the day and year first set forth above, as witnessed below by the parties involved.

_______________________________   _______________________________________

[Your Name] / "Composer"   [Commissioning Party Name] / "Commissioner"

_______________________________   _______________________________________

Date   Date

Index

About the Author

Steven L. Rosenhaus has a multi-hyphenate career as a composer, arranger, conductor, lyricist, educator and clinician, author, dramaturge for musicals, and performer. His 250+ original works and arrangements have been published and performed by such musicians as the New York Philharmonic, the U.S. Navy Band, the Band of His Majesty's Royal Marines Plymouth, the Meridian String Quartet, pianist Laura Leon, and many others. Dr. Rosenhaus taught music composition with specialties in concert music, musical theater, and songwriting at New York University for over thirty years. He is the author of *The Concertgoer's Guide to the Symphony Orchestra* and co-author with Allen Cohen of *Writing Musical Theater*.